Jean Piaget

An interdisciplinary critique

International Library of Psychology

General editor: Max Coltheart
Professor of Psychology, University of London

Jean Piaget
An interdisciplinary critique

Edited by

Sohan Modgil PhD
Reading in Educational Research and Development
Brighton Polytechnic

Celia Modgil PhD
Senior Lecturer in Educational Psychology
London University

and

Geoffrey Brown PhD
Professor of Education
East Anglia University

Routledge & Kegan Paul
London, Boston, Melbourne and Henley

Clark County Community College
Learning Resources Center
3200 E. Cheyenne Ave.
N. Las Vegas, Nevada 89030

First published in 1983
by Routledge & Kegan Paul plc
39 Store Street, London WC1E 7DD,
9 Park Street, Boston, Mass. 02108, USA,
296 Beaconsfield Parade, Middle Park,
Melbourne, 3206, Australia, and
Broadway House, Newtown Road,
Henley-on-Thames, Oxon RG9 1EN
Printed in Great Britain by
St. Edmundsbury Press Ltd,
Bury St. Edmunds, Suffolk
© Routledge & Kegan Paul 1983

NOV 9 1983

Library of Congress Cataloging in Publication Data

Jean Piaget, an interdisciplinary critique.

(International library of psychology)
"Proceedings of the conference, Jean Piaget (1896-
1980): a British tribute, the continuing debate, held
at Brighton Polytechnic on 22-23 May 1981" - Pref.
Includes bibliographical references and indexes.
1. Piaget, Jean, 1896-   - Congresses.
2. Cognition in children - Congresses. 3. Cognition
and culture - Congresses. 4. Knowledge, Theory of -
Congresses. I. Modgil, Sohan. II. Modgil, Celia.
III. Brown, Geoffrey, 1935-   . IV. Series.

BF109.P5J4 1983   155.4'13'0924   83-3096

ISBN 0-7100-9451-5

In memory of
Jean Piaget
1896–1980

Contents

Preface

This volume contains the proceedings of the conference 'Jean Piaget (1896-1980): A British Tribute - The Continuing Debate', held at Brighton Polytechnic on 22-23 May 1981. The collection of papers goes beyond a particular event which took place at a specific time. It stands on its own as a sustained inquiry as to how Piaget's theory is seen in relation to a range of areas of knowledge. Pairs of academics from various disciplines who have worked on aspects of Piagetian theory engaged in 'for and against' debates. The scope of the volume is therefore inter-disciplinary. A more distinguished team of British contributors could not have gathered to pay tribute to Professor Jean Piaget.

The conference was sponsored by Brighton Polytechnic Faculty of Education Studies and received the support of the staff in general and the assistance of a number of members who deserve special mention.

The Director, Geoffrey Hall, gave particular recognition to the event by welcoming the participants at the formal dinner. Kenneth Gardner, Dean of the Faculty, provided constant encouragement to the conference from its conception to conclusion and formally proposed the vote of thanks to all the contributors and partici-pants.

The many and varied administrative matters were handled by Dr Lyn Gorman, Faculty Officer, who ably anticipated the multiplicity of factors involved in conference co-ordination. Special gratitude is also extended to Malcolm Clarkson and John Pearce for their advice and to Hazel Cooke, Vicki Gardner and Kathleen Moxon for their generous involvement.

It would not have been possible to hold concurrent debates without the excellent chairing of the sessions by: Professor Neil Bolton, Dr Dennis Davis, Ron Hardie, Emeritus Professor Alastair Heron, Dr Roger Holmes, Dr John Radford, Dr John Versey and Dr Helen Weinreich-Haste. Gratitude is also extended to those staff and students who gave of their time and energy. A major contribution to the success of the conference was the excellence of the facilities of the Eastbourne Short Courses Centre of Brighton Polytechnic.

Acknowledgments

The undertaking of this enterprise was only possible in collaboration with the numerous distinguished contributors herein. We are greatly indebted to them for demonstrating their trust by accepting our invitation to join forces to pay tribute to Professor Jean Piaget.

Our confidence in the volume has been enhanced by the recognition given to it by its inclusion in the International Library of Psychology series. We thank Professor Max Coltheart, general editor.

We are further grateful to Routledge & Kegan Paul, publishers of the British and American editions. We express our gratitude to David Godwin, Stratford Caldecott, Elaine Donaldson and the Production team.

Sohan and Celia Modgil
May 1982

Contributors

Margaret Boden, Sussex University
Derek Boyle, Aberdeen University
Geoffrey Brown, East Anglia University
Peter Bryant, Oxford University
George Butterworth, Southampton University
Nicholas Emler, Dundee University
Michael Garfield, Manchester Polytechnic
S.H. Irvine, Plymouth Polytechnic
Peter Kutnick, Sussex University
Paul Light, Southampton University
Barbara Lloyd, Sussex University
Peter Lloyd, Manchester University
C.K. Mackay, Aberdeen University
Wolfe Mays, Manchester University
Celia Modgil, London University
Sohan Modgil, Brighton Polytechnic
James Russell, Liverpool University
John Sants, Sussex University
Janet Strivens, Liverpool University
Peter Tomlinson, Leeds University

Part 1

Editors' introduction

1 Jean Piaget (1896-1980): the continuing debate

Sohan and Celia Modgil

Piaget has devoted a lifetime's work to the formulation of a theory of knowledge: of how the individual comes to know his world. He did not confine epistemology to philosophy but more widely related it to the human sciences. His psychological investigations demonstrated the childhood origins of human knowledge in numerous spheres: logic, space, time, mathematics, science, morality, play and language. Concurrently, psychological processes, reasoning, perception, imagery, memory, imitation and action received analysis.

However, Piaget himself modestly claimed that he had 'laid bare a more or less evident general skeleton which remains full of gaps so that when these gaps will be filled the articulations will have to be differentiated, but the general lines of the system will not be changed' (Sinclair de Zwart, 1977, p. 1). That the theory will be open-ended and tentative and subject to revisions is, in part, a validation of it as a developmental theory which is developing.

Modgil (1974), Modgil and Modgil (1976), an eight-volume series, and Modgil and Modgil (1980) bear witness to the number of experts in a wide variety of fields who see the potential of Piagetian theory. However, after many euphoric years in accord with the predictions of Piaget, the discrepancies of aspects of the theory, the omissions, replicatory and related research and alternative interpretations are currently being highlighted.

Most critics of Piaget would agree with Boden (1979) that, 'despite all the criticisms, there is a rich store of psychological insights and theoretical speculations, and a profusion of intriguing empirical observations and remarkably ingenious experiments, to be found in Piaget's pioneering work'. Donaldson (1978) argues that the evidence now compels us to reject certain features of Jean Piaget's theory but acknowledges the positive influence of Piaget's views on her own psychological writings. Siegel (1978) identifies a unifying theme throughout her collection of critical essays: the consideration of theoretical viewpoints other than Piaget's. 'When Piagetian theory cannot explain a particular set of findings, it is obvious that other theories must be considered.'

It is, however, of interest that Siegel comments that 'no one theory predominates'.

It is the purpose of this introductory section to outline some of the elements of Piagetian theory which have been subject to initial questioning. However, as Boden (1979), Donaldson (1978) and Siegel (1978) suggest, it is difficult to present these criticisms without accompanying counter-arguments or acknowledgments of positive elements.

EXISTING ISSUES OF DEBATE

Methodology - performance/competence
The earliest criticisms of Piaget's work involved his sampling techniques and lack of statistical treatment. However, Piaget's clinical method can be seen to have redressed the balance in relation to quantitative and qualitative analysis of data. Siegel (1978) argues on the basis of experimentation that Piagetian results are primarily a consequence of the linguistic demands of the concrete-operational tests. Brown and Desforges (1979) focus on the various aspects of the demands of a task which might defeat a child and lead to an underestimation of his competence: 'Piaget's tasks are cloaked in language.' Boden (1979) draws similar attention: 'one of the methodological problems is to decide when a child's failure is due to a lack of Piagetian structures or general principles of thinking and when it is due to other factors (such as ignorance, incomprehension or short memory-span)'. Donaldson (1978) and Elliot and Donaldson (1982) have further focused on the misinterpretation of questions and instructions during Piaget-type interviews. In counter-argument, Sinclair de Zwart (1982) states that the various conservation concepts are key notions in physics, and that the history of science shows their gradual, often difficult, elaboration by scientists. The enormous bulk of data, both in verbal and non-verbal tasks, obtained with thousands of children speaking many different languages, show clearly the type of pre-theories children have about epistemologically important notions. The tasks were intended to study the epistemic development of certain concepts in the child, not as a set of tests to determine children's cognitive levels. Donaldson (1978) would favour the use of familiar materials as opposed to the standard Piagetian materials: children's capabilities are likely to be at their greatest in contexts that are most related to their experiences. Tamburrini (1982), however, focuses on the educational limitations of contextually bound competences. With reference to Donaldson's distinction between 'embedded' and 'disembedded' thought, she comments that disembedded thought must inevitably entail competences that are generalizable and stable, the competences that, it has been argued, are assessed by Piagetian tests, in contrast to situation-specific competences.

Highly abstract theory
Some critics object that Piaget's views are so vague as to be
irrefutable. Boden (1979) questions whether Piagetian terms
such as equilibrium, assimilation and accommodation offer
explanations of cognitive growth or polysyllabic descriptions
of it. An abstract, systematizing concept must be amenable to
significantly parallel specifications at more detailed empirical
levels - many would agree that his theory does not fulfil this
requirement. His account of the nature, preconditions and results
of the various mental transformations underlying cognitive
achievements is too broadly sketched to express or properly
differentiate between them. He does not specify in sufficient
detail precisely how the transformations he postulates are
effected, or precisely what the transformations are (Boden,
1979). It would seem, as cited above, that Piaget would not be
averse to these gaps being filled.

Stages
It is perhaps appropriate to suggest that the Piagetian stage
concept has received imbalanced attention, to the detriment of
other key factors in Piagetian theory. It is the aspect which has
most readily appealed to educational application attempts. The
notion most confounding the critics is Piaget's claim that the
developmental stages are qualitatively different, but at the same
time he states that the transitional process is gradual - 'horizontal
décalage'. It would be expected that such profound qualitatively
different structures would be apparent in all areas at the same
time.
   Brown and Desforges (1979) elaborate that the search for a
structure irrespective of content has led to generalities which
cannot be sustained. It would seem more appropriate to attempt
to locate cognitive structures within specific content domains
and subsequently to identify any generalities after sufficient
taxonomies have been pursued. The notion of 'stage' creates more
conceptual problems than it solves.
   It would seem that Genevan workers are intent to reduce the
importance of the stage issue: operational structures provide an
interpretive framework to infer the lower and upper limits of a
child's concepts, but cannot explain all facts of cognitive
behaviour (Karmiloff-Smith and Inhelder, 1975); the concept of
stage does not serve a central function in Piaget's theory (Gruber
and Vonèche, 1979); 'It is essentially a descriptive concept that
accounts for the fact that any change, in order to be perceived
at all as change must be dually composed of invariance and
transformation' - other descriptions of development do not
guarantee the principles of differentiation and hierarchical integration (Vonèche and Bovet, 1982).

Underestimation of the complexity of children's cognitive achievements
Emanating particularly from child development researchers is the accusation directed at Piaget of the underestimation of the competence of children at a given age; that he is unaware of the large variety of subtly different psychological processes that might contribute to a given achievement. Boden (1979) reminds, however, that this identification needs to be set against the fact that for many years it was Piaget himself who was outstanding in pointing out some of the structural complexities of behaviours that others saw as relatively simple skills. Boden reviews recent child development research and relates it to appropriate Piagetian stages.

Logical model
In addition to questions of the reliability of his logic by logicians (Parsons, 1960; Ennis, 1978), Piaget's expression of his theory of intelligence in a highly formalized manner in logical and algebraic terms has not always received appreciation. He has often been accused of overestimating the rationality of adult thinking and of concentrating too much on mathematical and scientific contexts. However, as Boden points out, Piaget was aiming for a precise and qualitative formal specification of the development and functioning of the structured mechanisms and transformational processes by which intelligence is generated. Piaget raised the questions of computational ideas for articulating the inner dynamics of psychological feedback and kept them alive in a period when the conceptual tools for their more precise and detailed formulations were not yet available.

Language
It is a common criticism that Piaget has not given sufficient attention to language. Sinclair de Zwart (1982) has acknowledged that Piaget's contribution to the understanding of language is small but emphasizes its importance because of the profound issues he has raised.

   This section has, therefore, been presented as a brief scenario from which will follow the tribute to Piaget. (More extended discussions can be obtained from: 'British Journal of Psychology', May 1982; Modgil and Modgil, 1980; and Modgil and Modgil, 1982.) This tribute will take the form of further debate in relation to the already stated and further issues in the continuing attempt to determine the validity and future relevance of Piaget's work.

CONTINUING THE DEBATE: THE STRATEGY OF THE BOOK

The volume provides theoretical analyses, supported by research, of aspects of Piaget's theory presented predominantly either negatively or positively by pairs of distinguished academics representing particular areas of knowledge. Each paper includes an introductory consideration of the area of knowledge involved, together with discussion and analysis comprising a clear statement of how significant aspects of Piaget's theory, within the framework of Piagetian theory in general, are seen predominantly either negatively or positively to relate to the represented discipline. Eight areas of knowledge are covered: cross-cultural psychology; education; educational psychology; language; moral development; philosophy; social psychology; and sociology.

Margaret Boden, in the introductory chapter, recalls Piaget's biologically grounded epistemology requiring interdisciplinary effort. She outlines recent research in biology, embryology and philosophy that is consonant with Piaget's epistemological aims.

In the area of cross-cultural psychology, Barbara Lloyd assesses the Piagetian contribution to cross-cultural studies, whereas Sid Irvine analyses the existing data on conservation tasks administered within a range of cultures. He focuses in particular on the necessity to consider language structure as the key cross-cultural variable in traditional Piagetian tasks.

Kenneth MacKay argues that Piaget's influence on education is only beginning to be felt; it is the unifying epistemological theory from which more precise psychological theories of development, learning and instruction may be derived. The real impact of Piaget's work has been in broadening and intensifying the educational debate. Following a review of weaknesses inherent in the application of Piagetian theory to education, Derek Boyle, noting Piaget's lack of attention to language, stipulates that linguistic experience is of prime importance and that more attention should be paid to using language more effectively as a means of instruction at all ages.

John Sants analyses Piaget's attitudes to education and concludes that it is his methods in new (particularly social) applications rather than his theories which will continue to be educationally productive. Geoffrey Brown argues that Piagetian theory is at odds with the educator's view of the world in many respects, and he particularly questions the relevance for education of operatory structures and the process of equilibration.

Peter Lloyd acknowledges the contribution of Piaget to the understanding of language but argues that such understanding profits more from his method than his theory. James Russell does not reflect Piaget's thesis that the child's early interactions with the concrete world build, at a nonconscious level, the foundations upon which later conceptual linguistic structures are established. Rather than regarding the structures as really active constructions as Piaget, Russell suggests they are elaborations of innate schemes. Among a number of assumptions made in this context is that cognitive structuring at an epistemic but non-verbal level does not alter with the acquisition of basic verbal concepts relevant to conservation: competence in conservation is present before such a judgment can be given in answer to a question.

Nicholas Emler illustrates Piaget's influence on the moral development sphere through outlining three themes emanating from Piaget's pioneering work. Emler gives particular attention to the theme he considers to reflect most accurately Piaget's original intentions: the treatment of moral development as a function of social relationships. This divergence of emphasis from individual thinker to special participant promises a fruitful integration between developmental and social psychology in this area. Peter Tomlinson, while acknowledging the relevant and conceptual resources in Piaget's work, argues that research in moral developmental issues will be enhanced through being informed by alternative constructs and paradigms from current cognitive psychology.

Following a philosphical examination of the justification of a range of criticisms directed to Piaget's theory, Wolfe Mays considers Piaget's notion of equilibrium as used by Piaget in his account of the mechanism of intellectual exchange in an attempt to determine whether Piaget's use of this notion is as confused as is sometimes alleged. Michael Garfield's title relates to his identification that Piaget's emphasis on the child's developing structures through his activity with the world seems to convey knowledge as an individualist activity: the concern of the paper is to examine the extent to which Piaget has succeeded in giving us an account of the development of knowledge which, while placing heavy emphasis on the construction of that knowledge by the developing person, does not thereby collapse into idealism; or, on the other hand, while seeing the world as some sort of constraint or limit on knowledge, can nevertheless pull back from a naive realist position. Has Piaget given us a third way between the two, or does he simply oscillate between them?

In the social cognition context, George Butterworth addresses himself to the critics of Piaget who argue that Piaget's writings reveal little concern for the social whether as a component of knowledge or as a factor in its acquisition. Such criticisms create dichotomies between aspects of learning which actually interpenetrate. Butterworth's paper shows various dichotomies in explanations proposed as alternatives to Piaget to be ill-founded. This is not to suggest, however, that Piaget's theory is beyond reproach. Paul Light argues that the fundamental character of Piaget's theory has led us to conceive of cognitive development in an ahistorical, acultural fashion, and that in consequence it has seriously distracted us from issues central to the study of social cognition.

Peter Kutnick's paper illuminates Piagetian theory applied to sociology. He illustrates Piaget's provision for the analysis of social/societal understanding which, he proposes, certainly stimulates if not facilitates our understanding of self and society. Janet Strivens, within a sociological context, reviews the commentaries on Piaget's work. However, she concludes by highlighting the difficulties faced by students in making sense of both sociological and psychological formulations and in relating either to the practical decisions they face in applied social fields. In different guises, the gulf between theory and practice continues, and this should be the concern of the radical critiques.

In the concluding chapter, Peter Bryant comments on the variegated content of the previous chapters - a book 'so full of contradiction'. He recalls the prominence of contradiction in Piaget's theory and examines the question of contradiction and Piaget's equilibration model in the light of recent Piagetian writings.

REFERENCES

Boden, M. (1979) 'Piaget'. Glasgow: Fontana.
Brown, G., and Desforges, C. (1979) 'Piaget's Theory: A Psychological Critique'. London: Routledge & Kegan Paul.
Donaldson, M. (1978) 'Children's Minds'. Glasgow: Fontana,
Elliot, A., and Donaldson, M (1983) Piaget on Language, in S. Modgil and C. Modgil (eds), 'Jean Piaget: Consensus and Controversy'. Eastbourne: Holt, Rinehart & Winston.
Ennis, R.G. (1978) Conceptualization of Children's Logical Competence: Piaget's Propositional Logic and an Alternative Proposal, in L.S. Siegel and C.J. Brainerd (eds), 'Alternatives to Piaget'. London: Academic Press.
Gruber, H. and Vonèche, J.J. (1979) 'The Essential Piaget'. London: Routledge & Kegan Paul.
Karmiloff-Smith, A., and Inhelder, B. (1975) If You Want to Get Ahead, Get a Theory, in 'Cognition', 3,3, pp. 195 212.
Modgil, S. (1974) 'Piagetian Research: A Handbook of Recent Studies'. Windsor: National Foundation for Educational Research (NFER).
Modgil, S., and Modgil, C. (1976) 'Piagetian Research: An Appreciation and Theory of Cognitive Development and Sensorimotor Intelligence', vol. 1. Windsor: NFER.
Modgil, S. and Modgil, C. (1976a) 'Experimental Validation of Conservation and the Child's Conception of Space', vol. 2. Windsor: NFER.
Modgil, S., and Modgil, C. (1976b) 'The Growth of Logic: Concrete and Formal Operations', vol. 3. Windsor: NFER.
Modgil, S., and Modgil, C. (1976c) 'School Curriculum and Test Development', vol. 4. Windsor: NFER.
Modgil, S., and Modgil, C. (1976d) 'Personality, Socialization and Emotionality and Reasoning among Handicapped Children', vol. 5. Windsor: NFER.
Modgil, S., and Modgil, C. (1976e) 'Cognitive-Developmental Approach to Morality', vol. 6. Windsor: NFER.
Modgil, S., and Modgil, C. (1976f) 'Training Techniques', vol. 7. Windsor: NFER.
Modgil, S., and Modgil, C. (1976g) 'Cross-cultural Studies', vol. 8. Windsor: NFER.
Modgil, S., and Modgil, C. (eds) (1980) 'Toward a Theory of

Psychological Development', Windsor: NFER.

Modgil, S., and Modgil, C. (eds) (1982) 'Jean Piaget: Consensus and Controversy'. Eastbourne: Holt, Rinehart & Winston/New York: Praeger.

Parsons, C. (1960) Inhelder and Piaget's 'The Growth of Logical Thinking', II: A Logicians Viewpoint, in 'British Journal of Educational Psychology', 51, pp. 75-84.

Siegel, L.S. (1978) The Relationship of Language and Thought in the Pre-operational Child: A Reconsideration of Non-verbal Alternatives to Piagetian Tasks, in S. Siegel and C. Brainerd (eds), 'Alternatives to Piaget'. London: Academic Press.

Sinclair de Zwart, H. (1977) Recent Developments in Genetic Epistemology, in 'Genetic Epistemologist', 6, pp. 1-4.

Sinclair de Zwart, H. (1982) Piaget on Language: A Perspective, in S. Modgil, and C. Modgil (eds), 'Jean Piaget: Consensus and Controversy'. Eastbourne: Holt, Rinehart & Winston.

Tamburrini, J. (1982) Some Educational Implications of Piaget's Theory, in S. Modgil and C. Modgil (eds), 'Jean Piaget: Consensus and Controversy'. Eastbourne: Holt, Rinehart & Winston.

Vonèche, J.J., and Bovet, M. (1982) Training Research and Cognitive Development: What do Piagetians Want to Accomplish?, in S. Modgil and C. Modgil (eds), 'Jean Piaget, Consensus and Controversy'. Eastbourne: Holt, Rinehart & Winston.

Part 2

Introduction

2 Interdisciplinary epistemology

Margaret Boden

To commemorate Piaget is above all to celebrate his rich legacy
to psychology; but we should also remember his deep commitment
to interdisciplinarity. He studied and wrote about many different
fields, but his approach was not a mere magpie-eclecticism. For
Piaget enjoyed a synoptic vision, a conviction that similar insights
and structural principles unite the various branches of human
knowledge. He looked forward to a day when the human and
biological sciences would form part of an integrated intellectual
enterprise, of which his own genetic epistemology would form the
seed. Should his seminal work achieve its full maturity, then, the
fruit would be more than a psychology of the growing mind, and
more than a principled pedagogy. It would be a biologically
grounded epistemology, within which the special sciences could
be systematically situated.

The need for a concerted interdisciplinary effort within the
human sciences is widely, if not universally, acknowledged.
Accordingly, a number of anthropologists and sociologists - and
even some philosophers - have taken notice of Piaget's work,
whether to accept or to criticize it. (I say 'even' philosophers,
because they commonly hold that empirical facts can give no
principled support to any philosophical position, so are epistemologically irrelevant.[1] This widespread philosophical view, which
was repeatedly criticized by Piaget, will be discussed later.)
For instance, two very recent examples of full-length books
drawing largely on Piaget's ideas are C.R. Hallpike's 'The
Foundations of Primitive Thought' and D.W. Hamlyn's 'Experience
and the Growth of Understanding'.[2] The former is an enthusiastic
(perhaps over-enthusiastic) application of his psychology to
anthropology, the latter a philosophical study which praises his
dialectical integration of empiricist and rationalist insights in
epistemology, but criticizes him for not taking sufficient account
of the essentially social nature of knowledge.

The need for co-operation between the human sciences and
biology is less commonly appreciated, and it is much to Piaget's
credit that he recognized it early in his intellectual life and kept
it in mind thereafter. His most fundamental and long-standing

interests concerned the biological grounds and development of knowledge, in both ontogeny and phylogeny. I shall therefore concentrate on some recently published work that is relevant to Piaget's vision of a biologically grounded epistemology.

Although none of these authors can be described as primarily inspired by Piaget, each of them cites Piaget as someone whose ideas are significantly consonant with his or her own work. (Because of space limitations, I can offer only pointers to their work rather than expositions of it: readers who are interested should consult the primary sources.)

Piaget distinguished two types of interdisciplinarity, one relating to common structures or mechanisms, the other to common methods. He saw the first type as exemplified by what he termed 'structuralist' principles in the various individual sciences, such as biology, anthropology and linguistics. The second is exemplified by information theory, which he described as 'a fundamental interdisciplinary instrument'. Indeed, both these aspects of interdisciplinarity may be involved together, as is suggested by his characterization of cybernetics as 'the general science of equilibration'.

The three main problems facing the human and biological sciences he identified as the production of new structures, self-regulation and communication or exchange. He pointed out that 'the study of these central problems is conducted more and more in the light of three instrumental methods . . . viz. games or decision theories, information theory in general, and cybernetics to the extent that it concerns communication, guidance or control'; and he predicted that 'these common logico-mathematical techniques are at once the best indication of the convergence that is called for and the best means of effecting a junction'.[3]

I have argued elsewhere that 'cybernetics' can play the role of a general science of equilibration only if we interpret it as covering all of information-science, including the recently developed theory of computation and artificial intelligence.[4] The concepts of classical cybernetics are not capable of expressing the rich variety of qualitative (structural) distinctions between different types of information-processing, or symbolic transformation, that characterize human thought. These can be expressed only (as far as we know) by specifically computational concepts. Piaget expressed sympathy with a programming methodology on several occasions, even saying that if he had been starting his work again as a young man he would have used it himself.[5] Since most of the computational work related to his writings, whether done by self-declared Piagetians or by critics of Piaget, is concerned with specifically psychological problems, I shall not discuss it here.[6] But we shall see that (much as he predicted) this methodology promises to clarify and enrich our understanding not only of psychological processes but of other life-processes too.

Some current work in theoretical biology is consonant with Piaget's hopes for a structuralist and cognitive biology. By a 'structuralist' biology, I mean one which conceives of biological phenomena on their own level, and which explains observed changes in terms of general principles of transformation expressed at this level rather than in the terms of biochemistry or molecular biology. This of course does not preclude attention to the underlying biochemical mechanisms wherever possible, but the main theoretical concern is with the systematic transformation of the patterned organization of the creature as a whole. By a 'cognitive' biology, I mean a biology in which the central theoretical terms include concepts drawn originally from the domain of knowledge and action.[7] Examples of such concepts include knowledge itself, as well as language, instruction, description, interpretation, information, code, message and control. These concepts are independent of their detailed embodiment in any particular mechanism, and they can be organized by computational principles of transformation, so that a cognitive biology is in principle a structuralist one.

C.H. Waddington, whose theoretical morphology Piaget so greatly admired, was among the first to suggest that biological systems be viewed on the analogy of linguistic structures. By a language, Waddington said, he meant 'a set of symbols, organized by some sort of generative grammar, which makes possible the conveyance of (more or less) precise commands for action to produce effects on the surroundings of the emitting and the recipient entities'.[8] As this quotation may suggest, it is no accident that the list of 'cognitive' terms given above contains items familiar in the context of the information-sciences, and of artificial intelligence in particular. To put it another way, and to cite a point made by Piaget in a different context,[9] more general principles of informatics underlie specifically linguistic phenomena, so that the Waddingtonian paradigm for biology should be thought of as information-processing rather than as natural language itself.

A student of Waddington's, whose special concern is with the development and regeneration of cells and organisms, has recently argued for an explicitly cognitive biology.[10] B.C. Goodwin explains morphological changes in terms of transformational principles concerning spatio-temporally organized fields, or interacting waves of metabolic activity. That is, he uses the same sort of concepts to describe the temporal organization of regeneration and embryonic growth as to account for the functioning of biological clocks (within cell, organ or organism). Waves of different periodic phase are responsible for different levels of integration in morphology and behaviour, and one and the same metabolite can convey different instructions (can have distinct biological meanings) at different stages of development. As regards the generation of behaviour from morphology (the theoretical continuity of activity and form), he suggests that it is because the time-phase of neural changes is extremely short that they lead to patterned activities, rather than to patterned forms.

Characteristically, Goodwin expresses this last point in cognitive terms:

> 'One might put it that the embryo is more a sculptor, the brain more a composer of music, both being very fine artists. This suggests that a necessary condition for the emergence of mind came about by the simple expedient of an increase in the rate of elementary embryonic processes, a result of membrane specialization, thus achieving an uncoupling of activity waves from the viscous 'drag' of matter which normally results in morphogenesis.[11]

In general, he relies heavily on notions of instruction, description and interpretation, and speaks of the cell or the cell-system as embodying knowledge of its environment and potential choices. And he notes various ways in which this manner of speaking is not a mere fanciful metaphor, but can suggest fruitful lines of theoretical and experimental inquiry that otherwise might be overlooked.

Goodwin draws attention not only to the relevance of artificial intelligence (as opposed to classical cybernetics, whose concepts are quantitative rather than qualitative in nature), but also to Piaget as someone who saw the need for a structuralist biology of this general type. Interestingly, Piaget spoke of the possibility of 'a comparative epistemology of time', which would ground the baby's schemas of time in the temporal organization of the embryo and ultimately in the more general phenomenon of biological clocks.[12] Also, of course, Piaget claimed that epistemological issues should be addressed by theoretical biology, that the notion of knowledge and its cognates should enter into the biologist's descriptions of all living things.

Piaget even looked for a biology that would be 'cognitive' in a stronger sense than this. For he had a strongly Lamarckian streak, and believed that his experiments on plants and animals had demonstrated Lamarckian inheritance. Even Waddington, who praised these experiments as exemplars of what he (and Piaget) termed 'genetic assimilation', rejected Piaget's appeal to an unspecified mechanism vaguely described by him as a 'progressive reorganization, or gradual change in the proportion of the genome'.[13] And biologists today are no longer willing to believe in Lamarckian evolution. Admittedly, the recent experiments of Edward Steele suggest that some inheritance of acquired characteristics may be possible, since an acquired immunological tolerance in mice can apparently be passed on to the offspring.[14] But although one can (and some biologists do) describe an antibody as expressing 'knowledge' of its antigen, and although acquisition of an immune response can often be regarded as favourable to the organism, this limited instance of the inheritance of acquired characteristics cannot justify Piaget's evolutionary progressivism.

Piaget on several occasions looked forward to a future science which he described as an 'embryology of reflexes'.[15] This would study perceptuomotor development in the womb, and correlate it with sensorimotor function on the one hand and neurological data about the developing brain on the other. Colwyn Trevarthen has recently reviewed the relevant embryological findings, especially those concerning the development of vision and visuomotor control, and relates them to the apposite (though admittedly programmatic) remarks of Piaget as well as to his studies of early cognition.[16]

In view of Piaget's emphasis on the role of the infant's own activities in prompting development after birth, a Piagetian approach to prenatal development would lead one to expect that there are processes of dialectical interaction within the interuterine environment, such that the embryo's own movements actively aid development of the growing neural structures. Trevarthen points out that attempts to identify such processes have failed; but these researches are in such an early stage, and their intrinsic difficulty is so great, that we cannot be sure that they will not succeed.

What is clear already is that amazingly complex neural patterns develop in the uterus, in an apparently autonomous fashion. These form the groundwork for an integrated behaviour-space (or perceptuomotor organization) within which the baby's cognitive functions are situated from the very moment of birth. The foetal sense organs are all protected from external stimulation, even from the stimulation potentially available within the womb. The eyelids are closed, and the ears and nostrils are obstructed by epithelial plugs. (Admittedly, one cannot be sure that no stimulation whatever is getting through – for instance, the difference between light and dark might be perceptible through closed eyelids, and it is not clear that the tactile receptors are nonfunctional.) Nevertheless, neural connections of extraordinary complexity and specificity develop, generating a visuomotor system whose basic biological functions are pre-programmed rather than having to be learned after birth.

From the earliest stages of neural growth, which are integrated by the basic somatic polarities, embryonic development is based on a body-centred neural field. Such a field could in principle act as a structural ground for perceptual guidance of the action of the body as a whole (though this is not to say that we understand just how it might do so). The body-centred neural field becomes gradually more differentiated with the (autonomous) growth of more specialized brain structures. Questions arise about whether certain reflexes of the foetus are functionally isolable from this overall structural scaffold, questions which find conceptual parallels in regard to observable behaviour after birth.

Trevarthen remarks on the striking fact that foetal activity seems to be only a very restricted part of what the circuitry of the foetal brain might reasonably have been expected to perform. In other words, innately determined physiology and neurology seem to prefigure actual behaviour. Postural and touch reflexes, and compensatory eye movements, appear very early in foetal development, and by the fourth month the foetus shows finely individuated face and hand movements. But the neuro-logical circuitry is already laid down that will mediate even more subtle control and co-ordination of body parts.

These results too are anti-Piagetian, in that they suggest that much of the sensorimotor integration necessary to the object-concept is already prefigured in the womb. For example, the various sensory modalities do not have to be integrated by the constructive activities of the baby, but are already poised to function in a concerted fashion before birth. And integration of perceptual functions with motor control is similarly present in schematic form. That is, the constructive activities of the baby have more to start from at birth than Piaget suggested. (This has of course been suggested also by psychological studies of neonates, but I am concentrating on non-psychological work here.)

But in another, important, sense these embryological findings are fundamentally consonant with Piaget's views. For they emphasize the biologically grounded and largely autonomous cog-nitive powers of the baby, in contrast to empiricist approaches to psychophysiology, which stress principles of conditioning and the like. Moreover, they show that even the earliest spontaneous movements of the foetus are patterned, or rhythmical. This is what one would expect on the basis of Lashley's pioneering dis-cussions of the serial ordering of behaviour,[17] and of Goodwin's ideas about the importance of temporal cycles of activity in the development of organisms. Even more to the point, it is also what one would expect on the Piagetian view: organizing structures are present from the start, and maturation involves the gradual differentiation of more and more specific and inter-articulated substructures. Were we able to achieve a clearer conceptual grasp of this differentiation and mutual articulation within one disciplinary area, we might be able to apply these conceptual insights to others. Understanding how an embryo, or a foetal brain, develops might help us to understand the differentiation of a child's intellectual schemata, and vice versa.

Turning from Piaget's first love, biology, to his second, philosophy, a recent epistemological study is of particular interest.[18] The main thesis of P.C. Churchland's 'Scientific Realism and the Plasticity of Mind' is that a realist interpretation of science is correct, and that this implies that our most familiar ontological assumptions might have to be given up in favour of others if they were shown by science to be faulty. Even our per-ceptual experiences and introspective access to our own minds are not theory-neutral, but involve spontaneous interpretations over and above the registration of sensory stimulation. Moreover, some of these interpretations, or intentionalities, are not intro-spectively evident, and are not clearly reflected in our verbal concepts or linguistically mediated perception. As he puts it, 'our familiar sensations simply teem with objective intentionalities over and above (or perhaps instead of) the familiar set commonly ascribed to them'.[19]

This theory-laden or intentional character of experience has the consequence that our common-sense ideas about the basic ontological structure of the world and of our own minds might be radically false, despite their admitted usefulness for our everyday purposes. It is conceivable, he says, that creatures with an essentially different perceptual and introspective experience could be seeing reality more truly. It is conceivable also that, by the assimilation of scientific discoveries, human experience might be essentially transformed so as to afford us a truer appreciation of reality. That is, we might conceivably come to see the world in terms of modern physics. (Churchland gives some intriguing suggestions about what this sort of perceptual experience might be like.) However, it is an empirical question how far such a change is actually open to us: we still see the sun rising and setting while the earth stands still, and it may be that some of the perceptual intentionalities established by our biological evolution cannot be 'over-written' by future scientific knowledge.

Since all our knowledge and experience is conditional on the judgments of science, says Churchland, epistemology must be scientifically based. An adequate account of the nature and limits of human (or animal) knowledge cannot rely on purely a priori arguments, independent of the facts of our embodiment and biological situation. We cannot safely assume that the units considered basic by current epistemologies are in fact those on which our minds are grounded (still less those which would offer the truest reflection of reality), or that the accepted principles of rational transition between epistemic states are indeed among those that are usable by intelligent creatures. If they are not, then any norms of rationality defined in terms of them must be irrelevant to our knowledge.

So although there is a distinction between descriptive and normative epistemology, the latter must take the former seriously if it is to be of any use. Like Piaget, then, Churchland chides most philosophers for their attacks on what they term 'psychologism' in philosophy, and for their failure to admit the epistemological relevance of facts about the development of knowledge (whether in the individual or in the species). It is not that psychology or biology can determine criteria of validity, for this is the job of the normative epistemologist. But empirical science can demonstrate possibilities (such as types of data structure or inference strategy) that may have been overlooked by philosophers, and can also show which symbolisms and strategies are actually used by living creatures. Only a philosophical epistemology, however, can legislate on how these (and other) symbolisms and strategies should be used.

As Churchland points out, there are strong reasons for doubting that the basic epistemic units of traditional epistemologies are well chosen. Briefly, most epistemologies are based on units defined in terms of natural languages, whether 'ideas' defined by verbal means or (more commonly) 'beliefs' and 'propositional attitudes' conceived of as sentential units. The assumption that rationality is basically linguistic in form (an assumption often stated explicitly) is narrowly parochial, in that it denies rationality to animals and even human babies. And it is incapable of expressing the continuity between infant – or, more problematically, animal – intelligence and adult human knowledge. Linguistic beliefs exist and are epistemologically important, but they are grounded in and develop on the basis of non-linguistic cognition. Instead of seeking a rational kinematics of sentences only, the epistemologist should aim at a systematic account of the operation of 'epistemic engines' generally.

One is reminded forcefully of Piaget's views about the priority of logic over language, and also of his hopes for a general science of cybernetics. Indeed, Churchland specifically complains of philosophers' failure to take account of Piaget's developmental psychology. He foresees a collaboration between empirical research into the development of cognition and philosophical epistemology, integrated by some new form of information-science dealing with self-improving epistemic systems in general.

Unfortunately, Churchland has little to say about what such an approach might be like. However, he sketches a simple mathematical model of the development of an internal tidal clock, and speaks of creatures incorporating such a model as having learned some astronomy, their internal states containing information in that regard. And he describes animals as 'informational sponges', saying:

> one need only suppose the overt behaviour of such informational sponges to be a systematic function of their information-bearing states to have outlined a conception of the internal activities of natural fauna that owes nothing to our usual cognitive concepts, and which places us on a continuum with animals, trees, and ultimately even beaches.[20]

In addition, he refers to the first oscillatory regime of his imaginary tidal clock as a basic informational framework in which development and epistemological differentiation can be grounded.

These remarks, sketchy though they are, are interesting in light of our previous discussion of Goodwin's theoretical biology. Like Churchland, Goodwin speaks of organisms as embodying knowledge, and he even describes evolutionary learning as an 'intelligent' process. Like Churchland too (but with considerable experimental backing), he outlines mathematically describable mechanisms incorporating vital functions also described in cognitive terms. And like Churchland (again, with good scientific evidence), he regards biological clocks as theoretically and phylogenetically basic.

Churchland's discussion also brings to mind computational approaches to psychobiology, for he emphasizes that the new

ways of thinking about minds and organisms that we need are
likely to be conceived in primarily informational terms. However,
he does not refer to psychologically relevant work in artificial
intelligence. Possibly, he would seek to dismiss such an approach
as merely another subclass of 'sentential' epistemologies (he dis-
misses J.A. Fodor's claims that cognitive psychology must be
computational on these grounds).[21] But the common view (sub-
scribed to also by Piaget) that the absence of social, verbal,
language implies the absence of any symbolic representation, or
language in a wider sense, has been forcefully rebutted by Aaron
Sloman, in relation to cognitive psychology and artificial intelligence.[22] Acquaintance with a computational methodology suggests
that the relatively unstructured, quantitative, mathematical
models sketched by Churchland (and elaborated in more detail
by Goodwin) are in principle incapable of expressing the structural and procedural distinctions needed to characterize epistemological phenomena.

Further, much of what Churchland says about 'non-inferential'
interpretative responses to sensory input suffers from the same
failing that characterizes J.J. Gibson's references to 'information
pick-up' in perception.[23] That is, because the computational transformations concerned are not linguistic and do not depend on
high-level concepts, they are assumed not to exist. Powerful
statements of the contrary viewpoint have been expressed by
Shimon Ullman and other members of David Marr's research
group, backed up by hypothetical algorithms for the visual
computations that may be being carried out by the retina and
early stages of the visual system.[24] These clear hypotheses are
an immeasurable advance on the vague metaphors employed by
Churchland: if animals are informational sponges, we need to
specify precisely which holes the different types of information
are going through, how the hollows are interconnected inside
the sponge, and what happens when the contents of two channels
meet.

Clearly, the interdisciplinary epistemological enterprise predicted by Churchland – and previously by Piaget – is much
needed. Even Churchland, sympathetic to empirical science
though he is, refers to very few studies by biologists, physiolo-
gists and psychologists, and none by computational theorists.
This illustrates what Piaget bemoaned as the 'tragic' splitting up
of courses among and even within university faculties, which he
saw as becoming more and more cut off from each other.[25]

Most of the authors I have cited regard Piaget as a sympathetic
or suggestive influence rather than a primary intellectual source.
This is not surprising, for – in contrast with the state of affairs
in psychology – there is no identifiably Piagetian programme of
interdisciplinary effort outside the International Centre in
Geneva. The reason is that there is no distinct methodological
tradition, comparable to that implicit in Piaget's corpus of psychological experiments, to act as a shared intellectual matrix for
discussion. So Trevarthen, for example, remarks that Piaget has

left us no precise directives for a neurobiological study of cognitive development, despite the embryogenic form of his theorizing, and concludes his paper with the admission that 'it would be dishonest to leave the impression that we see any more than the beginning of an adequate psychobiological theory of perception'.[26] Moreover, the views of these authors differ from Piaget's on various important points. But to share Piaget's hope for an interdisciplinary genetic epistemology is not necessarily to endorse all of his suggestions about how this might be achieved. Likewise, to acknowledge him as a creative psychologist of the first rank need not be to accept even the main outlines, still less the details, of his thought. Rather, it is to treat his oeuvre as a fertile source of suggestive ideas, theoretical questions and empirical observations, worthy of the attention required to confirm or to amend them.

In sum, Piaget's theory of development is a still-developing theory, with a potential for growth, modification and perhaps even metamorphosis. The examples I have discussed today indicate the continuing vitality of his interdisciplinary project, initially conceived at the time of the First World War, for they were all published within the last few years. It is a measure of Piaget's greatness that a commemoration of his life's work, even in areas other than psychology, can thus involve one in looking forward no less than looking back. This man born in the last century is still with us in this one – and he will surely be a living force in the next.

NOTES

1　For a clear expression of this view with particular reference to Piaget, see D.W. Hamlyn, Epistemology and Conceptual Development, in T. Mischel (ed.), 'Cognitive Development and Epistemology', New York, Academic Press, 1971. For a rebuttal see S. Toulmin's chapter in the same volume.
2　C.R. Hallpike, 'The Foundations of Primitive Thought', Oxford, Clarendon Press, 1979; D.W. Hamlyn, 'Experience and the Growth of Understanding', London, Routledge & Kegan Paul, 1978.
3　Jean Piaget, 'Main Trends in Interdisciplinary Research', London, Allen & Unwin, 1973, pp. 9, 13-14, 67.
4　M.A. Boden, 'Piaget', London, Fontana, 1979. ch. 7.
5　In conversation with T. Gouin-Decarie, for Radio Canada TV, 1979 (Jean Gascon, personal communication).
6　In addition to the references given in the chapter cited in the previous note, see a recent book by a longtime collaborator of Piaget's: Seymour Papert, 'Mindstorms: Children, Computers, and Powerful Ideas', Brighton, Harvester Press, 1980.
7　M.A. Boden, 'Minds and Mechanisms: Philosophical Psychology and Computational Models', Brighton, Harvester Press, 1981. See ch. 4, The Case for a Cognitive Biology.

8 C.H. Waddington (ed.), 'Toward a Theoretical Biology', vol. 4, Edinburgh University Press, 1972, p. 288.
9 Piaget, 'Trends', p. 8.
10 B.C. Goodwin, 'Analytical Physiology of Cells and Developing Organisms', London, Academic Press, 1976.
11 B.C. Goodwin, Embryogenesis and Cognition, in W.D. Keidel et al. (eds), 'Cybernetics and Bionics', Munich, Oldenbourg, 1974, p. 47.
12 Jean Piaget, 'Biology and Knowledge', Edinburgh University Press, 1971, p. 62.
13 Ibid., p. 304.
14 R.M. Gorezynski and Edward Steele, Inheritance of Acquired Immunological Tolerance to Foreign Histocompatibility Antigens in Mice, in 'Proceedings of the National Academy of Science', 77 (1980), pp. 2871-5.
15 E.g., Jean Piaget and Barbel Inhelder, 'The Psychology of the Child', London, Routledge & Kegan Paul, 1969, p. vii.
16 Colwyn Trevarthen, Neuroembryology and the Development of Perception, in F. Falkner and J.M. Tanner (eds), 'Human Growth', vol. 3, New York, Plenum, 1979, pp. 3-96.
17 K.S. Lashley, The Problem of Serial Order in Behavior, in L.A. Jeffress (ed.), 'Cerebral Mechanisms in Behavior', New York, John Wiley, 1951, pp. 112-35.
18 P.C. Churchland, 'Scientific Realism and the Plasticity of Mind', Cambridge University Press, 1979.
19 Ibid., p. 28.
20 Ibid., p. 143.
21 Ibid., p. 131; see also J.A. Fodor, 'The Language of Thought', Brighton, Sussex, Harvester Press, 1976.
22 Aaron Sloman, The Primacy of Non-Communicative Language, in M. McCafferty and K. Gray (eds), 'The Analysis of Meaning' (London, ASLIB and British Computing Society), 1979.
23 J.J. Gibson, 'An Ecological Approach to Visual Perception', Boston, Houghton Mifflin, 1978.
24 Shimon Ullman, 'The Interpretation of Visual Motion', Cambridge, Mass., MIT Press, 1979; David Marr, Visual Information Processing: The Structure and Creation of Visual Representations, in 'Sixth International Joint Conference on Artificial Intelligence', pp. 1108-26.
25 Piaget, 'Trends', p. 12.
26 Trevarthen, Neuroembryology, pp. 67, 79.

Part 3

Cross-cultural psychology

3 Cross-cultural studies of Piaget's theory

Barbara Lloyd

My task is to evaluate the Piagetian contribution to cross-cultural research. Before attempting this assessment it is useful to consider briefly the nature of cross-cultural studies and to examine the history of cross-cultural research using Piaget's theory.

Trained as a psychologist, it is tempting for me to focus immediately upon cross-cultural psychology and so claim Piaget as a developmental psychologist. But as Margaret Boden (1979) has argued, Piaget was a biologist and a philosopher first, and only second a developmental psychologist. Before examining cross-cultural psychology we need to look at cross-cultural research generally.

Speculation about other cultures has long been a feature of Western thought. The rise of evolutionary theory in the nineteenth century provided a scientific interest and appeared to offer an explanation of cultural differences. Cultural differences were quickly assimilated to an evolutional perspective. Cultural and racial differences were readily conflated and races were seen, akin to species, as forming an evolutionary continuum with Western civilization representing the most highly developed form and end point of social evolution.

In 1858 Gladstone proposed that the Greeks of the Homeric period could not have perceived colour with the same sensitivity as modern man. His evidence was linguistic, the colour terms of the Greek epic poems. By 1880 Geiger had provided an evolutionary account of these differences in colour vocabulary and in alleged visual acuity. A debate ensued and attempts were made to assess the visual acuity of peoples of different cultures and races, but it was some time before the entwined strands of linguistic, perceptual and biological evidence were disentangled.

As it emerged that language was not an adequate guide to perceptual abilities the need for evidence beyond that which might be furnished by armchair speculations became clear. At the turn of the century a Cambridge University group of scholars, today identifiable as anthropologists and psychologists, organized an expedition to the Torres Strait Islands between Northern Australia and New Guinea in order to investigate problems of a linguistic, social and psychological nature. Among their numbers was Rivers, who has since been claimed as one of the founding fathers of cross-cultural psychology. On his return he published an account in which he reported many linguistic and perceptual differences (Rivers, 1901). Rivers argued for an evolutionary sequence and also suggested that the differences he observed in the colour sensitivities of Murray Islanders and English men reflected underlying psychological differences related to skin and retinal pigmentation.

Psychologists challenged such claims and offered environmental or cultural explanations in opposition to biological accounts (Woodworth, 1910). By 1911 the anthropologist Franz Boas not only asserted that all human beings had the same mental potential but he also challenged the notion of unilineal cultural evolution which suggested that all societies were progressing through a series of stages which would ultimately result in a culture similar to our own. For nearly fifty years the position of Boas, known as cultural relativism, held sway. Anthropologists eschewed an evolutionary approach, and an ahistoric stance dominated social anthropology for many years.

Cultural comparisons invite explanation, and a negative reaction to biological accounts among many social scientists may reflect the use of biological explanations to support racism. The Nazis' 'final solution' to the Jewish problem was couched in biological terms of race, and discussions of black-white differences in education and achievement often invoke racial variables. Anthropologists have reacted by adopting a relativist stance which accepts each culture on its own terms and which makes comparisons problematic. Contemporary psychologists have also struggled with the interpretation of differences, and the very conduct of cross-cultural research is seen to be fraught with ethical problems. Why then should scholars pursue cultural comparisons?

Cultural diversity lies at the heart of anthropology, which defines itself as the study of man. Broadly speaking, all aspects of man's nature and his products are its domain. Man's biology is studied by physical anthropologists; his language is the concern of ethnolinguistics, his prehistory is the domain of archeologists; and man's cultural institutions are the province of social anthropology. Since its earliest days anthropologists have been concerned with the institutions and products created by man - in all their diversity.

The position of cross-cultural psychology is somewhat different. Although an area of study which employed comparative methods was identified by another of the putative founding fathers of cross-cultural psychology, Wundt (in his 'folkpsychologie') believed that cultural psychology differed from laboratory psychology. Its subject matter was complex processes of a cultural nature, and its methods were those of observation. The discipline, as viewed by Wundt, would lie somewhere between anthropology and experimental psychology.

This is not the contemporary view. Indeed, three very active
practitioners define cross-cultural psychology as 'a meta-method
with all of the areas of psychology as grist to its mill' (Bochner,
Brislin and Lonner, 1975, p. 7). Their argument is that cross-
cultural psychology is not a separate subdiscipline within
psychology but an approach, comparative in the sense that
cultures rather than species function as the independent variable.
Explanations for the regularities observed in dependent variables
are sought in psychological theories of great generality moder-
ated by specific cultural variables.

Further evidence that cross-cultural psychology is defined as
a meta-method taking all areas of psychology as its domain can
be found in the 'Handbook of Cross-cultural Psychology',
published in 1980. Its five volumes cover the theoretical history
and foundations of cross-cultural psychology, its methodology,
basic psychological processes, and developmental, social and
abnormal psychology. In his introduction the overall editor,
Triandis, argues that all psychological theories should strive for
universality and explains that each volume has a specialist editor
since no single psychologist could be an expert in the diverse
subdisciplines of psychology reviewed in the Handbook.

This contemporary view of the cross-cultural enterprise
entails a divorce from anthropology which is of recent origin.
The chapter on the cross-cultural method in the 1954 'Handbook
of Social Psychology' was written by the anthropologist John
Whiting, and it was his revision which appeared in the 1968
edition. Writing in the 1954 'Manual of Child Psychology',
Margaret Mead asserted that 'the history of the use to which
psychology has put data about primitive children and data about
primitive peoples when constructing theories of developmental
psychology is a history of the changing relationships between
anthropology and psychology' (1954, p. 735). In reviewing this
collaboration Mead noted that much of the early research had a
biogenetic slant which interpreted the behaviour of the child as
recapitulating the past history of the race. Later developmental
research was undertaken by anthropologists within a psychoanalytic framework and those involved in the multi-disciplinary
speciality known as personality and culture. The few psychologists engaged in cross-cultural studies often worked in these
traditions.

With the rise of cross-cultural psychology as an enterprise
distinct from psychological anthropology, the concerns of
psychologists working in other cultures came to reflect more
closely the interests of their professional colleagues engaged in
research in their own laboratories. In the historical account of
cross-cultural Piagetian studies I seek to show that the surge
of interest in cross-cultural studies about twenty years ago
reflects a more general rediscovery of Piaget by Anglo-Saxon
psychologists in the 1960s. The divorce between anthropological
and psychological concerns is evidenced by the anthropologist
Hallpike's recent evangelical attempts to persuade his anthro-

pological colleagues of the value of Piaget's theory in understanding primitive thought (Hallpike, 1976, 1979). The issues that this attempt to import Piaget into contemporary anthropology raises are complex and complicated by anthropologists' tendency to seek evidence of thought in terms of its products – language, classificatory systems and myths – while psychologists pursue their understanding in the thinking processes themselves. These issues arise in our discussion of cross-cultural Piagetian research and in an evaluation of the contribution Piaget's theory has made to the cross-cultural enterprise.

CROSS-CULTURAL PIAGETIAN RESEARCH

By now scores of investigators have pursued Piagetian concepts in a diversity of cultural settings. This review does not attempt to survey them. Instead, I look at the major questions to which the presence or absence of cultural differences have been addressed, examining a few studies typical of three distinctive eras of Piagetian-inspired cross-cultural research. In the early period, influenced by Piaget's books of the 1920s and 1930s, anthropologists and psychologists interviewed children and adults in primitive cultures to learn the nature of their thought: was it animistic or marked by moral realism? The second era reflected the rediscovery of Piaget by developmental psychologists, and cross-cultural evidence was sought to verify the universality of the structures and functions Piaget had described in his account of the ontogenesis of cognition. The third era has at least two new foci; psychologists' preoccupation with methodology, and a need to delineate, more fully than Piaget has done, the consequences of cultural diversity.

THE EARLY PERIOD

The first cross-cultural study to explore Piagetian theory was Margaret Mead's investigation of animism which she carried out in 1928-9 among the Manus people of the Admiralty Islands. Piaget's early books, 'The Language and Thought of the Child' (1926) and 'Judgment and Reasoning in the Child' (1928) were available to Mead when she set out, and by the time she published her findings in 1932, 'The Child's Conception of the World' (1929) and 'The Child's Conception of Physical Causality' (1930) had also been published in English. Mead viewed her research as drawing together the anthropologist Levy-Bruhl's hypotheses about the prelogical nature of primitive thought and the assumptions of Piaget that the child's thought, which he held to differ both in degree and kind from that of Western adults, was more closely related to that of primitive man than to that of civilized man. Specifically, she asked whether the characteristics which Piaget had identified in the thought of

civilized children - the use of animistic premises, anthropomor-
phic interpretations and faulty logic - were to be found in the
thought of primitive children. Her research, framed in the
Boasian tradition, asked further whether the characteristics
Piaget had described were the product of a special social
environment and what the impact of growing up in a milieau
congenial to primitive thought or one that was not informed by
Western scientific thinking would have on the thought of Manus
children.

According to a variety of measures, the Manus were indeed
different from Genevans. Mead reported that children showed
less spontaneous animistic thought than Manus adults and seemed
to prefer cause-and-effect explanations. She noted the lack of
figures of speech in the Manus language and the practical
upbringing of children, which exposed them to ritual and super-
natural beliefs only after puberty. These results, which Mead
described as directly contradicting Piaget, she believed to
require a cultural, rather than a purely psychological, explanation. She suggested that either we can postulate a universal
psychological substratum (today perhaps we might call it a competence) towards animistic thought which can be suppressed by
cultural beliefs and practices, or we can view animism as the
tendency of particular minds and observe their residues in
particular languages and social institutions. The presence or
absence of animistic thought was not, for Mead, an aspect of a
developmental progression but the result of certain cultural
forces.

Mead's study of animism is typical of the first period of cross-
cultural research in its choice of problem but her results were
atypical. Prior to the 1960s, concepts such as animism, causality
and morality, drawn from Piaget's books of the 1920s and 1930s,
provided the focus of research attention. Later investigators
challenged, on methodological grounds, Mead's failure to find
animism in the thought of Manus children and psychologists,
among them Dennis (1943) argued that Piaget's qualitative descriptions of the nature of children's thought were valid for all
societies and reflected universal mental immaturity and experiences in childhood. The differences Dennis found in Hopi children
were of a quantitative rather than qualitative nature. The Hopi
children he interviewed provided more animistic and morally
realistic explanations than white American children of the same
age. In seeking to explain the Hopi delay in development, Dennis
administered an intelligence test and found that Hopi boys were
superior to white norms. He concluded that the delay reflected
Hopi cultural beliefs and not a general retardation in Hopi
intellectual development. Piaget's qualitative description of
children's thinking appeared to apply to children around the
world.

THE UNIVERSALITY OF PIAGET'S STRUCTURAL THEORY

In the late 1950s and early 1960s Piaget's conservation tasks
and his study of number (Piaget, 1952) were becoming more
widely known, as was his formal description of intellectual
development in terms of operational structures (Piaget, 1950).
The focus of cross-cultural research shifted from the qualitative
analysis of the nature of thinking and reflected Piaget's interest
in structure. This is not the place for a detailed account of the
rediscovery of Piaget by developmental psychologists. The
decline of behaviourism, a renewed interest in internal processes
and the publication of Flavell's (1963) thorough summary of
Piaget's work, making it accessible to Anglophones, may all have
contributed. Cross-cultural research reflected this resurgence of
interest.
    Among the earliest of this new breed of cross-cultural studies
was Price-Williams's (1961) investigation of Tiv children, in which
local materials were ingeniously used to test conservation of
continuous and discontinuous quantities. In asking whether children in cultures around the world were able to provide conserving
responses in the face of perceptual transformations of initially
equivalent materials, theoretical issues about children's use of
operations of identity, reversibility and reciprocity were being
raised. The conservation tasks are important as indicators of the
transition from pre-operational to concrete operational thinking.
Their popularity in cross-cultural research may reflect the ease
with which they could be assimilated to the rigorous demands of
American psychological methodology (Goodnow, 1969). Indeed,
the conservation tasks were eventually used by non-Genevans,
in a standardized format akin to intelligence tests (Tuddenham,
1971).
    The unified structure of the concrete operations, formalized
by Piaget in the eight groupings, was held to develop simultaneously and to imply that the various conservations on which
they were based would develop at the same time. But in research
with Genevan children Piaget found that on some conservation
tasks children provided evidence of concrete operational thinking
earlier than they had on others. Piaget called this progression in
the acquisition of the different conservations a horizontal 'décalage'
and among Genevan children reported that quantity was conserved first along with space and that these were followed by
weight and then volume (Piaget, 1950). Another dimension was
added to cross-cultural investigations with this further question
about the order in which conservations were acquired.
    During this period Piaget was invited to contribute to a new
publication, the 'International Journal of Psychology', which had an
editorial policy that encouraged trans-national and trans-cultural
research. Piaget's paper, published in the first issue, dealt with
the necessity and significance of such research and offers Piaget's
own evaluation of the enterprise (Piaget, 1966). It reflects the
dominant interest of this second period in its discussion of con-

servation and concrete operational thinking.

Piaget began his exposition by distinguishing his field, genetic psychology, from developmental psychology. He made clear his concern with the ontogenesis of cognition and his use of psychological investigations of development to reveal and explain psychological processes. He differentiated adequately conducted genetic psychological research, which revealed structures and operational functioning, from standard intelligence testing, which he described as concerned with performance. Piaget also identified four sets of factors which influence cognitive development and these have since been widely quoted. He described two of these factors as individual and two as socio-cultural and asserted that through cross-cultural research their relative effects could be assessed.

I can do little more than name the four factors Piaget identified; to explain them would require a paper on its own. The first set of individual factors was described by Piaget as biological and linked with the epigenetic system. Their influence was particularly relevant in the maturation of the nervous system. The second set, or equilibration factors, are involved in the general co-ordination of actions; Piaget views the operations of intelligence as the highest form of these regulations. The two socio-cultural factors entail a distinction between aspects of social and inter-personal activity which are common to all cultures and those which vary from one society to another. The latter Piaget labelled factors of educational and cultural transmission.

It is artificial to isolate these factors, since development, for Piaget, is seen as a function of the interaction of these four sets of forces.

In demonstrating how cross-cultural studies could identify the differential effects of these four factors, Piaget drew extensively on Mohseni's doctoral research carried out in Iran and Europe (Mohseni, 1966). Piaget framed two general questions for cross-cultural research: (1) Do we always find the same stages of development? and (2) Do we always find them at the same ages? Somewhat hypothetically, given the data then available, Piaget argued that the cross-cultural constancy of the sequential order of stage development supported the importance of epigenetic factors, but that a positive answer to the second question concerning the particular ages at which they appeared would be required to support the importance of maturation or the biological factors. Differences in the ages at which rural and urban Iranian children acquired conservation underlines the importance of socio-cultural factors, but Piaget speculated on the role of maturation in the development of sensorimotor and early semiotic functioning.

Rather than pursue in greater detail Piaget's efforts to dis-entangle the effects of his four factors, let us look at Dasen's (1972a) review which skilfully summarized cross-cultural re-search of this second era. In his focus upon issues of structure and problems of concrete operational thinking, Dasen captures the spirit of the second period of cross-cultural Piagetian research; in considering the effects of schooling, Westernization, urbanization and other socio-cultural factors, and in arguing for quasi-experimental studies which might link operational development to particular cultural variables, he foreshadows research of the third period.

Dasen suggested that general questions about the universality of the sequential succession of stages and the ages at which they appeared obscured three related points about Piaget's stage theory. He identified these as: (1) the global sequence of sensorimotor, pre-operational, concrete and formal operational development; (2) the sequences through which the same operational structures are applied to different concepts such as the horizontal décalage of quantity, weight and volume already mentioned in connection with conservation; and (3) the sequence of substages characteristic of the acquisition of particular concepts as assessed by specific tasks.

Dasen's first question has direct relevance to Piaget's genetic theory, and the evidence he marshalled supported Piaget's own prediction that the reasoning of adults in primitive societies would only reach concrete operational development. Formal operational thought, reflecting in Piaget's theory characteristics of Western scientific thinking, could not be expected universally.

Dasen's second and third questions, relating as they do to issues of research technique, suggest a psychological preoccupation with methodology becoming evident in Piagetian studies. Piaget's genetic theory neither predicted nor adequately explained the horizontal décalages observed in Western and non-Western studies. Dasen's plea for more individual data or the reanalysis of existing data in order to resolve the contradictions seen in descriptions of horizontal décalages in different cultures is that of a psychologist and not a genetic epistemologist. Worries about the failure of cross-cultural studies to find discrepancies in substage development are generally of a methodological nature, but Dasen's suggestion that investigators may be guilty of an ethnocentric bias in neglecting to pose alternative classifications foreshadows a growing unease with Piaget's commitment to Western scientific thought as the end point of development. All of these issues were elaborated in the decade which followed.

CULTURE AND COGNITIVE DEVELOPMENT

Piagetian studies of the last decade were influenced by cross-cultural psychologists who studied cognition from other theoretical perspectives. In a widely quoted article Cole and Bruner (1971) argued against a deficit interpretation of cultural differences, noting that in the United States it reflected a belief that 'middle-class behaviour is a yardstick of success' (p. 874). They employed the distinction between competence and performance current in linguistics to argue the need for clear understanding of the research context within which competence or capacity could be assessed and the relationship between that context and the wider social milieu of the individuals being studied. The distinction between competence and performance has been employed in recent summaries (Dasen, 1977a; Dasen and Heron, 1981). Its use has enabled psychologists to maintain their commitment to universal Piagetian structures (competences) while at the same time allowing them to explain observed cultural differences (performance) in terms of the particular demands of assessment procedures or of the cultural setting in which different individuals live.

As interest in situations and in cultural contexts increased in this era, Piaget's theory was repeatedly attacked for being ethnocentric. At one extreme Buck-Morss (1975) condemned the Piagetian project, asserting that it reflected the industrial, capitalist society in which it had originated. The end point of development – formal operational thought – she held to be a product of that system, characterized by its values, and she saw Piaget's ontogenetic theory as a justification of it.

The end point of development in operational thinking has been the concern of other psychologists not as sweeping in their condemnation. This interest may also reflect the accumulating evidence that in some societies many adults fail to achieve concrete operational thinking, particularly when measured using the conservation tasks (e.g., Dasen, 1974 among Australian Aborigines; Bovet, 1974 in Algeria). Cole (1975) and Jahoda (1980) have questioned the validity of the Piagetian approach in so far as it leads to the characterization of whole societies as predominantly pre-operational in their thought.

Arguments have been presented in response to this attack. Dasen and Heron (1981), bearing in mind the issue of competence and performance, note that it is unfortunate that the major diagnostic tool used to determine concrete operational thinking has been the conservation tasks. They also point out that adherence to the view of concrete operations as a unified structure sustains the interpretation that individuals who fail to conserve are also unable to deal conceptually with actions and their reversible operations. Referring specifically to Cole's example of Australian Aborigines, Dasen and Heron note that Aborigines find water with uncanny skill in harsh desert conditions but that they have not been concerned with the manner in which water is stored. They argue further that quantitative comparisons of amount of liquid may not have ecological importance but that spatial skills of a sophisticated order are both necessary for survival and demonstrable in Piagetian tasks.

A somewhat different, revisionist, defence of Piaget was provided by Greenfield (1976) in her discussion of the end point of development. She argued that the lesson of Piaget's approach to studying development is the need to identify its end point at the outset. She suggests that Piaget's own views about the end point may have changed, and that Western scien-

tific thought may no longer hold sovereign sway. She uses
Piaget's 1972 paper on diversities in formal operational development in adolescence, its revisions and his suggestion of 'new and
special structures that still remain to be discovered and studied'
(p. 11) to imply a shift to a cultural relativist position. To
buttress this interpretation Greenfield cites Bovet's Genevan-
supported cross-cultural research in which different end points
of operational development framed in terms of social roles are
suggested for Algerian men and women. The use of social roles
to define the end point of development is a major revision, and it
is not clear to me how far it may have gained Piaget's support
or represented his views.

Before drawing this brief and partial historical account to a
close I will discuss only one more of the many innovations in
this recent era, the concern with methodology. In his 1972
review, Dasen quoted Piaget's warnings about the pitfalls of
comparative research, but in the interest of offering conclusions
about the status of Piaget's structural theory he had eschewed
further discussion of technique. The issue was taken up by
Kamara and Easley (1977) in a volume on cross-cultural Piagetian
research edited by Dasen. They provide a thorough discussion
of problems, including the absence of reliable records of age,
the difficulty of working in an unfamiliar language and the
appropriateness of statistical techniques in evaluating stage
development. In keeping with the spirit of this era, they
suggest that too many investigators have treated the test situation in a standardized manner which has inhibited the discovery
of new structures. It is worth noting that not even Piaget and
his collaborators were exempt from their criticism. The past
decade has been one of doubt and reformulation.

SUMMING UP

What, then, can be said about Piaget's impact on cross-cultural
studies? Our conclusions necessarily reflect the criteria we use
in undertaking our evaluation. I should like to begin by suggesting that we must judge a theory as ambitious in its scope as that
of Piaget not by asking whether it is true or false, but by considering whether it is fertile or sterile in stimulating thought and
research.

Even from my incomplete historical survey, it seems to me that
there can be little doubt that Piaget has provided cross-cultural
psychologists with a great deal of grist to their mill. It is difficult to think of another theorist who has provoked quite so much
comparative research. Witkin's theory of psychological differentiation and its ecological elaboration with Berry is the closest runner
up (Witkin et al, 1962; Witkin and Berry, 1975). Dasen has com-
bined these two approaches in recent years, thus bringing
together Piaget's theory, which is aimed primarily at identifying
universal aspects of development, with that of Witkin, which

seeks to identify aspects of cognitive style in particular features
of socialization (Dasen, 1974).

It is more difficult to predict what the impact of Piaget's work
will be on future cross-cultural research. In preparing this paper
I recently asked two promising cross-cultural psychologists,
products of the past decade, what was new in cross-cultural
Piagetian research. Their replies, offered independently, suggested that the excitement was no longer in Piagetian studies but in
an attempt to bring the psychological study of cognition and
cognitive development more closely together with the everyday
concerns of cultural life (B. Rogoff and D. Wagner, personal
communications, April 1981). Their appraisal of the current
state of research mirrors the impact of Michael Cole's (1975;
Laboratory of Comparative Human Cognition, 1979) persuasive
proposals for an ethnographic psychology. Cole (1978) recently
lamented that standard laboratory procedures usually fail to
capture important aspects of intelligent behaviour, yet in turning
to anthropology he has found that anthropologists have studied
products such as language, myth and kinship, but not the
thought processes which he as a psychologist is interested in
learning more about.

Kinship is a universal puzzle; societies may differ in their
solutions, the degree of relationship they choose to recognize in
behaviour and in according verbal labels, but it is surely a
salient dimension of cultural life. In the past decade a number of
researchers, going back to Piaget's studies of the 1930s, examined
kinship cross-culturally (Greenfield and Childs, 1977; LeVine
and Price-Williams, 1974; Price-Williams, Hammond, Edgerton and
Walker, 1977). In fact, Greenfield compared the usefulness of
insights gained from Piaget's own studies of children's understanding of kinship and a formal, componential analysis deriving
from cognitive anthropology and reported that she found Piaget's
theory most useful in analysing children's developing understanding of kinship.

My two informants' comments reflect another theme from the
last decade. Responding to my pressure for information about
people doing cross-cultural work, one of them supplied the name
of a Genevan psychologist and mentioned that he spoke fifteen
languages. I already noted that Kamara and Easley (1977) produced an influential paper dealing with methodological issues in
comparative research and discussed at length the problems in
working in a second language and an alien culture. Speaking
personally, I have found the matter of language virtually insol-
uble. At one time I relied upon a system known as back translation - getting material translated, in my case, into Yoruba,
and then back into English by another Yoruba speaker. I could
then compare the two English versions - my original and that
which the Yoruba translation had yielded. While this system may
be useful in many situations, I am uneasy about using it to
diagnose cognitive competences. I wonder whether the intense
concern with method of the last decade - and an appropriate

concern, I believe – may have discouraged some investigators.

But I do not wish to end on such a pessimistic note. In the last year or two, Hallpike (1979) published an impressive book arguing the usefulness of Piaget's theory in providing anthropologists with a universal framework with which to order their highly diverse and sensitive descriptions of other cultures, and Seagrim and Lendon (1980) have produced a sophisticated report of their Piagetian-inspired studies of Australian Aboriginal intellectual development.

I have chosen to conclude my evaluation with Seagrim and Lendon's study because it provides a number of reasons for being optimistic about the future of cross-cultural Piagetian studies. It has acknowledged origins in the work of de Lemos (1969) and Dasen (1972b) in the second era of Piagetian research. Somewhat uniquely in the cross-cultural field, Seagrim and Lendon have built upon the work of their predecessors and at a general level supported Piagetian claims for universality. In their own words (Seagrim and Lendon, 1980, p. 181),

> This lays to rest finally, for us at least, the issue of competence: they have the same capacity to acquire the forms of knowledge of the physical world that Piaget has ascribed to white middle-class children brought up in a Western culture. However, they matched white children in these regards only if they are subjected to a total immersion in white culture for a duration and at ages we have not been able to specify.

With this statement Seagrim and Lendon settled one of the major controversies of the second era: the universality of Piaget's theory. In the qualifying sentence which follows they echo the concerns of the past decade. Despite their modesty about their understanding of cultural factors, they have made a major contribution to the issues of the past decade. Rather than viewing Piaget's theory as a psychological statement to be tested for its truth or falsity, they are careful in recognizing genetic psychology as epistemology. They use Piaget's analysis of the epistemic subjects' understanding of conservation – entailing qualitative and quantitative identity to direct their attention to those aspects of aboriginal life which would support or inhibit the development of quantitative understanding.

If future generations of cross-cultural psychologists build upon studies such as that of Seagrim and Lendon, informed as it is about the hazards of cross-cultural research and enriched as they are by a thorough understanding of Piaget's complex and fertile theory, cross-cultural studies of cognition should continue to thrive.

ACKNOWLEDGMENTS

I am grateful to G. Duveen and M. Scaife and especially to
P. Lloyd for reading and commenting on this paper. An earlier
version was presented to the Psychology Department at
University College, Cardiff.

REFERENCES

Bochner, S., Brislin, R.W. and Lonner, W.J. (1975) Introduction,
  in R.W. Brislin, S. Bochner and W.J. Lonner (eds), 'Cross-
  cultural Perspectives on Learning'. New York: Halsted, pp.
  3-36.
Boden, Margaret A. (1979) 'Piaget', London: Fontana.
Bovet, M.C. (1974) Cognitive Processes among Illiterate Children
  and Adults, in J.W. Berry and P.R. Dasen (eds), 'Culture
  and Cognition: Readings in Cross-cultural Psychology'.
  London: Methuen, pp. 311-34.
Buck-Morss, S. (1975) Socio-economic Bias in Piaget's Theory
  and its Implications for Cross-cultural Studies, in 'Human
  Development', 18, pp. 35-49.
Cole, M. (1975) An Ethnographic Psychology of Cognition, in
  R.W. Brislin, S. Bochner and W.J. Lonner (eds), 'Cross-
  cultural Perspectives on Learning'. New York: Halsted, pp.
  157-75.
Cole, M. (1978) Ethnographic psychology of cognition, in G.D.
  Spindler (ed.), 'The Making of Psychological Anthropology'.
  Berkeley: University of California Press, pp. 614-31.
Cole, M. and Bruner, J.S. (1971) Cultural Differences and
  Inferences about Psychological Processes, in 'American
  Psychologist', 26, 867-76.
Dasen, P.R. (1972a) Cross-cultural Piagetian Research, in
  'Journal of Cross-Cultural Psychology', 3, pp. 23-40.
Dasen, P.R. (1972b) The Development of Conservation in
  Aboriginal Children: A Replication Study, in 'International
  Journal of Psychology', 7, pp. 75-85.
Dasen, P.R. (1974) The Influence of Ecology, Culture and
  European Contact on Cognitive Development in Australian
  Aborigines, in J.W. Berry and P.R. Dasen (eds), 'Culture and
  Cognition: Readings in Cross-cultural Psychology'. London:
  Methuen, pp. 381-408.
Dasen, P.R. (1977a) Are Cognitive Processes Universal? A
  Contribution to Cross-cultural Piagetian Psychology, in N.
  Warren (ed.), 'Studies in Cross-cultural Psychology', vol 1.
  London: Academic Press, pp. 155-201.
Dasen, P.R. (ed.) (1977b) 'Piagetian Psychology: Cross-
  cultural Contributions'. New York: Halsted.
Dasen, P.R. and Heron, A. (1981) Cross-cultural Tests of
  Piaget's Theory, in H.C. Triandis, A. Heron and E. Kroeger
  (eds), 'The Handbook of Cross-cultural Psychology' ('Develop-

mental Psychology', vol. 4). Boston: Allyn & Bacon.
Dennis, W. (1943) Animism and Related Thought Tendencies in Hopi Children, in 'Journal of Abnormal and Social Psychology', 38, pp. 21-36.
Flavell, J.H. (1963) 'The Development Psychology of Jean Piaget'. Princeton, NJ: Van Nostrand.
Geiger, L. (1880) 'Contributions to the History and Development of the Human Race' (trans. D. Ascher). London: Trübner.
Gladstone, W.E. (1858) 'Studies on Homer and the Homeric Age', vol. 3. Oxford University Press.
Goodnow, J.J. (1969) Problems in Research on Culture and Thought, in D. Elkind and J.H. Flavell (eds), 'Studies in Cognitive Development: Essays in Honour of Jean Piaget'. New York: Oxford University Press, pp. 439-62.
Greenfield, P.M. (1976) Cross-cultural Research and Piagetian Theory: Paradox and Progress, in K. Riegel and J. Meacham (eds), 'The Developing Individual in a Changing World', vol. 1. The Hague: Mouton, pp. 322-33.
Greenfield, P.M. and Childs, C.P. (1977) Understanding Sibling Concepts: A Developmental Study of Kin Terms in Zinacantan, in P.R. Dasen (ed.), 'Piagetian Psychology: Cross-cultural Contributions'. New York: Halsted, pp. 335-58.
Hallpike, C.R. (1976) Is There a Primitive Mentality? in 'Man', 11, pp. 253-70.
Hallpike, C.R. (1979) 'The Foundations of Primitive Thought'. Oxford: Clarendon Press.
Jahoda, G. (1980) Theoretical and Systematic Approaches in Cross-cultural Psychology, in H.C. Triandis and W.W. Lambert (eds), 'Handbook of Cross-cultural Psychology' ('Perspectives', vol. 1.). Boston: Allyn & Bacon, pp. 69-141.
Kamara, A.J. and Easley, A. (1977) Is the Rate of Cognitive Development Uniform across Cultures? in P.R. Dasen (ed.), 'Piagetian Psychology: Cross-cultural Contributions'. New York: Halsted, pp. 26-63.
Laboratory of Comparative Human Cognition (1979) What's Cultural about Cross-cultural Cognitive Psychology? in 'Annual Review of Psychology', 30, pp. 145-72.
de Lemos, M.M. (1969) The Development of Conservation in Aboriginal Children, in 'International Journal of Psychology', 4, pp. 255-69.
LeVine, R.A. and Price-Williams, D. (1974) Children's Kinship Concepts: Cognitive Development and Early Experience among the Hausa, in 'Ethnology', 13, pp. 25-44.
Mead, M. (1932) An Investigation of the Thought of Primitive Children with Special Reference to Animism, in 'Journal of the Royal Anthropological Institute', 62, pp. 173-90.
Mead, M. (1954) Research on Primitive Children, in L. Carmichael (ed.), 'Manual of Child Psychology', 2nd ed. New York: Wiley, pp. 735-80.
Mohseni, N. (1966) La Comparaison des réactions aux épreuves d'intelligence en Iran et en Europe. Unpublished thesis,

University of Paris.
Piaget, J. (1926) 'The Language and Thought of the Child',
(trans. M. Gabain). London: Routledge & Kegan Paul.
Piaget, J. (1928) 'Judgment and Reasoning in the Child' (trans.
M. Warden). London: Routledge & Kegan Paul.
Piaget, J. (1929) 'The Child's Conception of the World' (trans.
J. and A. Tomlinson). London: Routledge & Kegan Paul.
Piaget, J. (1930) 'The Child's Conception of Physical Causality',
(trans. M. Gabain). London: Routledge & Kegan Paul.
Piaget, J. (1950) 'The Psychology of Intelligence' (trans. M.
Piercy and D.E. Berlyne). London: Routledge & Kegan Paul.
Piaget, J. (1952) 'The Child's Conception of Number' (trans.
C. Gatlesno and F.M. Hodson). London: Routledge & Kegan
Paul.
Piaget, J. (1966) Need and Significance of Cross-cultural
Studies in Genetic Psychology, in 'International Journal of
Psychology', 1, pp. 3-13.
Piaget, J. (1972) Intellectual Evolution from Adolescence to
Adulthood, in 'Human Development', 15, pp. 1-12.
Price-Williams, D.R. (1961) A Study Concerning Concepts of
Conservation of Quantities among Primitive Children, in 'Acta
Psychologica', 18, pp. 297-305.
Price-Williams, D.R., Hammond, D., Edgerton, C. and Walker,
M. (1977) Kin Concepts among Rural Hawaiian Children, in
P.R. Dasen (ed.), 'Piagetian Psychology: Cross-cultural
Contributions'. New York: Halsted, pp. 296-334.
Rivers, W.H.R. (1901) Primitive Color Vision, in 'Popular
Science Monthly', 59, pp. 44-58.
Seagrim, G. and Lendon, R. (1980) 'Furnishing the Mind:
A Comparative Study of Cognitive Development in Central
Australian Aborigines'. Sydney, Australia: Academic Press.
Tuddenham, R.D. (1971) Theoretical Regularities and Individual
Idiosyncrasies, in D.R. Green et al (eds), 'Measurement and
Piaget'. New York: McGraw-Hill, pp. 64-74.
Whiting, J.W.M. (1954) The Cross cultural Method, in 'The
Handbook of Social Psychology', vol 1. Cambridge, Mass:
Addison Wesley, pp. 523-31.
Whiting, J.W.M. (1968) Methods and Problems in Cross-cultural
Research, in G. Lindzey and E. Aronson (eds), 'The Hand-
book of Social Psychology', 2nd ed. vol. 2. Reading, Mass:
Addison-Wesley, pp. 693-728.
Witkin, H.A. and Berry, J.W. (1975) Psychological Differentiation
in Cross-cultural Perspective, in 'Journal of Cross-cultural
Psychology', 6, pp. 4-87.
Witkin, H.A., Dyk, R.B., Faterson, H.F., Goodenough, D.R.
and Karps, A. (1962), 'Psychological Differentiation'. New
York: Wiley.
Woodworth, R.S. (1910) The Puzzle of Color Vocabularies, in
'Psychological Bulletin', 7, pp. 325-34.

4 Cross-cultural conservation studies at the asymptote: striking out against the curve?

S. H. Irvine

FOCUS AND LIMITS

The definition of a concept is often achieved by illustrating both what it is and what it is not. The title suggests that the shape of Piagetian conservation research resembles a curve that has reached asymptote. The question is explored by examining research on conservation of quantity, weight and volume in young children reared in different cultures. Particular attention is given to work that claims to show that conservation increases with age to 50 per cent of the age group, but remains at that level even with age increase. Studies reporting this apparent phenomenon have been carried out in Australia, West Africa and Canada by Dasen (1972a, 1974, 1975). Heron and his associates claimed replications for weight conservation in Zambia (Heron and Simonsson, 1969; Heron, 1971) and in Papua New Guinea (Heron and Dowel, 1973). An earlier and influential account by Greenfield (1966) of research with village Wolof children also shows only 50 per cent attaining quantity conservation. She concluded that traditional belief systems strongly influenced the children's interpretation of transformations carried out by the experimenter. As her clinical methods have come under close scrutiny lately (J. Irvine, 1978; Greenfield, 1979), her 1966 work illustrates some issues in the clinical method that are unique to cross-cultural studies, and others that are general to psychology.

Reanalyses of existing material is the main method of the paper; and its emphasis is on construct validity. The issues addressed are those of the reliability of the dependent variable; and difficulties of establishing convergent validity and discriminant validity in the cross-cultural use of Piagetian tasks (PGTs). Before embarking on the reanalyses that form the bulk of the argument, it is necessary to specify the restraints that should be placed on its conclusions. First, doubts that are entertained concern only conservation research in cross-cultural contexts. Next, the more general issues raised at the end of the paper and the comparisons made with current attempts to verify cognitive models do not imply criticism of all previous work across cultures using PGTs. Current cross-cultural cognitive research has developed only because the pioneering work reviewed here was so well and fully described. Finally, the reanalyses are themselves a function of a particular view of what logical constraints are imposed by the use of PGTs in any context; and also by a view of the limitations of the clinical method in cross-cultural experiments. These views, and how they illuminate construct validation of Piagetian tasks, are described next.

GENERAL CHARACTERISTICS OF PIAGETIAN MEASUREMENT

Any outsider's concept of a very specialized field of human assessment should include an attempt to understand the data base: in particular, how data are collected and what their metric and logical properties are. Although one such attempt has already been made in the context of known assessment traditions in cross-cultural research (Irvine and Carroll, 1980, pp. 184-91), a second effort might still prove helpful here. Piagetian approaches to human assessment are based on a relatively small number of complex cognitive tasks applied individually to subjects whose chronological ages are the criteria for their assignment to groups. The subsequent verbal (or behavioural, as proxy for verbal) responses of individual subjects to these tasks are used to infer the presence or absence of logical mental operations in their thinking. Such responses are measured not in relation to group means, but as indicators of individual progress through certain stages of mental activity. The exact placement in these universal stages of an individual subject is a function of the experimenter's interpretation of a verbal response to an item or item-series. Just as a person who can jump will certainly be able to sit, crawl, walk and run, so a person who conserves quantity, weight and volume will be able to perform operations antecedent or necessary to conservation itself. Piagetian scales are absolute, and should be distinguished from psychometric test measurements, where any individual score may be relatively described as a moment around a mean, allowing products of moments, correlations and factor analysis for any group on which more than one measure exists.

Although that simple (or perhaps simplistic) account ought to offer some clues about the difficulties of relating variables derived from one kind of measurement to variables derived from another kind, it also offers some rather difficult construct validity puzzles to users of Piagetian tasks. One of these puzzles concerns the administration of a small number of items to a small sample. Whatever the *nature* of the measurement (absolute or relative), the number of items and the size of the sample or group eventually determine the amount of confidence in any judgment about the presence or absence of mental operations in a group of subjects. In example, if two yes-no items are administered to a group of size N, the number of subjects who could get two right by chance guessing would be $0.25N$. The observed proportion judged correct on the two items would require testing against the expected chance allocation.

The confidence limits of judgments involving responses to one, two, three or k items can be estimated. These confidence limits are crucial whenever developmental curves are drawn on the proportion of subjects meeting a criterion of competence within an age group. One of the general characteristics of Piagetian measurement has been the lack of reports publishing these confidence limits (Price, 1978). These limits are, of course, equally essential whenever comparison of proportions within age groups is made with a norm established in any experimental location. If between-group comparisons are made, incidentally, one must observe that absolute PGT measurements for individuals are invariably summed to provide success percentages for single age groups. These percentages are then compared in relative fashion, even by parametric statistics such as analysis of variance. An interesting paradox. In any event, proportions of conservers established in any group have chance limits and standard errors that are direct functions of how many items are used in relation to group size.

A second problem attends the accepted context for the use of PGTs, the clinical method. If a given response is taken to mean one thing in one culture, for example conservation or not conservation, but in effect means, or even could mean, something quite different in another, the basis of the clinical method's validity is threatened by yet another variable: what the experimenter thinks it means. Hence, in conferring developmental status on subjects, the experimenter's interpretations of what the subjects say or do, or refuse to say or do, are themselves variables. When language and culture are the same in the experimenter and in the particular group of subjects assessed, the probability of a correct interpretation of behaviour is greater than when either language or culture, or both, are different. As the experimenter's interpretation of a response is part of the method of establishing the validity of the construct assessed, that interpretation has to be correct.

In short, the standard method of using PGTs as measures of cognitive operations employs only a few items in small samples, in a number of different contexts. This implies that any classification of a group of individuals has large chance limits. An experimenter seeking to interpret results that arise from such procedures must first establish that the results could not have occurred by chance. That step seems essential whenever PGTs are administered. Any argument resting on the assertion that, although results are within chance limits, they are nevertheless valid because the clinical method increases reliability, must establish that the clinical method itself introjects no further unreliability. Within any single culture that assertion may never be disproved, since it is not capable of disproof. Across cultures, however, the clinical method is a priori suspect whenever the experimenter's cultural background or language is different from the subject's. The burden of that proof, especially when results fall within chance expectations, always rests with the experimenter. Now the focus is sharpened on specific studies dealing with conservation asymptotes in conservation in groups tested in Africa, Australia, Canada and Papua New Guinea. In particular, the necessary assumption that the asymptotes are indeed real phenomena, and not due to chance, is examined.

CONSERVATION AND CHANCE

Many reviews of attempts to employ PGTs across cultures exist, the most recent and critical being Brown and Desforges (1979) and Dasen and Heron (1981). Neither Brown and Desforges nor Dasen and Heron are satisfied with the progress of Piagetian conservation measurement. However, the contributions of cross-cultural fieldwork to mainstream theory are generally held to rest in variations or perturbations in rates of development through Piagetian stages whose sequence is largely confirmed. In particular, 'the rather odd but consistent finding, that in some populations a proportion of the children and adults do not seem to reach the last sub-stage of the concrete operational stage, which constitutes an important limitation to the universalist position' (Dasen and Heron, 1981, p. 296). Dissatisfaction with progress is not uncommon in cross-cultural assessment, but as Irvine and Carroll (1980, p. 194) point out, cross-cultural psychology, even as a discipline of verification, is so new that in the short term 'any particular scientific observation is subject to various biases arising from the researcher's theoretical perspective. Influenced is not only the choice of problem to be investigated, but also the method of investigation itself'. If one accepts this proposition, it is possible to ask if the finding of asymptote, which, if correct, is certainly as important as Dasen and Heron suggest, could itself be a function of that self-same short-run trial and error in cross-cultural theory and method. Whereas some errors, of course, may be carried over from those that already may be built into established Piagetian measures and experimental methods, other types of error may arise from the additional problems set by using PGTs in cultural contexts for which they were not originally intended. Both classes of error, involving the operationalization of the theory in its tasks and the interpretation of subject responses, may be resolved by construct validity studies. Until these are satisfactorily concluded, the interpretation of comparative developmental curves, and the reasons for them, may be impossible. This paper now sets out to examine the empirical base for the assumption that asymptote conservation curves are veridical, and that the experimenters' attributions of cause for observed failures to conserve in other cultures are valid.

The most difficult problem in mental measurement is the interpretation of observed group differences in test performance,
even when the number of items in a task is large, and the number
of subjects in any sample even larger (Irvine and Sanders, 1972;
Irvine and Carroll, 1980). Piagetian measurement is peculiarly
susceptible to challenges based simply on the number of items
in any single conservation task and the number of subjects in
any one sample. Both are unusually small. A uniquely cross-
cultural finding based on small item sizes and small sample
studies is asymptote in conservation in the concrete operations
stage around the 50 per cent mark in any age group. Does this
finding survive scrutiny of the number of items used to classify
subjects into stages, and also the number of subjects in an age
group used to establish developmental curves? As these are
empirical questions, two series of results are examined. The
first, by Dasen, employs the clinical method. The second, by
Heron, avoids the clinical issue by relying on behavioural response frequencies to a number of items. At this point in the
discussion the clinical method itself is not the subject of scrutiny,
although it will be later. The concern is simply the relationship
between the number of items used in the assessment, the size of
the sample, and confidence limits.

Dasen's studies

These studies are eminently suitable for reanalysis because of
the full reports of results and the consistency of the experimental procedures carried out by Dasen himself. Tasks of conservation of quantity, weight and volume were performed by
purposive samples of Australian aborigines at Hermannsburg and
Areyonga, by West African subjects at Adiopodoume, Ivory
Coast, and by Eskimos at Cape Dorset, Canada.

Particularly careful to preserve his tasks and his method of
administering them, Dasen conducted his experiments on samples
of approximately ten children in each age group from eight to
sixteen years. He administered two tasks on quantity, two on
weight and two on volume conservation. Table 4.1 summarizes
his results for each of these locations, listing the frequencies
judged to be conservers. The results can now be reanalysed
to discover how many observations survive a test of chance,
assuming that on a single yes-no item the chance probability of
success is 0.5, and on two successive items, 0.25.

In a group of given size, one-quarter of its members could be
classified as conservers by chance. This proportion has confidence limits based on the group's size. Dasen's samples contained ten children, and this means that any proportion from
zero to 0.52 lies within two standard errors. In short, six
children in every ten would have to be classified as conservers
before one could be certain that the chance limits set by the
number of tasks and the sample size were exceeded. The figures
in Table 4.1 show that only a few classifications exceed those

Table 4.1 *Dasen's Conserver Frequencies compared against chance*

Age group	Quantity				Weight				Volume			
	8	10	12	14	8	10	12	14	8	10	12	14
Ivory Coast (IC)	1	2	8*	9*	0	2	6*	6*	0	1	6*	4
Cape Dorset (CD)	0	6*	4	6*	0	3	3	2	0	5	5	3
Hermannsburg (HE)	2	3	5	7*	1	1	2	2	0	3	2	2
Areyonga (AR)	2	0	2	3	1	1	1	1	3	2	1	3
Lowest column frequency	0	2	2	3	0	1	1	1	0	1	1	2
Frequency for significant X^2	5	5	8	9	5	7	7	7	5	7	7	8
Reached in comparing	–	$AR/_{CD}$	$AR/_{IC}$	$AR/_{IC}$	–	–	–	–	–	–	–	–

Note: Frequencies in upper half of the table are compared with the probability that $0.25N$ could be assigned conserver status by chance responses to two items. Frequencies of 6 or more satisfy this criterion with 10 in each group. The lower half of the table shows the lowest column frequency, and below it the minimum frequency in any other sample of 10 subjects that would be required for a chi-square test of the differences between samples to reach significance.

chance limits. A second matter concerns the confidence that can be placed in any proportion of conservers in a group of size ten compared with any other proportion in another group. If, for example, one asserts that children from culture X develop conservation skills at a faster rate than children for culture Y, we must be sure that the points of comparison - proportions within age groups - differ significantly from each other. Without that certainty, the points on the curve could be random fluctuations around a population mean. The observed differences would not then be capable of serious interpretation. Table 4.1 also shows that only three out of a possible eighteen inter-group comparisons reach significance, when subjected to chi-square tests.

Reanalysis, then, reveals that little confidence can be placed in the results listed so far. Only the oldest groups are classified beyond chance limits, in quantity, weight and volume. These are always the same groups, and the final number classified is invariably greater than the 50 per cent 'asymptote'. Whatever the true population value, we know that the present classifications have a single standard error of more than 13, and confidence limits of nearly 27 per cent: sobering thoughts for those who might be tempted to generalize from such results. Finally, Dasen (1975) himself has used these very results to support Berry's (1976) ecological press theory of cognitive development, based on cultural habitats. One has to conclude that Dasen's results lend support to no theoretical position at present, since reliable comparisons of cognitive development rates cannot emerge from data with such large standard errors of measurement.

Heron's Zambian studies
Heron's work on conservation in Zambia is pivotal, first because it has often been cited as evidence for conservation asymptote; and also because it is one of the few series where subjects were not required to substantiate, in clinical situations, their signalled responses to stimulus items by answering questions put to them by a foreign experimenter. Heron, in fact, developed a sign-mime[1] procedure for classifying responses to a series of thirteen yes-no items. These were administered to groups of black and white children. Classification as a conserver of weight rested on signalled responses to three critical items (Heron and Simonsson, 1969, p. 284). As each item that was wrong on first presentation was also administered on a second occasion, the probability of getting any one of these three items correct by chance is 0.75. Hence, three critical items could have been guessed correctly by a proportion of 0.422 of the sample. Table 4.2 now examines the observed frequencies of African children classified in each age group against the expectancy that these frequencies are not significantly different from what could be expected from chance response to three critical items. Only one χ^2, and that for the youngest group, approaches significance. If the same exercise is repeated for the much smaller samples of white children, tested at the same time in Zambia as the black

group, the null hypothesis is supported only for eight- and nine-year-olds.

Table 4.2 Zambian conservers by age groups (reanalysed from Heron and Simonsson, 1969)

Age	7	8	9	10	11	12	13	14	15	Overall
Judged conservers	1	9	10	11	13	20	5	12	8	89
Expected chance frequencies*	5	9	11	9	10	16	8	8	5	76
Totals	11	21	25	21	24	37	20	20	12	181

*Note: Expected chance frequencies based on probability that 0.422 of total may get three items correct when the possibility of any single correct item is 0.75. No entry in the table reaches significance when subjected to a chi-square test, nor indeed do the entries overall.

To conclude, the procedures adopted by Heron produced non-chance classification in groups of white children culture-consonant with the original standardization sample for the task (Heron and Simonsson, 1969, p. 285). In culture alien groups of black children, classifications occur at the chance level, irrespective of age. Moreover, these classifications bore no relationship to other cognitive measures that intercorrelated well with each other (Heron, 1971). Knowing, as we do from many cross-culture test validation studies, that individual items do not travel well from one culture to another, not even the simplest of them (Irvine and Sanders, 1972; Poortinga, 1971; van der Flier, 1975), it is reasonable to conclude that the results provide less evidence for asymptote conservation than they do for task unreliability.

If the tasks are unreliable outside their culture or language, results around the chance level are to be expected, irrespective of the number of replications. If one requires an analogy, the roughly 50 per cent head or tails seen in coin tossing, irrespective of currency, culture or language, is attributable to the fact that a coin has two sides, not to dispositional qualities in humans that engineer the result.

QUESTIONS OF VALIDITY

While some valid measurements are possible even if unreliable measures are used (one will hit the target occasionally but unpredictably), the major task in psychological assessment is that of steady validation of the measures that mark key constructs. Pressing problems of construct validity associated with the use of PGTs are evident in Heron and Dowel's work on conservation in Papua New Guinea. Construct validity can be discussed conveniently under three headings - generalizability, convergent validity and discriminant validity - and the results in Papua New Guinea fortuitously demonstrate unresolved issues in each area.

Generalizability
When subjects are classified consistently by different measures from the same methodological tradition (say, two intelligence tests constructed by different psychologists), this is taken as evidence of valid measurement. The debate over the order of the appearance of conservation of quantity, weight and volume in individual and groups reveals that conservation tasks do not always classify the same subjects as conservers (Dasen, 1972b, pp. 32-3). Nevertheless, Heron and Dowel produce what seem to be strong evidence for PGT generalizability when they first administer two items by Dasen's method, and then compare that classification by cross-tabulation, with results of seven (not three, as formerly in Zambia) actual items administered to subjects in Papua New Guinea (PNG). The resulting agreement of 83 per cent is very high indeed, and would refute charges that conservation tasks did not generalize across subjects because they are unreliable.

Examination of Heron's procedures shows, however that the two items administered under Dasen's clinical conditions are also involved in Heron's total of seven correct in order to be classified as a conserver. We are now dealing with the correlations of a (two items), with $a + b$ (these two plus another five). If the variance in a is small (it should be if the items are given twice), and if the correlation between these two (a) and the other five (b) is large, the correlation between a and $a + b$ approaches unity. Unfortunately, Heron provides no item indices, but some attempt to reconstruct these (Table 4.3) shows that the high agreement between Dasen's and Heron's classifications is plausibly explained by correlating two easy items with the same two plus another five that are closely correlated with these. In fact, one would be very surprised if, under these conditions, anything less than close agreement existed.

Convergent validity
Conservation tasks have been difficult to relate to measurement procedures that are not Piagetian. Heron twice (Heron, 1971; Heron and Dowel, 1973) tried to relate conservation status to problem-solving skills, using figural analogy items of 'matrices' origin. The Zambian results were no better than the PNG results. Conservation status was not related to superior problem-solving ability in academic attainment in either experiment, although moderate and significant correlations between figural analogy totals and school attainment were reported. It is difficult,

then, to produce evidence for conservation status apart from the small number of conservation tasks themselves; and, as was noted earlier, conservation tasks appear specific to quantity, weight and volume, with no clear evidence of generalizability across all three types.

Table 4.3 Hypothetical item difficulties and correlations with classification as conserver (based on Heron and Dowel, 1973)

Item	7	6	5	4	3	2	1
Conservers	1.0	1.0	1.0	1.0	1.0	1.0	1.0
Non-conservers	0.0	0.14	0.30	0.38	0.54	0.68	0.84
Overall (difficulty)	0.50	0.57	0.65	0.69	0.77	0.84	0.92
Phi-coefficient	1.0	0.87	0.73	0.67	0.55	0.44	0.29

Note: Each entry in the top half of the table is a hypothetical proportion of subjects correct for a perfect scale of seven items. This could mean that all conservers got each item of the seven correct, but that non-conservers got progressively fewer items correct. The non-conservers' proportions are twice the difference between 50 per cent (the number of conservers) and the hypothetical item difficulties, which range from 92 per cent correct on the easiest item, to 50 per cent on the most difficult. It is unlikely that the Heron and Dowel items did in fact form a perfect scale, but the argument is not invalidated, far from it, by that assumption for purposes of illustration.

Discriminant validity
If a task measures conservation, it must be demonstrated that it does not also measure something else. This is the essence of discriminant validity. One has to substantiate a claim that a task measures X, and not X plus Y or even Z. The Papua New Guinea report by Heron and Dowel produces a fine illustration of the PGT dilemma.

In a quest for greater reliability in the classification of conservers, Heron increased his criterion from three critical items (Zambia) to seven critical items (PNG). He lists the frequencies of subjects with all seven correct down to none correct (Heron and Dowel, 1973, p. 212). If, for a moment, one assumes that these frequencies had represented a perfect scale of seven items, Table 4.3 is the result, along with hypothetical item indices. The point of the illustration is that, even in optimum scale conditions, the most difficult item in a small number of tasks defines the total number of conservers. Next, the intercorrelation of that item with all others determines how well conservation is defined by the measure of seven items. Ironically, in Table 4.3, the most difficult item correlates perfectly with the status of conserver (it has to), but the easier the items, the less they correlate with conserver status. That happens to be an experimental fact, or artefact. In short, the most difficult item determines the final number of conservers, but because it also has the greatest variance around the 50 per cent mark it is liable to be measuring not just conservation, but a lot else besides that could be quite specific to the item but have no relation to conservation whatsoever. Given that finding, we realize that the 54 per cent of PNG subjects classified as conservers may indeed contain some conservers, but there is no guarantee that they are all conservers or, far more likely indeed, that those excluded are not also conservers. Once again, the asymptote of 54 per cent conservers is a function of experimental conditions, in which discriminant validity checks have not been evident, and unreliability seems the inevitable consequence.

These cross-cultural conservation studies offer empirical veri-fication of the view advanced by Irvine and Carroll (1980) that PGT use in non-Western contexts has shown some generalizability, little or no convergent validity and no discriminant validity. There emerge three conclusions, easily researched for their generality by scrutiny of other studies, from the Dasen and Heron work in conservation. First, the asymptote phenomenon does not survive the plausible hypothesis that it is a function of experimental error. Next, if the chance hypothesis is to be refuted, it will require more attention to the metric properties of items than has characterized PGT research hitherto. Last, unresolved problems of generalizability, convergent and dis-criminant validity cloud the use of PGTs, whatever the culture, but particularly in non-Western contexts.

THE CLINICAL METHOD ACROSS CULTURES

All clinical methods compound issues of reliability and validity because the experimenter processes the subject's response and makes a judgment about it. This procedure is difficult enough to replicate and cross-validate when culture and language differ-ences between experimenters and their subjects are non-existent. An important observation about Dasen's work in conservation is that chance frequencies are much less when he is working with French-speaking West Africans. French is Dasen's own language, and it is the original language of the PGT tasks. Outside that context chance frequency allocations are the norm. The clinical method seems particularly suspect when transplanted from the experimenter's native soil. Until recently, however, evidence of disagreement among cross-culture PGT users about the meaning of subject behaviour in clinical contexts has been hard to find. Nevertheless, a debate between Greenfield (1966, 1979) and Judith Irvine[2] (1978) about what subject responses among the Wolof might mean casts even more doubt about the validity of conservation classifications in experimenter-alien contexts. The

issue in the debate between Greenfield and J. Irvine boils down
to the different meanings given by the two experimenters to
identical responses from subjects. The debatable responses from
Wolof subjects in the same village, visited by each experimenter
independently, were 'You poured it' and silence. Greenfield
interpreted a 'You poured it' explanation of transformation of
water levels as the attribution by Wolof subjects of 'magic-
action' or benign sorcery on the part of the experimenter. She
also interpreted this verbal response as evidence of non-conservation, as she did silence.

J. Irvine adopted a different clinical method, in which she
posed as a language learner having difficulty with Wolof
expressions such as 'equal to', 'level with' and 'same as', which
as Greenfield herself reports (1966, p. 232) are both confusing
and confused. J. Irvine produced her beakers only after some
months of residence in the village above, with no assistants.
On receiving the reply 'You poured it' she feigned bewilderment,
and said she did not understand. Almost invariably, the subjects
followed up by offering conservation responses.

*Table 4.4 Discriminant validity in clinical methods of classifying
conservers in other cultures*

Subject response	'You poured it'	Silence
Greenfield (1966) variables	belief in magic action vs conservation	conservation vs non-conservation
Judith Irvine (1978) variables	politeness/silence vs rudeness/garrulousness	politeness vs rudeness

The expression 'You poured it' was a laconic way of saying
that, although the levels were transformed by pouring, the
quantity of water remained the same as before. The Wolof,
continues J. Irvine, do not value garrulousness, among either
themselves or their children. Silence shows politeness to a
superior, if one has already spoken. It does not always mean
failure to comprehend. Table 4.4 illustrates the dilemma of the
clinical method. Here are identical responses: Greenfield thinks
they mean one thing, J. Irvine says they mean something else.
For lack of any theory to guide our judgment, the debate is
worth pursuing. Greenfield's (1979) response to J. Irvine's
challenge is that Irvine's clinical methods are not identical with
her own and that Irvine's results are 'quite dubious'. But, once
the clinical method is allowed, it can never be too clinical, since
the validity of the experimenter's judgment depends not on the
clinical method's strictness of form but on its capacity to get at
the truth from the subject. It may, in consequence, seem odd
that a clinical method should lay claim to experimental rigour as

a defence. To categorize the problem as one of discriminant validity is helpful, since the subject's response is said to measure one thing, when it could be said to measure something else entirely. Greenfield, then, is left with the problem of vindicating her claim to measure conservation in unschooled Wolof subjects against the anthropological veto. One piece of evidence helpful to Greenfield would be non-chance classification of village subjects. Unfortunately, Greenfield's classifications of conservers among unschooled village subjects fail to survive chance tests based on two items given once, either within each age group or, when collapsed, across age groups. If, as J. Irvine suggests, Greenfield's interpretation of the subjects' responses in the village is incorrect, and what she was measuring was not conservation and was unrelated to it, allocations around the chance level would be predictable.

How far the anthropological veto extends to other cross-cultural conservation studies is unknown, although it has been applied often enough in the name of 'competence'; but the psychological dilemma is real enough. Standardized procedures may increase grounds for comparing results from different groups. Across cultures, that very standardization may ensure the existence of attribution errors, yet idiosyncratic clinical work increases the probability of experimenter biases. The foreign experimenter, working in a foreign culture, with few items on small samples, has an unenviable scientific task.

Interpreters and reviewers of results, on the other hand, have to decide what results gained under such conditions add to our knowledge of cognition. As a counsel to caution, a recent survey of conservation studies in Africa (Unesco, 1974) shows that only five of twenty-five were undertaken by psychologists indigenous to the culture and language of the subjects.

CULTURE AND COGNITION POST-PIAGET

Finally, it would be a mistake to believe that the ills of cross-cultural conservation studies could be solved if only there were enough indigenous psychologists to administer PGTs to subjects in their own language. That seems too naive and all-embracing a cure. A recent article by Price (1978, pp. 17-18) reviewing conservation studies in Papua New Guinea offers good prima facie evidence that the language of the subject in any given culture is a variable operating on PGT performance. It is easier for subjects to explain conservation responses in some PNG languages than in others. We have already noted that Dasen's results with older French-speaking West African subjects exceed chance levels. The most telling experimental evidence linking logical tasks with structural language characteristics has, surprisingly, been available in the cross-cultural literature for some time. Gay and Cole (1967, pp. 67-83) relate the group variability of concept formation involving conjunction, negation

and disjunction, to the characteristics of Kpelle and English.
As the Kpelle language has a special structural characteristic
for dealing with disjunction, Kpelle subjects do much better in
disjunction concept formation tasks than English-speaking
subjects. On the other hand, Kpelle subjects find implications,
involving 'if . . . then' propositions, hard to do, and equivalence
almost impossible. As PGTs in conservation involve both
implication and equivalence - 'If I pour the water in here will
I have more, less, or will the amount be the same?' - we know
that the form of the question is structurally difficult for the
subject. Kpelle responses to such questions then need discriminant validity studies in order to find out what is being
assessed by the question. Conservation competence is only one
of several plausible alternatives. Stimulus identity in the ver-
nacular does not guarantee either equivalent performance or
identical strategies or similar control processes when subjects
solve logical problems posed by the stimuli.

Language variation offers clues to cognitive structure when
the nature of the variation is known and performance that is
language-bound is predictable. Although no evidence of experi
menter use of structural differences in language has appeared in
cross-cultural conservation research since 1967, the work may
continue meaningfully if language variation becomes a cultural
variable of the future. In the past, culture and language variables have been confused, lacking precise hypotheses based
on knowledge of the language characteristics of Eskimos,
Aborigines, Papuans, Zambians, to name only a few. A second
condition for continuing conservation studies, it seems, must
also be satisfied. The original PGTs are being replaced by
others, as better theory becomes evident. Research by Bryant
(1974) and by Wallace (1972) has already produced alternatives.
Any elementary cognitive task that is eventually employed in a
search for conservation must be constructed from sound experimental theory, and subjected to consistent validity studies.
Recent work in cross-cultural assessment, involving elementary
cognitive tasks (Irvine, 1979; Irvine and Reuning, 1981;
Irvine, Schoeman and Prinsloo, 1980) reveals that simple
additive encoding process models are robust across cultures,
age ranges and symbol types. The theoretical advance from
these experiments is small in proportion to the amount of work
needed to verify it. So it might also be, for modified Piagetian
tasks.

Language structure, then, may be a cultural variable that is
heuristic enough to use as an independent variable. In conjunction with cognitive tasks that have evolved from criticism of
Piagetian theory, conservation studies across cultures might
not be unprofitable. As they stand at the moment, however,
they have some way to go before offering any direct challenge
to traditional views of cognitive development in children. It is
difficult, therefore, to be optimistic about the value of future
cross-culture PGT research on conservation in a quest for a

general theory of intellect. Cautious judgment compels a view of cross-cultural PGT assessment as that short-run trial and error behaviour characteristic of the beginnings of a new science. To claim more than this would be to do psychology itself a disservice.

NOTES

1 Heron refers to this as non-verbal. The signal is non-verbal, but it is doubtful whether the cognitive operations exclude use of verbal symbols.
2 Hereafter referred to as J. Irvine, who is, incidentally no relative or associate of the present writer.

REFERENCES

Berry, J.W. (1976) 'Human Ecology and Cognitive Style'. New York: Halsted Press.
Brown, G. and Desforges, C. (1979) 'Piaget's Theory, a Psychological Critique'. London: Routledge & Kegan Paul.
Bryant, P. (1974) 'Perception and Understanding in Young Children'. London: Methuen.
Dasen, P.R. (1972a) Etude preliminaire du developpement cognitif chez l'enfant ivoirien, Baoule et Ebrie. Mimeographed report, University of Geneva.
Dasen, P.R. (1972b) Cross-Cultural Piagetian Research, a Summary, in 'Journal of Cross-Cultural Psychology', 3, pp. 23-9.
Dasen, P.R. (1974) The Influence of Ecology, Culture and European Contact on Cognitive Development in Australian Aborigines, in J.W. Berry and P.R. Dasen (eds), 'Culture and Cognition'. London: Methuen, ch. 24.
Dasen, P.R. (1975) Concrete Operational Development in Three Cultures, in 'Journal of Cross-Cultural Psychology', 6, pp. 156-72.
Dasen, P.R., and Heron, A. (1981) Cross-Cultural Tests of Piaget's Theory, in H.C. Triandis and A. Heron (eds), 'Handbook of Cross-Cultural Psychology', vol. 4. Boston: Allyn & Bacon, ch. 7.
Gay, J. and Cole, M. (1967) 'The New Mathematics in an Old Culture'. New York: Holt, Rinehart & Winston, ch. 10.
Greenfield, P.M. (1966), 'Studies in Cognitive Growth'. New York: Wiley, ch. 11, pp. 225-56.
Greenfield, P.M. (1979) Response to 'Wolof "Magical Thinking" Culture and Conservation Revisited' by Judith T. Irvine, in 'Journal of Cross-Cultural Psychology', 10, pp. 251-6.
Heron, A. (1971) Concrete Operations, 'g' and Achievement in Zambian Children, in 'Journal of Cross-Cultural Psychology', 2, pp. 325-36.
Heron, A. and Dowel, W. (1973) Weight Conservation and

Matrix-solving Ability in Papuan Children, in 'Journal of Cross-Cultural Psychology', 4, pp. 207-19.

Heron, A. and Simonsson, M. (1969) Weight Conservation in Zambian Children: A Non-verbal Approach, in 'International Journal of Psychology', 4, pp. 281-92.

Irvine, J. (1978) Wolof 'Magical Thinking': Culture and Conservation Revisited, in 'Journal of Cross-Cultural Psychology', 9, pp. 300-10.

Irvine, S.H. (1979) The Place of Factor Analysis in Cross-Cultural Methodology and its Contribution to Cognitive Theory, in L. Eckensberger et al. (eds), 'Cross-Cultural Contributions to Psychology'. Lisse, Netherlands; Swets and Zeitlinger.

Irvine, S.H., and Carroll, W.B. (1980) Testing and Assessment Across Cultures: Issues in Methodology and Theory, in H.C. Triandis and J.W. Berry (eds), 'Handbook of Cross-Cultural Psychology', vol. 2. Boston: Allyn & Bacon. ch. 5, pp. 181-244.

Irvine, S.H., and Reuning H. (1981) 'Perceptual Speed' and Cognitive Controls: Tasks in Reconstructing Group Test Theory and Practice Within and Across Cultures, in 'Journal of Cross-Cultural Psychology', 12, pp. 425-44.

Irvine, S.H., and Sanders, J.T. (1972) Logic, Language and Method in Construct Identification Across Cultures, in L.J. Cronbach and P.J.D. Drenth (eds), 'Mental Tests and Cultural Adaptation'. The Hague: Mouton, pp. 425-6.

Irvine, S.H., Schoeman, A. and Prinsloo, W. (1980) Putting Cognitive Theory to the Test: Ability Testing Reassessed using the Cross-Cultural Method. Paper given at Fourth International Symposium on Educational Testing, Antwerp, June 1980.

Poortinga, Y. (1971) 'Cross-Cultural Comparison of Maximum Performance Tests'. 'Psychologia Africana' Monograph Supplement no. 6.

Price, J.R. (1978) Conservation Studies in Papua New Guinea: A Review, in 'International Journal of Psychology', 13, pp. 1-24.

Unesco (1974) 'The Development of Science and Mathematics Concepts in Young Children in African Countries'. UNESCO-UNICEF, printed by University of Sussex.

Van der Flier, H. (1975) The Comparability of Individual Test Performances, in 'Nederlands Tijdschrift voor de Psychologie', 30, pp. 41-9.

Wallace, J.G. (1972) 'Stages and Transition in Conceptual Development'. Slough, Bucks: National Foundation for Education Research, ch. 7.

Part 4

Education

5 Piaget and education: a positive comment

C.K. Mackay

I think it was Voltaire who observed that the art of being boring consisted in leaving nothing out. While I cannot guarantee that this present contribution will not be boring, I can guarantee it will not be for that reason. It would take more than a short paper like this even to catalogue the wealth of literature relating to Piaget's contributions to education, and I certainly don't intend to try to do so. Instead, I want to look at three areas of relevance: Piaget's direct contribution to education; some applications of his theoretical formulations to educational practice; and finally, what I consider to be Piaget's most important and enduring contribution, the provision of a multi-disciplinary and developing theoretical framework from which precise psychological theories of development, learning and instruction may be derived.

Let me begin with some comments on Piaget's direct involvement with educational practice. Reviews of this aspect are widespread; two short but enlightening biographies are given by Lunzer (1976) and Ginsburg and Opper (1979). Let me simply remind you here that Piaget was addressing himself to specifically pedagogical problems as early as the 1930s; in the 1940s and 1950s he was chairman of the International Bureau of Education, and, as Lunzer (1976, p. xiii) has it, 'His astonishing grasp of the problems of education on a world scale emerges most clearly in the two essays "Science of Education" and the "Psychology of the Child" (published in one volume by Longman, 1971), one of which was written in 1935 and the other thirty years later.' His direct contributions to education are well summarized in these essays. What I find as an attractive feature of them is that Piaget comes across not as an insulated guru, but as a man who has intimate knowledge of both children and the processes of education. Consider his comments on his visit to Susan Isaacs at the Malting House school in Cambridge (Piaget, 1971, p. 169):

But the impression that my visit to this astonishing experimental school made upon me was twofold. On the one hand, even these exceptionally favorable circumstances were insufficient to erase the various features of the child's mental structure and did no more than accelerate their development. On the other hand, some form of systematization applied by the adult would perhaps not have been wholly harmful to the pupils.

Or the commendation with which he refers to the 'wisdom of the Canadian school inspector who divided every class into two rooms, in order, he said, that the children should have time "to work", and that the teacher would not talk to all of them together the whole day long' (Piaget, 1971, p. 169). His wide experience of schools in Eastern Europe gave him valuable insights into the promotion of activity methods and vocational education. In Scotland he singled out Moray House for especial praise in its attempts to train university graduates together for both primary and secondary school teaching. At the same time, he was not unaware of the defects of the training provided even by that centre of excellence. He recalls with approval (1971, p. 77) that

> Claparède had already expressed the opinion, in his day, that a sufficient period in a teacher's training should always be given over to practice in animal training, since when that training fails the experimenter is bound to accept that it is his own fault, whereas in the education of children failures are always attributed to the pupil.

This latter comment was made during a discussion of the merits and demerits of teaching machines which Piaget appeared to accept as being of undeniable service where it is necessary to transmit facts or even in the comprehension of systems. But in the major enterprise to which education is wedded, that is the development of intelligence rather than the mere stocking of memory, or, as Piaget (1971, p. 51) has it, 'to produce intellectual explorers rather than mere erudition', the teaching machine is of little value; indeed, its use to promote inventiveness seems to be counter-productive.

I want to leave this area at this point. Let me make it absolutely clear, however, that I recognize I have done justice to neither Piaget's erudition nor his brilliance. Others more competent than I have done so on many occasions. What I have tried to do is to show that this brilliant scholar was also a man of practical experience and wisdom. While I want to argue that his theoretical insights have the most profound implications for educational practice, I want to begin by asserting that Piaget was, unlike many educational theorists, himself knowledgeable of the practical problems educationalists face.

The second area I want to consider is that of the application of Piagetian theory to educational practice. There is again a vast and rapidly expanding literature on this topic, and again it is

beyond my powers to summarize it (see, e.g., Gallagher and
Easley, 1978; Ginsburg and Opper, 1979; Murray, 1979; Schwebel
and Raph, 1974; Varma and Williams, 1976; Wadsworth, 1978).
I want to look at a few highly selected examples and then make
some general comments. The examples come from early schooling
and from science and mathematics teaching.

Two of Piaget's fundamental propostions are

(1) that learning is secondary to development; and
(2) that learning is most effective when the learner is
    actively involved.

Both these propositions have had enormous influence in the field
of early education. Teachers of young children have been given
guidance, in the first case, on what it might be appropriate to
teach and, in the second, on how what is appropriate might be
taught. Similarly, in the field of science teaching, the application of these Piagetian principles has led in Britain to the
development of Science 5-13, in Australia to the Australian
Science Education Project, and in the United States to the
Science Curriculum Improvement Study (see Lovell and Shayer,
1978, for a critical evaluation of these developments). In mathematics teaching, the Dienes' approach and the Nuffield Mathematics Project make explicit their debt to Piagetian theory.
Collis (1975) and Easley (1978) give further consideration to
the influence of Piagetian ideas on mathematics teaching.

But however successful these direct applications of Piaget's
theory may prove to be in the fullness of time, we have to admit
that they tend to be overshadowed by a host of misapplications.
It may be that our North American friends are somewhat more
impetuous than we in calling for improvements in education; it
may be that their system allows the individual teacher less chance
to choose her own teaching methods than is usual in Britain.
Whatever the reason, it would appear that, particularly in the
field of early education, Piaget's theory has been used to justify
a range of pedagogical nonsenses. An excellent summary of
these in North American practice is provided by De Vries (1978).
In this paper I want to consider some of the blunders due to
misunderstandings of the two principles already stated. Some
teachers either have been led to believe that, since all development is spontaneous, their role is reduced to that of custodial
care, or they have been forced to the belief that Piaget is wrong.
Both these absurd conclusions are, in my opinion, the result of
misunderstandings of Piaget's use of such concepts as spontaneity
and equilibration.

You will recall that Piaget (1970) posits four factors as being
involved in development: maturation, physical experience
(including logico mathematical experience), social interaction
(including language), and equilibration. The contribution of
each of these factors is essential for normal development, as
Piaget makes clear. Development is 'spontaneous' only in that

the contributions of maturation and physical and social experience are taken as necessities of a normal environment. It is the self-regulating character of the equilibration process that is unusual in Piaget's scheme, but the postulation of this feature does not in any way remove the necessity for the contribution of each of the three classical factors of development. It does mean there are limits to how far a child's logico-mathematical experience can be meaningful to him at any one time; it does mean that assimilation of new knowledge is regulated by what is already known; but by stressing this aspect of developmental influence, Piaget is in no way denying the fundamental importance of other factors. The teacher's role is therefore crucial in providing the appropriate experiences and contradictions to promote and indeed provoke development. The suggestion that the teacher's role is reduced to that of custodial care is nonsense.

The alternative to this collapse of morale owing to the misunderstanding of Piaget's view is that the teacher rejects Piaget's view. Many psychologists have tried to show that the basic principles of Piaget's theory outlined above are untenable. Engelmann, for example, agrees that the Piagetian observations of what children typically can and cannot do at certain ages are generally accurate, but at least in one place (Green, Ford and Flamer, 1971, p. 125) he explicitly rejects the theory derived from these observations. Children develop cognitively, according to Engelmann, not through the autoregulations or equilibrations that Piaget stresses, but through the specific experiences they encounter. Quite simply, if you want children to be able to do something, you teach them to do it. Engelmann has produced evidence from a number of experiments to support the view that children can be taught general rules which will result in changed performance over a wide variety of tasks. But changed performance is not what Piagetians judge cognitive development by. The ability to apply rules is not the same as a process of formal thinking. Beilin has likened such post-training performance to the activation of an algorithm which works only if the data are in a form consistent with the algorithm; an operation, on the other hand, is flexible and can accommodate to various inputs. The teacher who rejects Piaget's theory because he finds he can teach children to give correct answers to questions on, say, specific gravity before they understand conservation of amount across changes in shape has profoundly and fundamentally misunderstood Piaget's ideas.

Another area of confusion arises from Piaget's conception of action as the basis of all thinking and his belief that activity methods and the harnessing of the child's interest are essential for effective teaching. Piaget (1971) identifies two principal misconceptions: that activity necessarily involves manipulation of objects or the exercise of large musculature, and that a proper education for life requires drill in dreary chores.

In the first case, I think there would be few now who would quarrel with Piaget's view that it is necessary for young children

to manipulate objects in order to derive the elementary properties
of these objects and their relationships. This part of Piaget's
teaching is unremarkable except in that it appears that, for
many teachers of young children, it stops there. Thus we have
the cult of the activity school, the sand tray, the climbing
bars, the milk bottles, and a desperately dis-interested (and
frustrated) teacher. What seems to be forgotten in such est-
ablishments is that logico-mathematical knowledge is not derived
simply from the manipulation of objects. It is necessary for
young children to act directly upon objects, but the logico-
mathematical properties are derived not from the objects themselves but from the co-ordination of the child's actions upon
them. The ten-ness of the different arrays of pebbles (see
Piaget, 1971, pp. 37-8) which Piaget's mathematician discovered
as a young child is due not to the properties of the pebbles
but to the co-ordination of the child's actions upon them.
    At this elementary level, action upon objects is still a
necessary and integral part of the learning process. As the
child progresses through primary school and into secondary
school, this requirement fades. Quite obviously, learning
becomes more and more dependent on verbal interchange, on
manipulation of the representations of objects, on abstractions
from objects and their representations, and finally on reflective
abstraction such as might be found in the contemplation of mathematical truths which have no existence in reality. Let me quote
Piaget (1971, p. 68) on this point:

> At other levels the most authentic research activity may take
> place in the spheres of reflection, of the most advanced
> abstraction, and of verbal manipulations (provided they are
> spontaneous and not imposed on the child at the risk of
> remaining partially uncomprehended).

With regard to the second misapprehension (that of the
necessity for drill in dreary chores), although Piaget is insistent
on tying the child's learning to his interests, he clearly recognizes the need for a certain amount of what he calls 'imposed
labour'. He sees the cardinal problem of pedagogy encapsulated
in the question, can two types of knowledge be equated? For
example, do the same problems and techniques apply to the
teaching and learning of a number system and a mathematical
truth? If I interpret him correctly, he is saying that the latter,
the mathematical truth, will in appropriate cases depend upon
a mastery of the former, the number system, and, further, that
the number system may be mastered largely through drill at the
appropriate time. But that drill is for a specific purpose; it is
not drill undertaken for its own sake to train the mind or discipline the soul. I have argued at greater length elsewhere
(MacKay, 1979) that rote learning may not be incompatible with
Piaget's views. For example, it may be true that number is
reliably conserved only when the operations of ordination and

cardination are mastered and integrated and this occurs characteristically around seven or eight years of age. But that does
not imply that number teaching is inappropriate before concrete
operations are attained. There is nothing incompatible with the
skills approach illustrated by, say, Schaeffer, Eggleston and
Scott (1974), with the progressive integration of subitizing,
counting and estimating operators proposed by Klahr and Wallace
(1973), and with both these and the traditional Piagetian view.

It may be that, in the application of these ideas to the teaching of numbers to young children, markedly different practices
arise. In my opinion, these differences are due to misunderstandings of the Piagetian position and not to any error in that
position. Piaget is reporting what must be achieved before numbers can be reliably conserved. The other approaches attempt
to describe how that point may be reached. Thus I would argue
that a rote-learning, skill-building approach to conservation
attainment not only may be not incompatible with Piaget's
approach, it may indeed be thoroughly consonant with it. I
think the crux of the matter is that drill is here seen as part of
a process and can be related directly to that process. It goes
without saying, of course, that attempts to harness the child's
interest to necessary drills are commendable. As usual, Claparède
has summed it up pithily in the statement that the child should
not do what he likes but should like what he does. The point I
am making is that Piaget's views are not inconsistent with the
necessity for labour being imposed on the child. Nor is it restricted to the young child. There is drudgery attaching to every
worth-while enterprise; but that drudgery can only be useful
if it can be seen to relate to that enterprise. And that I believe
to be true at all levels.

Let me now turn to my third area of comment. I believe that
simply cataloguing the applications and misapplications of this
theory is missing the major source of impact of the theory for
education. I do not believe that it is legitimate to ask a general
theorist to provide immediately and directly applicable prescriptions for education. Piaget's theory relates to the development
of an idealized average, the epistemic subject; teaching is about
individual children. It would be unlikely if we were to find
direct applications of Piaget's theory to classroom teaching; it
would be highly likely, however, that we would find important
implications for classroom teaching. I agree with Ausubel and
Robinson (1971, p. 21) that

> the most important contribution of educational psychology
> comes through providing the teacher with a *theoretical struc-*
> *ture* from which he may formulate his own hypotheses as to
> how to cope with new problems which may arise from day to
> day. It is the possession of a sophisticated, integrated theory
> . . . which provides the teacher with that degree of flexibility
> which . . . (characterizes) . . . the way a professional
> approaches his work.

However, I am not claiming that Piaget is an educational psychologist in this sense. Rather, I think of him as, among other
things, a great educational theorist in the tradition of such as
Comenius, Rousseau, Pestalozzi, Froebel, Herbart, Dewey and
Montessori. But he is unique among these theorists in that the
educational prescriptions he proposed are derived from a theory
based on meticulous observation and ingenious experimentation.
Piaget has himself noted the major differences between these
illustrious forebears and between them and himself (Piaget, 1971,
pp. 9-10), and Kamii (1974, p. 202-4) has supported that
analysis.

Piaget's theory is not, in my opinion, an educational psychology
theory. Indeed, I would agree with Bruner et al. (1966) and
with Pascual-Leone et al. (1978) that it is not even an adequate
psychological theory of development. It is a multi-disciplinary
theory of development aimed principally at the solution of
epistemological questions. Genetic epistemology is interested in
solving different questions from those posed by developmental
and educational psychology. The overlap of interest is great,
however, and the relevance of genetic epistemology to developmental psychology is obvious. I believe the relationship is aptly
and cogently stated by Pascual-Leone et al. (1978), who suggest
that Piaget's theory should be seen by developmental and educational psychologists as a meta-theory. It is the unifying
epistemological theory from which more precise psychological
theories of development, learning and instruction may be
derived. Already the theory has had enormous impact in
broadening and intensifying the educational debate. I think its
future impact will be in the encouragement of research of the
type described by Pascual-Leone and his colleagues.

I believe too that Piaget's theory will be modified by that
research. Unfortunately, he is no longer with us to spearhead
that endeavour. But it is entirely within the spirit of his own
work to believe that developments will and should occur. In his
own words,' "Piaget's theory" is not completed at this date and
the author of these pages has always considered himself one of
the chief "revisionists of Piaget" ' (Piaget, 1970, p. 703).

REFERENCES

Ausubel, D.P. and Robinson, F.G. (1971) 'School Learning'.
    London: Holt, Rinehart & Winston.
Bruner, J.S., Olver, R.R., Greenfield, P.M. et al. (1966)
    'Studies in Cognitive Growth'. New York: Wiley.
Collis, K.F. (1975) 'A Study of Concrete and Formal Operations
    in School Mathematics: a Piagetian Viewpoint'. Melbourne:
    Australian Council for Educational Research.
De Vries, R. (1978) Early Education and Piagetian Theory:
    Applications versus Implications, in J.M. Gallacher and J.A.
    Easley (eds), 'Knowledge and Development', vol. 2. New York:
    Plenum.

Easley, J.A. (1978) Four Decades of Conservation Research, in
    J.M. Gallacher and J.A. Easley (eds), 'Knowledge and Develop-
    ment', vol. 2. New York: Plenum.
Gallagher, J.M. and Easley, J.A. (eds) (1978) 'Knowledge and
    Development', vol. 2. New York: Plenum.
Ginsburg, H. and Opper, S. (1979) 'Piaget's Theory of Intellec-
    tual Development'. Englewood Cliffs, NJ: Prentice-Hall.
Green, D.R., Ford, M.P. and Flamer, G.B. (1971) 'Measurement
    and Piaget'. New York: McGraw-Hill.
Kamii, C. (1974) Pedagogical Principles Derived from Piaget's
    Theory. In M. Schwebel and J. Raph (eds), 'Piaget in the
    Classroom'. London: Routledge & Kegan Paul.
Klahr, D. and Wallace, J.G. (1973) The Role of Quantification
    Operators in the Development of the Conservation of Quantity,
    in 'Cognitive Psychology', 4, pp. 301-27.
Lovell, K. and Shayer, M. (1978) The Impact of the Work of
    Piaget on Science Curriculum Development, in J.M. Gallagher
    and J.A. Easley (eds), 'Knowledge and Development', vol. 2.
    New York: Plenum.
Lunzer, E.A. (1976) Jean Piaget: A Biographical Sketch, in
    V.P. Varma and P. Williams (eds), 'Piaget, Psychology and
    Education'. London: Hodder & Stoughton.
MacKay, C.K. (1979) Vom Voroperatorischen zum konkret-
    operatorischen denken, in G. Steiner (ed.), 'Die Psychologie
    des 20. jahrhunderts', vol. 7. Zurich: Kindler Verlag.
Murray, F.B. (ed.) (1979) 'The Impact of Piagetian Theory'.
    Baltimore: University Park Press.
Pascual-Leone, J., Goodman, D., Ammon, P. and Subelman,
    I. (1978) Piagetian Theory and Neo-Piagetian Analysis as
    Psychological Guides in Education, in J.M. Gallacher and
    J.A. Easley (eds), 'Knowledge and Development', vol. 2.
    New York: Plenum.
Piaget, J. (1970) Piaget's Theory, in P.H. Mussen (ed.),
    'Carmichael's Manual of Child Psychology', 3rd ed. vol. 1.
    New York: Wiley.
Piaget, J. (1971) 'Science of Education and the Psychology of
    the Child'. London: Longman.
Schaeffer, B., Eggleston, V.H. and Scott, J.L. (1974) Number
    Development in Young Children, in 'Cognitive Psychology',
    6, pp. 357-79.
Schwebel, M. and Raph, J. (eds) (1974) 'Piaget in the Class-
    room'. London: Routledge & Kegan Paul.
Varma, V.P. and Williams, P. (eds) (1976) 'Piaget, Psychology
    and Education'. London: Hodder & Stoughton.
Wadsworth, B.J. (1978) 'Piaget for the Classroom Teacher'. New
    York: Longman.

6 The myth of Piaget's contribution to education*

Derek Boyle

In 1964 a symposium entitled 'Piaget Rediscovered' (Ripple and Rockcastle, 1964) debated the value of Piaget's ideas as a basis for education. A priori it would seem that the most valuable feature of Piaget's theory in this regard is the idea of stages, according to which a teacher can relate what he wishes to teach to what the child is capable of learning. This, unfortunately, is one of the most worrying aspects of the theory, primarily because of the well-known 'décalages'.

Flavell (1971) discusses the problem of stages and argues that a stage theory 'entails qualitative rather than quantitative changes in thinking'. That is to say that we must define a stage in terms of when certain types of thinking (such as reversibility) appear, rather than when earlier types (for example, sensory-motor thinking) disappear. Even mature adults under certain conditions display immature thinking, but we do not deny that they have attained a higher stage than children. Despite such defences, many commentators remain unconvinced. Among them, significantly, is Smedslund (1977).

Smedslund is significant because he is thought of as a supporter of Piaget's system, but more recently he has expressed doubts. He says: 'My conversations and dealings with children never quite convinced me that their behaviour could be adequately described as reflecting the presence or absence of certain operatory structures.' In the same symposium as Smedslund two other commentators, Brown and Desforges (1977) are critical of the concept of stage, and argue that a better model of development would be one based upon the integration of skills.

One major problem for the Piaget critic is that Piaget's theory is self-contained and not readily amenable to empirical criticism. Piaget's conception of cognitive development is essentially one of a necessary progression towards a state of thinking that is the ultimate outcome of evolution, and this aspect of the theory is the central concern of the critique by Rotman (1977). This does not, prima facie, seem the sort of theory that can underpin the process of education. I want now to examine the nature of Piaget's theory.

69

Piaget's primary concern is, of course, epistemology, and he claims that we can understand the nature of knowledge only by understanding the nature of thinking (Piaget, 1970). Piaget's conception of epistemology is rather different from that held by most philosophers. Epistemology is generally understood to be a study of how we think about what we know, and epistemologists make a clear distinction between what we know and how we know. Admittedly, following Kant, we must agree that the ways in which our minds work largely determine how we know things, but there is a clear distinction between thought processes and the contents of thought. Piaget's approach to the problem confuses the two to no clear advantage. His claim that genetic epistemology seeks to explain how the mind goes from one state of knowledge to another judged to be superior confuses 'knowledge' with 'structure of the mind', a confusion that has damaging consequences for an educationalist attempting an assessment of a child's specific attainments as against his general ability, as I shall attempt to show later with examples.

The conception of the growth of knowledge as a progression from inferior to superior states is the main focus of the criticism by Rotman (1977). Rotman is a mathematician, which makes his criticism particularly pertinent in view of the fact that Piaget's fundamental model is one of symbolic logic, and that he makes frequent reference to the group of French mathematicians known collectively as 'Bourbaki'. Rotman argues that Piaget misconceives the nature of mathematics and, in particular, the role of proof in mathematical progress. The body of mathematics is a coherent structure, but the techniques of proof are not part of that structure. He says that 'mathematics really consists of justifying assertions about structure . . . only an impoverished view of language, and mathematical language in particular, could support the analysis that Piaget gives' (Rotman, 1977, p. 64).

We may summarize Rotman's argument as follows. Individual mathematicians exchange ideas through the medium of language. As a result of discussion they agree upon forms of expression of mathematical notions, but these forms of expression may change in the course of time. Piaget undervalues the language that mathematicians use, preferring to invoke the epistemic subject, to which the very notion of language is hardly applicable. Rotman's point is relevant to much more than mathematics. In all fields it is the case that 'the viewpoints of others are public entities, made meaningful to an individual subject through the inter-subjective agreements and conventions embodied in language' (Rotman, 1977, p. 154). A lack of treatment of linguistic interchange is a severe limitation on any theory of cognitive development. Much of our development takes place through linguistic interchange, much of it between children and their teachers. To base the practice of education on a theory that reduces linguistic interaction to a negligible role is to base it upon a theory whose influence must be pernicious. Piaget's theory is not concerned with how individual children develop intellectually, either alone or in interaction with others: it is concerned with the development of the postulated 'epistemic subject', of which the workings of any individual mind can afford only an illustration. This is an extremely bizarre basis for the practice of education, which is ineluctably concerned with the development of individual children.

Piaget is dedicated to a belief in historical inevitability, this inevitability being a reflection of the way in which the mind must develop. In support of this view, he proposes a version of Auguste Comte's recapitulation hypothesis and argues that intellectual ontogenesis must reflect the development of thinking from Neanderthal times to the present day. There is no way in which this proposition could be tested, so presumably it is a metaphysical statement that expresses Piaget's viewpoint on intellectual progress. That viewpoint, as I suggested earlier is that there is a historical inevitability in progress from inferior to superior states of knowledge, or modes of thinking, which for Piaget seems to mean the same thing. Teachers may well ask themselves why, if progress is inevitable, they are in business at all.

Inevitability of progress apart, there is another feature of Piaget's theory that has worrying consequences for any pedagogy based upon it. Professor Inhelder (1964) wrote:

> Piaget is quite willing to label himself a 'relativist', because his interest is neither in the knower nor in the known, but in the *relation between knower and known;* it is this relationship, which changes in the course of development, that is the material of Piaget's genetic studies.

It is the belief that Piaget's theory is concerned with the 'relation between the knower and the known' that is at the basis of attempts to use Piaget's theory as a guide to the development of the child's intellect. These attempts are mistaken because Piaget's attitude to knowledge and the knower is fundamentally misleading. Knowledge for Piaget means how knowers think, which is not what most people mean by knowledge. To talk about a relation between knower and known in Piaget's terms is to talk about two aspects of the same thing, which is not at all what most people mean when they talk about knowers and knowing.

I shall illustrate some of the confusions that may arise when teachers attempt to base instruction on Piagetian theory by reference to three books written to illustrate such attempts. The first is by Furth and Wachs (1974) and concerns the 'Tyler Thinking School' in Charleston, West Virginia, where they have created an environment 'to implement Piaget's theory by providing the child with experiences best designed to develop his thinking'. They distinguish development (i.e., 'general mechanisms of action and thinking') from learning ('the acquisition of specific skills and the memorising of specific information'). They call 'learning' the result of teaching that does not basically alter the child's intelligence; and 'development' the result of teaching that brings about intellectual change. In practice, of course, one cannot teach without transmitting specific skills, but Furth and Wachs claim that the conceptual distinction between general and specific changes has value. However, it does appear from what they say that development can be brought about by teaching, and their conceptual distinction is valuable only in maintaining the Piagetian dogma that development is spontaneous.

Let us pause to consider what spontaneous development might mean. Piaget's model is that of maturation of the neuro-muscular system. A baby deprived of the opportunity to walk will nonetheless develop the neuromuscular apparatus to make this possible at a certain age. Can we really believe this to be true of the intellect? Would a child growing up without direction, in however intellectually rich an environment, develop into a skilled thinker? Is it not more likely that he would formulate faulty hypotheses and draw wrong conclusions? We cannot experiment to find out, but we conduct the business of living on the assumption that our errors are corrected by the interchange of ideas through language. This is the whole purpose, not only of schooling, but also of publishing books, scholarly papers and rebuttals, and of holding conferences at which contentious issues are debated.

An example makes clear the disastrous consequences of a determination to fit data into a Piagetian framework. An eight-year-old living in Washington, DC at a time when the mayor was named Washington believed that the mayor of Philadelphia would be a Mr Philadelphia. Furth and Wachs assumed that the child 'would have been capable of thinking at a more mature level if . . . motivated to do so' (1974, p. 17). It is quite unwarranted to describe this thinking as 'low-level' and the result of inadequate motivation. The boy was drawing an inference from facts at his disposal, and he was wrong because the facts were insufficient. On the basis of those facts the inference was quite reasonable. Being right or wrong could have nothing to do with motivation in this instance; improvement in the child's performance (if, indeed, the idea of improvement has any meaning here) would be contingent upon an increase in the sort of factual knowledge that would allow the boy to realize that his first experience of towns, mayors and their names embodied a coincidence.

My second book for discussion is by Schwebel and Raph (1974) and is a collection of chapters by different authors. The one I have singled out is by Sinclair, and I have chosen it because it clearly illustrates the tendency of the Piaget shop-floor to use words in their own special way. Here is a quotation (1974, pp. 57-8):

Piaget and his collaborators did not conclude that any kind of

learning procedure would be useless. . . . [They] meant
only that empirical methods, whereby the subject has to accept
a link because this is imposed upon him, do not result in
progress; progress results only when the subject himself discovers the link. This active discovery of links is what happens
in development; it is therefore called spontaneous - maybe
unfortunately - for development is always the result of interaction. . . . Learning is dependent on development, not only
in the sense that certain things can be learned only at certain
levels of development, but also in the sense that in learning -
that is, in situations specifically constructed so that the
subject has active encounters with the environment - the same
mechanisms as in development are at work.

I maintain that this argument is little short of dishonest. In
the first place, there is a false dichotomy between imposition of
a link and discovery of that link. Most teachers, if not all, would
regard effective teaching as the explanation of links, but Piaget's
theory requires Sinclair to hold that whatever is not discovery is
imposition. Presumably if a teacher successfully explained a link
to a child this would count as the child's having discovered it!
Sinclair's reference to 'activity' amounts to no more than saying
that intellectual development occurs only when children understand what they are doing, a proposition with which few would
disagree, whatever their persuasion. This trumpeting of banal-
ities as if they were logical implications solely of Piaget's theory
is typical of the narrowness and arrogance of the Piaget factory.
As for the reference to 'spontaneous' development (another
Piagetian sacred cow), this shows that 'spontaneous' development
is not spontaneous at all, but is dependent upon the environment provided by the teacher. The advice to teachers to provide environments in which children can discover things for
themselves is not exclusively Piagetian.
My third example (Wadsworth, 1978) confirms the suspicion
that the major activity of the Piaget-for-education industry is
sticking its own label on other people's tried and tested goods.
Wadsworth, a Piagetian scholar, and a teacher, attempts to
apply Piaget's theory to the practice of education, calling on the
theory 'only to the extent necessary to provide a rationale for
the teaching practices and principles presented'. He claims that
'Piagetian methods are a more efficient set of methods than
traditional methods for acquiring skills and knowledge'. If we
ask what these methods are, we have great difficulty in discovering precisely what is Piagetian about them. For example;
'Reading about and talking about things are not neglected,
though they are not emphasised to the exclusion of everything
else, as in traditional classrooms.' What tradition is this that
excludes everything except reading and talking? Where are
these classrooms? Certainly not in Britain, where Froebel and
Montessori had exercised a liberating influence long before
Piaget became a cult figure; nor, I suspect, in many parts of

Europe where, of course, they were influential even earlier.

Piaget has recognized that the stress on activity is not new. Writing on the genesis of the 'new methods' (Piaget, 1971), he acknowledges that the importance of activity was recognized by Montessori, Froebel, Pestalozzi, Rousseau and even Socrates. He conceives his own unique contribution as being the objective establishment of the truth of the principle that activity is vital. Unfortunately the truth of this principle has recently been questioned.

Anthony (1977), writing in the same symposium as Smedslund, who has already been mentioned, argues that Piaget's claim that children need actively to manipulate objects is not supported by empirical research. Nor, as Anthony points out, does Piaget's commitment to this view appear to be shared by his close collaborators (Inhelder and Sinclair, 1969; Inhelder, Sinclair and Bovet, 1974). While some active handling can be beneficial, Anthony concludes that 'The extreme Piagetian insistence on physical activity has been excessive.'

Here is part of the quotation from Inhelder, Sinclair and Bovet (1974) which Anthony (1977, p. 25) uses to make his point:

> being cognitively active does not mean that the child merely manipulates a given type of material; he can be mentally active without physical manipulation, just as he can be mentally passive while actually manipulating objects. Intellectual activity is stimulated if the opportunities for acting on objects or observing other people's actions or for discussions correspond to the subject's level of development.

The clear implication of this is that there can be physical activity or intellectual activity, and that intellectual activity is more important. To talk of 'intellectual activity' is to talk figuratively; it means that the child must think about what he is doing if he is to learn from any experience, a proposition that is hardly a revelation. Piaget does not seem to be referring to intellectual activity when he says (Schwebel and Raph, 1974, pp. ix-x):

> It is absolutely necessary that learners have at their disposal concrete material experiences (and not merely pictures), and that they form their own hypotheses and verify them (or not verify them) themselves through their own active manipulations. The observed activities of others, including those of the teachers, are not formative of new organisations in the child.

While what Piaget says does not rule out the requirement that the child be intellectually active, he is adamant that the child must actively manipulate material, 'with all the tentative gropings and apparent waste of time that such involvement implies' (Schwebel and Raph, 1974, pp. ix-x). This unambiguously means that insight cannot arise from observation, a proposition that is not confirmed by empirical studies, as Anthony demonstrates.

As Anthony points out, the importance of physical manipulation is not a logical deduction from Piaget's theory, but it is a principle that has been made the basis of some teaching techniques. Herein, I think, lies a great danger. If it should become an accepted dogma that physical manipulation is essential for learning, then able children who could learn efficiently and quickly from demonstration and explanation would be held back by the insistence on frustrating and time-wasting activities. Of course there must be activity at some stage: children must be encouraged actively to apply their knowledge. However, there has long been a distinction made in psychology between learning and performance: improvement in performance certainly requires practice, but chimpanzees can learn by observation, and even rats can learn while apparently doing nothing. There is no reason to suppose that children are less gifted.

Human beings have a great advantage over animals in that language makes observation more efficient, because it can be accompanied by verbal explanation. Unfortunately in the Piagetian scheme of things actions come first, words a very poor second. Recommending that children be made to discover things through active manipulation rather than by talk and discussion is tantamount to refusing to accept the essentially verbal nature of human intellectual functioning. The recommendation would, if widely applied, be intellectually stultifying to our brightest children.

Earlier in this paper I discussed Rotman's criticism of Piaget's account of the development of mathematical thinking. An important point made by Rotman is that Piaget gives an inadequate account of the social role of language in the development of mathematics. A number of Piaget's critics have emphasized the importance of language in problem-solving, and I myself have just indicated my belief in the essentially verbal nature of human intellectual functioning. I want to devote the rest of this paper to the question of language in mental development.

In his classic paper on the manipulation of a matrix of glass varying in the dimensions of height and diameter, Bruner (1964) stressed the importance of language in solving the problem, which consisted of reconstructing the matrix after the shortest, thinnest glass had been moved from the south-west corner of the grid to the south-east. The children then had to construct a mirror image of the original grid. Seven-year-olds usually succeeded, whereas most of the younger children (five and six years) failed. Success or failure on the task was related to the language that the children used to describe the glasses. There were three linguistic modes. In the dimensional mode, the children singled out two ends of an attribute, e.g., 'That one is higher, and that one is shorter'. In global usage, the children would say 'That one is big and that one is little'. In confounded usage, children would use non-matching descriptions, such as 'That one is taller and that one is little'. (My copy of Bruner's paper gives the examples for global and confounded usage the other way about, but I take that to be the result of misprints, so I hope I have made the appropriate correction.) The children with the confounded usage had the greatest difficulty with the transposition task, and made twice as many errors as children using the dimensional or global modes. Bruner concluded that improvement in language should aid this type of problem-solving; and certainly the activation of the child's previously acquired language habits should improve performance. This is in agreement with the work on the role of language in problem-solving reported by Luria (1961).

More recently the work of Donaldson (1978) has emphasized that children can often understand far more than Piagetian experiments suggest. What appear to be failures in reasoning are frequently failures of understanding. It would be impossible here to summarize the numerous investigations made by Donaldson's students, McGarrigle and others, and I expect that the work is familiar to most readers, so I will simply remind you that a very slight change in the experimental technique had a very great effect upon the success rate in Piagetian-type experiments. In one experiment McGarrigle used four toy cows, three black and one white, all laid on their sides to indicate that they were sleeping. Children of an average age of six years were asked two questions:

(1) Are there more black cows or more cows?
(2) Are there more black cows or more sleeping cows?

Three out of twelve children correctly answered the first question (which is the standard Piagetian form), whereas eleven out of twenty correctly answered the second; the difference is statistically highly significant ($p = 0.01$). Similar studies have confirmed the dramatic effect that a change in one word can have on the outcome.

I want to conclude by discussing some modest investigations of my own.[1] Most studies in this area have been concerned with individual children, but I am interested in how children influence each other, so I asked three five-year-olds of my acquaintance to sit round a table with me to solve a variety of problems. I was particularly interested in the language that the children used, so we made a videotape of the activity. The children were perfectly at ease both with me and with the television cameras and technicians - all have been delighted to 'be on TV' with me both before and since. My observations confirmed what every teacher of young children knows, namely that children learn from each other, and often learn the wrong solution to a problem if the dominant member of a group has the wrong idea. This point may seem banal but it is worth making because so much of what Piaget says appears to imply that this will not happen. Another point worth making is that Piaget's subjects all appear to speak grammatically correct, if rudimentary, French. Other investigators' subjects seem to speak perfect English. My three little girls - all daughters of university lecturers - spoke what appeared, on close analysis, to be a foreign language. I shall give two examples to illustrate what I mean.

We started by discussing lies.

(E)	Do you know what a lie is?
(All - in chorus, emphatically)	No!
(E)	Does anyone ever say you mustn't tell lies?
(All)	Yes!
(E)	Then do you know what a lie is?
(All)	Yes!
(E)	Suppose I said '2 and 2 are 5'. Is that a lie?
(All)	No.
(E)	Why is it not a lie?
(Catherine - one of the three)	Because it's only 4 really.

My next example is from conservation of number. I spread out six 10p pieces and six 1p pieces, lining them up in the familiar way. Then I questioned them:

(E)	See those silver coins there and copper coins here: are there as many copper coins as there are silver ones?
(Catherine)	Yes.
(Helen)	No.
(Kirsten was puzzled and said nothing.)	
(E)	You said 'No', Helen?
(Helen)	Because there's the same number.
(E)	The same number?
(Catherine)	Five here and six here.

When I had got agreement that there were as many copper coins as silver (and that there were six of each) I pushed one of the sets of coins together and asked if there were still as many copper as silver. As the experiment progressed it became clear that Catherine believed that there were, while Helen thought that when one group (either copper or silver, for we did it both ways) was pushed together, there were more of one than the other. Towards the end of the experiment Catherine had changed her mind and was agreeing with Helen, and so was Kirsten (who seemed to have no firm views of her own). When they insisted that there were more copper coins when the copper coins were pushed together, I asked:

'How has it become more copper? Count them and tell me.' They did and agreed that there were six of each. Then followed this exchange:

(E)	So, is there more silver or more copper?
(All)	More copper.
(E)	But they both came to six didn't they?
(All)	Yes.
(E)	But there's still more copper?
(Helen and Kirsten)	Yes.
(Catherine)	They're equal.

Following this I got an unexpected insight into the girls' command of our numerical system. They spontaneously began totalling the money, starting with the 10p pieces. The counting (in unison) began like this: Ten, twenty, thirty, forty, fifty, sixty.

| (E) | What about the copper ones? |
| (All - in unison) | Seventy, eighty, ninety, twenty, twenty-one, twenty-two. |

Is it surprising that, with so little command of the verbal and numerical systems in terms of which adults communicate, children give apparently irrational answers to questions about difficult matters like class inclusion? If a perfectly rational, highly educated adult were asked Piagetian-type questions in a language with which he was not perfectly familiar he would, I suggest, give answers not unlike those given by Catherine, Helen and Kirsten. The fact that the language used by children in Piagetian situations does not always appear to make such sense does not necessarily mean that they are thinking irrationally. It means that we cannot confidently make inferences from what children say, to what they think.

An obvious implication of what I have been saying is that we should pay far more attention to what children actually say, both in the classroom and in the experimental situations in which we observe them. Unless we listen very carefully to what the children tell us we can be seriously misled about their intentions. For instance, in a standard task of conservation of liquid volume with three-year-olds, I was using green food-colouring dye so that the contents would show up clearly on television, as my intention was to use the demonstration for teaching purposes. I asked Jane, a forthcoming and articulate child, if the identical dolls I was using had the same amount to drink. When she agreed that they had, I poured the contents of one glass into a vessel of a different shape and asked her if the dolls still had the same amount to drink. She said they had. Since all the other three-year-olds in the experiment were clear that the amount changed, this looked like a remarkable instance of early conservation. However I asked Jane: 'How do you know it's still the same?' To this she replied: 'Because they've both got green'. No doubt every other investigator in this field has obtained similar answers, but we seldom hear about them. Even 'anti-Piagetian' investigators usually limit themselves to telling us how many children, under what conditions, 'solved' a problem: without the detailed protocols we can seriously misunderstand what is going on.

I believe that we misunderstand children more often and more drastically than is supposed, which implies that they very frequently fail to understand us. In view of the vast amount of educational failure, the widespread semi-literacy and numerical incompetence of our society, I deduce that failures of communication in schools are on a monumental scale. If we are to ensure that misunderstandings in education are kept at the lowest possible level, we need a programme devoted to analysing precisely what children say, from which we may deduce what they understand their teachers to mean.

This recommendation certainly does not follow from Piaget's theory. In fact, as far as education is concerned, very little follows at all. McClinton and Meier (1978, p. 341) tell us:

> Many schools claim a Piaget-based curriculum. Since Piaget did not endorse specific educational practices, these schools vary considerably. In some schools, skills studied by Piaget, such as classification, measurement, and matching, are taught. In other schools these skills are benignly neglected on the assumption that children eventually learn them on their own.

However, they list eight characteristics of the focus of 'most Piagetian schools' as follows:

(1)   mental traits important for learning, such as independence, curiosity and confidence;
(2)   interaction among children and opportunities for children to resolve their own conflicts;
(3)   co-operative and egalitarian attitudes;
(4)   co-ordination of physical actions;
(5)   respect for a child's ideas, even if they are 'wrong';
(6)   mild challenges to egocentric thought;
(7)   play as a method of education;
(8)   learning by doing rather than by seeing or hearing.

With the best will in the world, I cannot see what is specifically Piagetian about these points, which are the commonplaces of primary school education. Of course, the authors I have referred to are writing in the USA where, for all I know, primary school education in general is not what it is in Britain, and reformers have indeed set up new types of school in which the benign influence of 'child-centredness' is attributed to Piaget. But liberalism in education cannot possibly be derived from a theory that is essentially about a postulated neo-Aristotelian essence called the 'epistemic subject', only incidentally about how individual children develop, and hardly at all about learning.

Even if we could, by the use of special pleading, forge a link between Piaget's theory and the recommendations that Furth and

Wachs, Schwebel and Raph, Wadsworth, and McClinton and Meier make, ostensibly on the basis of that theory, there would still be no guarantee that children taught by allegedly Piagetian methods would grow up literate and numerate, which presumably is a criterion by which most people would judge the success of pedagogical methods. Indeed, Piaget's argument that actions are more important than words, with its consequent neglect of the role of language, would seem to ensure precisely the opposite.

However, I feel that we have no reason for alarm. So far as I can tell, in Britain at any rate, Piaget has not significantly influenced primary school education. For that we can all be profoundly thankful.

NOTES

* This chapter is a revised and updated version of a chapter entitled Piaget and Education: A Negative Evaluation, in S. Modgil and C. Modgil (eds), 'Jean Piaget: Consensus and Controversy'. Eastbourne: Holt, Rinehart & Winston, 1982.
1 This material is presented at greater length in Modgil and Modgil, op. cit.

REFERENCES

Anthony, W.S. (1977) Activity in the Learning of Piagetian Operational Thinking, in 'British Journal of Educational Psychology', 47, pp. 18-24.

Brown, G. and Desforges, C. (1977) Piagetian Psychology and Education: Time for Revision, in 'British Journal of Educational Psychology', 47, pp. 7-17.

Bruner, J.S. (1964) The Course of Cognitive Growth, in 'American Psychologist', 19, pp. 1-15.

Donaldson, Margaret (1978) 'Children's Minds'. Glasgow: Collins.

Flavell, J.H. (1971) Stage-related Properties of Cognitive Development, in 'Cognitive Psychology', 2, pp. 421-53.

Furth, H.G. and Wachs, H. (1974) 'Thinking Goes to School: Piaget's Theory in Practice'. New York: Oxford University Press.

Inhelder, Barbel (1964) Piaget's Genetic Approach to Cognition, in J. Cohen (ed.), 'Readings in Psychology'. London: Allen & Unwin.

Inhelder, B. and Sinclair, H. (1969) Learning Cognitive Structures, in P. Mussen, J. Langer and J. Covington (eds), 'Trends and Issues in Developmental Psychology'. New York: Holt, Rinehart & Winston.

Inhelder, B., Sinclair, H. and Bovet, M. (1974) 'Learning and the Development of Cognition'. London: Routledge & Kegan Paul.

Luria, A.R. (1961) 'The Role of Speech in the Regulation of

Normal and Abnormal Behaviour'. Oxford: Pergamon Press.
McClinton, Barbara S. and Meier, Blanche, G. (1978) 'Beginnings
    Psychology of Early Childhood'. St Louis: Mosby.
Piaget, J. (1970), 'Genetic Epistemology' (the Woodbridge
    Lectures at Columbia University in 1968). New York: Columbia
    University Press.
Piaget, J. (1971) 'Science of Education and Science of the Child'.
    London: Longman.
Ripple, R.E. and Rockcastle, V.N. (eds) (1964) Piaget Redis-
    covered: Report of the Conference on Cognitive Studies and
    Curriculum Development, in 'Journal of Research in Science
    Teaching', 2.
Rotman, B. (1977) 'Jean Piaget: Psychologist of the Real'.
    Brighton: Harvester Press.
Schwebel, M. and Raph, Jane (eds) (1974) 'Piaget in the Class-
    room'. London: Routledge & Kegan Paul.
Smedslund, J. (1977) Piaget's Psychology in Practice, in 'British
    Journal of Educational Psychology', 47, pp. 1-6.
Wadsworth, B. (1978) 'Piaget for the Classroom Teacher'. London:
    Longman.

Part 5

Educational psychology

7 Piaget's attitudes to education

John Sants

In his later years, when interviewed as the world-famous child psychologist, Piaget was fond of saying that he was not really very interested in education. Such detachment always surprised the interviewer: Piaget was, after all, among teachers, just about the best known of all child psychologists. Piaget's further claim - that as a genetic epistemologist he had nothing to say about pedagogy - appeared disingenuous, or just downright mischievous. Was he trying to stir things up? How did a psychologist claiming to be uninterested in education become so influential? A remark by Piaget in one of those interviews with Jean-Claude Bringuier, 'Conversations with Jean Piaget', gives hints of how the puzzle may be resolved.

'Any adult you choose,' said Piaget, 'whether cave-man or Aristotle, began as a child and for the rest of his life used the instruments he created in his earliest years.' What instruments did Piaget create in his earliest years? And how did they form his ideas of childhood and education? Fortunately, Piaget, as a good genetic epistemologist, has left us some excellent accounts of his childhood as he remembered it. The most useful of these is his (1952) chapter in 'The History of Psychology in Autobiography', vol. IV. Piaget exactly caught the spirit of the exercise of trying to give 'the elements of an explanation of the author's work', limiting himself to 'the scientific aspects' of his life. Furthermore, he was excited at the prospect because in looking over the writings of his youth, especially his novel, he had discovered how little his ideas had changed. To be more precise, he realized that he had only ever had a single personal idea' which he had striven all his life to express without ever fully succeeding. Piaget's one idea,

'developed under various aspects in (alas!) twenty-two volumes, has been that intellectual operations proceed in terms of structures-of-the-whole. These structures denote the kinds of equilibrium toward which evolution in its entirety is striving; at once organic, psychological and social, their roots reach down as far as biological morphogenesis itself.'

Piaget wrote that around 1950 when he was fifty-four. Most of the elements of Piaget's theories can be seen in one form or another in the words describing his 'single personal idea'. Piaget goes on to give an account of the childhood experiences which help to explain the creation of his idea. In what follows, I shall be using the chapter in 'The History of Psychology in Auto-biography' (Piaget, 1952) together with the first chapter in 'Insights and Illusions of Philosophy' (Piaget, 1965), in which Piaget once again describes his formative educational experiences. As other sources I shall be using the earliest of Piaget's books because in them from time to time he recalls his childhood and earliest influences. In his later works there is less digression from the topic in hand.

Piaget begins the autobiographical explanation of his work with carefully formulated descriptions of his parents. His father was still alive in 1951 when he wrote the chapter in the 'History'. His father, a medieval historian, was, Piaget explained,

> a man of painstaking and critical mind, who dislikes hastily improvised generalizations . . . he taught me the value of systematic work, even in small matters. My mother was very intelligent, energetic, and fundamentally a very kind person; her rather neurotic temperament, however, made our family life somewhat troublesome. One of the direct consequences of this situation was that I started to forgo playing for serious work very early; this I obviously did as much to imitate my father as to take refuge in both a private and a non-fictitious world. Indeed, I have always detested any departure from reality, an attitude which I relate to the second important influential factor of my early life, viz. my mother's poor mental health; it was this disturbing factor which at the beginning of my studies in psychology made me intensely interested in questions of psychoanalysis and pathological psychology. Though this interest helped me to achieve independence and to widen my cultural background, I have never since felt any desire to involve myself deeper in that particular direction, always much preferring the study of normalcy and of the work-ings of the intellect to that of the tricks of the unconscious.

I have quoted this lengthy passage in Piaget's own words for two reasons: first, because every word was chosen with care by Piaget to explain important aspects of his work; and, second, because the passage is an authentic recollection of his childhood. It is the authenticity and not the accuracy of recall that matters. Piaget has himself given an amusing account of how memories of childhood can be false. He 'remembers' how he was nearly kidnapped from his pram in the Champs-Elysées. He has a vivid recall of someone trying to grab him, the nurse getting scratched in his defence and a policeman coming to the rescue. But the whole story had been invented by the nurse, told to him by her when he was seven or eight, and explained to be a lie by his

mother when he was fifteen. What matters, however, is that it
was all remembered by Piaget as part of his childhood, to be
revived and recorded for ever in an interview in Piaget's old
age, and also to be included in a lecture to the American
Society of Psychoanalysis and published in 'The Child and
Reality' in 1972.

In comparing his mother and father Piaget is making a number
of important contrasts of qualities. The opposing qualities were
for ever present in himself, and in conflict with each other. His
father was rational, his mother irrational. His father a stickler
for evidence, his mother given to imaginative speculation.
Piaget, like Freud, was always aware of this tug of war between
his speculative and scientific sides. When he retreated to the
mountains to write, his 'Dionysian excitement ended in intellectual
activity'. His father, as he tells us, disliked hastily improvised
generalizations and demanded that they be tested with evidence.
In these early examples are the origins of Piaget's life-long preoccupation with scientific methods in the service of imagination.
The problem is dealt with on many occasions. In 'Insights and
Illusions', Piaget (1965) talks of the conflict he felt within himself between 'the habits of verification of the biologist and the
psychologist, and speculative reflection which constantly tempted
me'. He knew that speculation was 'bound up with the whole
personality of the thinker' and therefore susceptible to 'one's
unconscious desires'. He concedes the need for a 'publicly veri-
fiable method of testing', and, as we will see later, his early
apprenticeship as a biologist instilled in Piaget a permanent respect for the methods of scientists. Yet, as many of his critics
have contended, Piaget's Dionysian excitement so often ran
away with him.

The imaginative nature which Piaget shared with his mother
had its darker side. Unconscious desires may generate original
thinking but they may also generate instability. His mother's
neurosis aroused Piaget's interest in psychoanalysis. Piagetian
theory in modern textbooks is often given as if it were an alternative to psychoanalytic theory, with the two theories having
nothing to do with each other. Yet Piaget's debt to Freud is
profound. In later years references to Freud tend to disappear
from Piaget's books, but they were there in some number at the
start. Piaget's lecture on Freud, given in 1920 when he was a
youthful twenty-four, is a little gem. It was given to teachers
at Dr Simon's suggestion because at that time in France teachers
knew nothing of Freud's work. Piaget had just come back from
a year in Zurich where he spent some time in Bleuler's psychia-
tric clinic. 'The aim of psychoanalysis', Piaget told his audience
of teachers, '. . . consists in rediscovering . . . hidden tendencies which guide the person without his knowledge.' 'Psycho-
anlysis', he continued, 'is a sort of individual history, an
embryology of the personality.' The whole lecture has the air
of being given by a young man believing in psychoanalysis. It
has nothing of the sceptical report about it.

Scattered throughout Piaget's lecture on 'Psychoanalysis in its Relations with Child Psychology' are numerous hints of his beliefs about the child. Among others is the view that there is in the child 'the desire to grow, and to be in all ways like grown-ups'. This belief is based on the assumption (a cornerstone of Adler's thinking, as Piaget pointed out) that 'the child necessarily suffers from feelings of inadequacy . . . .'. Here perhaps is a harbinger of the belief, implicit in all Piaget's later theorizing, that childhood is something for the child to grow out of. But there is one lesson above all that Piaget learned from psycho-analysis and the psychiatrist, Bleuler. In 'Judgment and Reason-ing in the Child', Piaget (1924) declares that 'it is to the lasting credit of this science (i.e. psychoanalysis) that it has discovered two ways of thinking: one, social, communicable, guided by the need for adapting oneself to others, "logical thought"; the other, personal uncommunicable as such, "autistic thought"'. The dis-tinction was to remain fundamental for Piaget, in his life and in his work.

In order to understand why the distinction meant so much to Piaget, one has to go back to his own childhood and recall that his mother's neurosis frightened him into giving up play very early in favour of serious work. Personal undirected thinking could lead to madness. Salvation lay in communicating one's thoughts to others. This revelation was not only of value to Piaget in search of his personal mental health: it was to be the foundation of his educational theories. The idea crops up again and again and is of course related to Piaget's concern about the two sides of his character, the speculative and the scientific. On the one hand is speculation with the dangers of madness. On the other, social reality testing, with the dangers - as Piaget saw in his philosophizing - of undue dependence on current ideologies. In 'Judgment and Reasoning' Piaget puts it rather well: 'We are constantly hatching an enormous number of false ideas, conceits, utopias, mystical explanations, suspicions, and megalomaniacal fantasies, which disappear when brought into contact with other people.' Sharing our thinking is at 'the root of our need for verification. Proof is the outcome of argument'. Piaget's interest in egocentrism (whatever it may have become) began as a problem in his own personality development.

False ideas, fantasies and the like nearly gained the upper hand in the later stages of Piaget's adolescence. In the 'History' he explains how, when he was about eighteen and preparing for his baccalaureate in formal education, while at the same time getting on with his own biological research on molluscs, his intensive private reading in philosophy and religion all began to affect his mental health. He had 'to spend more than a year in the mountains filling my forced leisure time with writing a sort of philosophical novel which I was imprudent enough to publish in 1917'. 'Recherche' was published as fiction because Piaget feared the reception his ideas might get from scientists; yet the novel was really a formulation of his theories of development and contained among others his 'single idea'. It was in adolescence that Piaget discovered personal stability and the nature of his life's work. It was a radical and satisfactory cognitive and emotive reorganization at the end of childhood. In adolescence he had encountered the extreme consequences of undirected, non-communicable thought. In 'The Language and Thought of the Child' he writes of the 'inextricable chaos of adolescent thought as a result of bottling up one's own thoughts and not even thinking in terms of other people'. With such a dramatic personal adolescence one might have expected this stage of development to figure more prominently in Piaget's theory. One has to look hard for such an emphasis, but in 'Six Psychological Studies' (1964) there is a discussion of the importance of 'the metaphysics peculiar to the adolescent'. It is at this stage, Piaget asserts, that the 'real preparations for personal creativity occur, . . . examples of genius show that there is always continuity between the formation of personality, as of eleven to twelve years, and the subsequent work of the man' (p. 69). Note that the link is between personality and adult theorizing.

So far I have been concerned with parental influences in Piaget's recollections of childhood. Did he think his teachers mattered? Teachers, Piaget conceded, had some bearing on the formation of his single idea; but the important teachers were not those he found in school. The classroom was a frustrating place. In a passage tucked away in 'The Moral Judgment of the Child' (1932, p. 352) Piaget recalls his 'little class in a little town in Switzerland'. There were three kinds of boys in the class: lazy, conscientious, and those 'who were only moderately good pupils in school, but who went in for "interesting things" at home – chemistry, the history of aviation, zoology, Hebrew, anything you like except what was on the curriculum'. The list of interests for the third group leave little doubt about which group Piaget himself belonged to. The educational lesson for Piaget from this little class of his was that the conscientious boys became civil servants or 'filled minor academic posts', the lazy did no worse. Piaget's group were forever being told: 'If only you spent on your homework a quarter of the time you spend on your personal pursuits, you would do exceedingly well.' On looking back, he could only wish that he had spent even more time on interests of his own choosing instead of those chosen for him by his teachers. To be fair, he added, there were some good teachers who encouraged the pursuit of personal interests. Self-regulation, it can be seen, had appealed to Piaget at a very early age.

The teachers who influenced Piaget were not in school at all. One was Paul Godet, the director of the Natural History Museum, who was so impressed by that now famous one-page article on the partly albino sparrow (spotted, claimed the ten-year-old Piaget, in the park in Neuchâtel) that he gave the boy the job of sticking labels on his collections of shells. Piaget assisted Godet until the latter's death five years later. He never ceased

to recall his debt to the man who took him on as an apprentice
in biology. Henceforth, as a scientist, Piaget was to have some
protection 'against the demon of philosophy'. The second
influential teacher in Piaget's boyhood was his godfather.
Piaget's mother, as a devout Protestant, had 'insisted' he take
religious instruction when he was fifteen, the year Paul Godet
died. This authoritarian insistence was the kind of parental
interference Piaget was to deplore when he became a child
psychologist. Piaget's father encouraged scepticism in religion,
so that, not for the first time, Piaget was pulled in opposite
directions by his parents. Fortunately for him he went to stay
with his godfather, spent happy hours walking and fishing, was
introduced to books by Bergson, and finally (with unlikely help
from a godfather) resolved his religious dilemma with the realization that God was life itself. Biology could explain all knowledge.
The lesson was never forgotten. The third influential teacher
in Piaget's youth was the logician, Arnold Reymond. After a
particular lesson with Professor Reymond, Piaget first formulated
his ideas about systems and equilibria as a way of dealing with
the relationship between parts and wholes 'in all fields of life'.
    Piaget takes some trouble to explain how all aspects of his work
originated. Adults were of some help in his education, but the
real work was done by Piaget himself. A pattern of learning
tends to be repeated: Piaget is troubled by two irreconcilable
ideas or tendencies: science and speculation, biology and God.
He finds his resolution in social exchange. The formula is often
recommended by Piaget in his writings on education. Most of
Piaget's conflicts had been resolved by the time he emerged from
his adolescent chaos. When he wrote his novel 'Recherche' in
1917 he set down his 'life plan'. In his essay on The Mental
Development of the Child, published as the first of the 'Six
Psychological Studies', Piaget dwells on the important resolutions
made in adolescence which, for Piaget himself, lasted a lifetime:
'The adolescent makes a pact with his God, promising to serve
him without return, but, by the same token, he counts on play-
ing a decisive role in the cause he has undertaken to defend.'
Once made the pact is best left alone. Piaget's recovery of his
equilibrium, by his own efforts in adolescence, was another
lesson he did not forget. Out of the experience came his belief
that 'we really possess only what we have conquered by ourselves'.
    That quotation comes from Piaget's discussion on education at
the end of 'The Moral Judgment of the Child'. The repeated
burden of this discussion is the folly of trying to transform the
child's mind from the outside by authoritarian means: 'It is
idle . . . to try and transform the child's mind from outside,
when his own taste for active research and his desire for cooperation suffice to ensure normal intellectual development' (p. 392).
The formula from Piaget's own experiences is that activity, hard
thought and companionship promote the healthiest development.
The combination yields the happiest equilibrium within the grow-

ing child. Parental 'mistakes' can only too easily disturb. Much better for the child's social interaction to be with 'collaborators'. There are deep 'psychological tendencies which urge [the child] to work with others'. Other children can best provide the conditions to moderate egocentricity, and provide the necessary testing against social reality; but if an adult teacher does wish to intervene he or she had best do it as an 'elder collaborator . . . a simple comrade' and not as an authoritarian 'priest'. Paul Godet, Piaget's comrade in education, had been the ideal teacher, never to be forgotten. He at least did not encourage verbalism. The cardinal sin of teachers, in traditional schools, as Piaget tells us with some passion in 'Moral Judgment', is that they do encourage egocentric verbalism in the child, i.e., 'the imaginative interpretation of imperfectly understood words'. Piaget's reluctance to view language as one of the good things of development goes back to his early suspicion that it is the language of adult constraint which confines the child within himself: 'The prestige of the spoken word triumphs over any amount of active experiment and free discussion.'

The book I have quoted from was written when Piaget was in his thirties, while his memories of childhood were still fresh and active. How did he see education and teachers in his later years, when he had become an established priest in child psychology with all the accompanying authority of the office? It cannot be said that Piaget found it easy to admire teachers in traditional schools. His most explicit discussion of education in his later years is of course Education and Teaching since 1935, written in 1965, as Piaget approached his seventieth year, and published as the first part of 'Science of Education and the Psychology of the Child'. Piaget's complaint is a familiar one: schools try to impose knowledge from above. As a result, teachers are trained to be no more than 'mere transmitters of elementary and only slightly more than elementary general knowledge, without allowing them any opportunity for initiative and even less for research and discovery'. Having castigated schools and teachers in what Piaget considers to be the traditional system, he goes on to tell us what teachers should be, and how they should be trained. Unfortunately, in doing this Piaget for once sounds tetchy and authoritarian. His book on pedagogy – or rather on the profession of pedagogy – is far too authoritarian to be influential. It is easier for teachers to find inspiration in his earlier books on children.

Piaget's influence on teachers and others involved in education has gone through many stages since 'The Language and Thought of the Child' was first published in English in 1926. A teacher getting hold of that book on publication had no difficulty in capturing the spirit of Piaget's enchanted exploration of children's thinking. In books like that Piaget makes you want to go out and find a child to talk to. When Piaget visited Susan Isaacs's school there must have been an immediate rapport between psychologist and teachers. Since the war, however, Piaget has

become part of the teacher's curriculum. This has been his un-
doing. Teachers struggling with books published since 1950
try as best they can to memorize his terms and definitions. They
may even get as far as memorizing the names of the stages of
child development. At best they may get hold of some form of
the 'Piagetian' description of cognitive development. Only if they
are lucky will they get the hang of what Piaget had to say about
what goes on as a child grows up. Piaget's influence now that he
is no longer writing will, I suspect, derive once again from his
earlier books. Writing as a young man, Piaget did not avoid the
importance of social relationships in the world of the child. In
his own childhood he had learned how to harmonize activity and
reflection in companionship. 'The whole problem', he wrote in
'The Moral Judgment of the Child', 'is therefore how to take the
child out of his egocentricity and lead him to cooperation.'
Piaget the distinguished genetic epistemologist rather took his
eyes off the educational problem he found so challenging as a
young man. In adolescence he had made a satisfactory 'life-plan'
to keep him clear of a return to chaos. I don't think he ever
quite understood how he had managed to unite his intelligence
and affectivity; but he preferred not to dig around in the 'tricks
of the unconscious' to find out.

The egocentricity which had worried Piaget as an adolescent
was a self-centredness in which affect dominated intellect. The
result was chaos. In Piaget's novel (in which he found his
personal solution to the problem) the hero extricates himself
from emotional chaos by setting himself to work: Sebastian tack-
led the biological problem of the variation of species. Fifty years
later, in conversation with Bringuier, Piaget expressed the
solution in lighter vein: 'You can make life's little irritations
disappear by burying yourself in your work.' Piaget's life-plan,
in which work dominated affect, served him well enough. Yet
in his autobiography he had said that the best equilibrium is
achieved when there is 'reciprocal preservation of the parts and
of the whole'. In his little lecture on psychoanalysis Piaget ended
by proclaiming, with all the optimism of youth,

> There remains, therefore, an extremely instructive psycho-
> logical task to be undertaken in order to determine in each
> individual the relations between the state of his intelligence
> and the state of his autistic or unconscious life. And certainly,
> psychoanalysis is already full of insights in this regard.

Again, many years later, in the address to the American Society
of Psychoanalysis (reprinted in 'The Child and Reality'), Piaget
ended with a belief that general psychology should be 'based
simultaneously on the mechanisms discovered by psychoanalysis
and on the cognitive operations'. The simultaneous attack on
affectivity and intellect, however, was to elude him. He was
even in old age inclined to say that affectivity was no more than
a problem for neurology and endocrinology. Yet in his younger

days he thought he caught a glimpse of how these two aspects of human life – so often at odds within himself – could and should be reconciled in the ideal equilibrium. 'Let us therefore try to create in the school', he wrote in 'The Moral Judgment of the Child', 'a place where individual experimentation and reflection carried out in common come to each other's aid and balance one another'(Piaget, 1932, p. 392). There is enough in Piaget's idea to make it worth resurrecting as an educational objective.

REFERENCES

Bringuier, Jean-Claude (1980) 'Conversations with Jean Piaget'. University of Chicago Press.
Piaget, Jean (1918) 'Recherche'. Resume in Gruber, Howard E. and Vonèche, J. Jacques (1977), 'The Essential Piaget', London: Routledge & Kegan Paul.
— (1923) 'The Language and Thought of the Child' (English translation, 1926). London: Kegan Paul, Trench Trubner and Co.
— (1924) 'Judgment and Reasoning in the Child' (English translation, 1928). London: Routledge & Kegan Paul.
— (1932) 'The Moral Judgment of the Child' (English translation, 1932). London: Routledge & Kegan Paul.
— (1952) 'A History of Psychology in Autobiography', vol. IV, ed. E.G. Boring et al. New York: Russell and Russell.
— (1964) 'Six Psychological Studies' (English translation, 1967). New York: Random House.
— (1965) 'Insights and Illusions of Philosophy' (English translation, 1972). London: Routledge & Kegan Paul.
— (1969) 'Science of Education and the Psychology of the Child' (English translation, 1971). London: Longman.
— (1972) 'The Child and Reality' (English translation, 1973). New York: Grossman.

8 Piaget's theory and educational psychology

Geoffrey Brown

If one searches for a definitive statement of what constitutes a good theory, one is likely to be disappointed. There doesn't appear to be a handy template which one can hold against a formulation and say 'Yes, that's a good theory.' A number of authorities offer views however (Kuhn, 1970; Lakatos and Musgrave, 1970; Marx and Goodson, 1976), and they have much in common.

Among the criteria they cite are the following.

(1) Breadth of application: does the theory account for only a very narrow range of activities, or does it have general application?
(2) Testability: do the formulations generate predictions which can be shown to be true or false?
(3) Parsimony: how many assumptions must be made, or how many hypothetical constructs erected, in order to achieve a certain breadth of application?
(4) Fruitfulness: does it provide a framework upon which further research can be built?

There are others; the terminology varies from source to source, but the gist is the same.

On some of these criteria Piaget's theory gets a shining 'good theory' seal of approval. There can be little doubt that the breadth of application, in relation to the number of basic concepts invoked, is quite prodigious. To encompass play, mathematics, speech, morality, etc., within a basic model comprised of a few stages of cognitive development, operating in accordance with relatively few underlying logico-mathematical structures, is an accomplishment of the highest order. Furthermore, there can be little doubt that over the last five decades the spread of Genevan-type research theses and publications has assumed almost epidemic proportions. True, much of it cannot really claim to further the theory, or to test it in any serious way, but if activity is the criterion, it is certainly a fruitful theory. And, of course, there has also been a strong thread of genuinely original empirical work and commentary woven through these decades too.

This leaves the criterion of testability; and it has been left until last because it deserves special attention. Can the theory be tested? As we have suggested elsewhere (Brown and Desforges, 1979), there may be different answers for different aspects of the theory. For those aspects which can be tested, do the tests support the theory? It is suggested that often they do not. Yet it is contended that this is the criterion which should hold primacy over the others. For what benefit is to be derived from a theory, however parsimonious, however broad in field of application, however stimulating as a source of further work, if, when tested, it does not accord with the world as we find it. If, in other words, there is a very good chance that it is wrong.

Educational psychology is concerned with many facets of the learner, the context and the teacher. This paper will focus upon one very central concern, facilitating a child's learning of some curriculum item. In order to accomplish this it is necessary to know a number of things, and every teacher in training is made aware of these needs. They may be presented as a sequence of requirements:

(1)   to discover the present level of knowledge and under-
      standing possessed by the learner;
(2)   to find a way of organizing and presenting the new
      information in a way compatible with the present level of
      understanding; and
(3)   to then engage the learner and the task.

It is recognized that classroom practices are many and varied and the strategies adopted by learners are by no means uniform, but the sequence proposed still characterizes a great deal of classroom activity in Britain, even if Professor Bennett has withdrawn his support.

At each point in the sequence the Piagetian model appears to offer guidance, yet on closer inspection insuperable difficulties prevent implementation.

The standard Genevan position is that language development is preceded by cognitive development. That is, a child must possess certain operatory structures before he creates language forms which denote these operations, although Piaget has admitted that this may not always be the case and that parallel developments may occur (Ferreiro, 1971). Yet the traditional position is maintained; language is neither a sufficient nor a necessary condition for the development of operations. So if the teacher wishes to ascertain whether a child possesses certain forms of thought she might be misled into false negative errors if she listens to the explanations, or so the theory seems to indicate.

The status of language in Piagetian studies has led to criticism on a number of counts. At the most basic level, the method of critical exploration requires a unique dialogue with each subject.

While this may 'raise the hackles' of the 'experimental control' brigade, it probably has much to be said in its favour. However, some other issues are not so readily dismissed.

Smedslund (1977) has pointed out that, in order to decide whether a child is behaving logically, we must take for granted that he has correctly understood all the instructions. Yet the only way in which we can determine this is by observing his behaviour and taking it for granted that it is logical with respect to his understanding. So the method of critical exploration obliges the researcher to choose which he will take for granted and which he will study.

A second issue concerns the criteria by which operations are identified. The Genevan protocols demand that the presence of an operation be confirmed by the child's correct judgment and accompanying explanations; 'special attention should be paid to the child's justification of his answers. . . . ' (Inhelder and Sinclair, 1969). They even go so far as to criticize the 'judgment only' criterion used by others as not demonstrating true operations. Siegel (1978) comments that 'it would seem to be a paradox to postulate the independence of language and thought and then to rely on language to infer the existence of certain kinds of thought'. She perhaps overstates the case, for there is no claim to 'independence', but even if we substitute 'possible asynchrony' there is still a paradox. If language is not a sufficient or even a necessary condition for cognitive acquisitions, why is it a necessary criterion to establish their presence?

Siegel's results indicated a marked difference between three- and four-year-olds - the former were uninfluenced by linguistic cues, but not the latter. Furthermore, three-year-olds more frequently passed a concept attainment task and failed an associated language task. Only one or two children succeeded on a verbal task and failed the associated concept task. The author concluded that there was, therefore, no reason to require judgment plus explanations from the three-year-olds, but also that there was strong evidence that the relative independence of operations and language were disappearing in the four-year-olds. Thus, the traditional criteria would give reasonably accurate assessments of four-year-olds, but many false negative classifications for three-year-olds.

The problematic nature of child language is intensified by the recent work of Annette Karmiloff-Smith (1979). Her analyses of the ways in which young children used language suggested that it was inappropriate to analyse their utterances in terms of adult usage.

So there is some confusion. Is one to adopt judgment plus explanation as the criterion? If so, on what grounds? That language and operations are isomorphic? And by what criteria shall we judge the explanation? Maybe one should suppose that judgment will be in advance of explanations, and ignore the Genevan convention.

If this criterion problem is resolved, by using either judgments or judgments plus explanations, according to preference or habit, the teacher may assess the presence of an operatory structure. The notion of 'structure d'ensemble' proposes that, at any given point in time, a child's behaviour across a wide range of activities will be characterized by a particular logico-mathematical structure. So that, if the presence of a particular stage is determined by certain tasks, the level of performance on many other tasks may be predicted with reasonable probability. Yet what constitutes 'reasonable probability'? The theory acknow-ledges the likelihood of fluctuations during transitional stages, and because of the 'resistance' of certain materials. Yet the espousal of a structuralist approach demands the basic integrity of the stage notion.

So 'structure d'ensemble' leads to an expectation of high cor-relations between measures of a particular operation. Contrary evidence abounds (see Brown and Desforges, 1979; Pascual-Leone, 1970; Sigel and Hooper, 1968), and the evidence appears in every year of childhood and adolescence. Hamel (1974) gave a battery of multiple classifications and multiple seriation tests to groups of children between the ages of five and a half and nine years. Correlations varied from +0.39 to +0.72. Neimark (1975) traced the transition from concrete to formal operations with a longitudinal study of children between the ages of nine and twelve. While there was a reasonable degree of concurrency in her data, test-retest correlations were only of the order of +0.4, and the intra-subject variability led her to conclude that various aspects of formal operations did not appear concurrently.

Wason's demonstration that undergraduates could solve a logic problem in an everyday context but not in a formal and abstract form (Wason and Johnson-Laird, 1972) is another well-known example of lack of structure. It is now suggested that even the everyday context is irrelevant for today's undergraduates (Golding, 1981). Whatever the fluctuations over time and between contexts, it is clear that the concept of a formal operational stage has little to commend it in these circumstances.

Examples abound, and Flavell and Wohlwill (1969) chose to interpret Piaget's structures as descriptions of competence, as the only way of coping with the apparent lack of homogeneity. This may be an elegant theoretical ruse, but for the purposes of informing the practice of education it effectively rules the notion out of court. The task for educational psychology then becomes one of defining those psychological variables which intervene between competence and performance. When one considers how little is known of the ubiquitous 'resistance' used to explain some forms of 'décalage', it would seem that Piaget has said little to illuminate that area.

Even Flavell (1971), possibly the greatest expositor of the theory, conceded that the only version of 'stage' which he could countenance was that which denoted an emergent function. That is, the first indication of a particular structure would denote that, under certain conditions, it could be deployed. In view of

Harris's claim that 'modus tollendo tollens' (if $p.q$; $\bar{q}$; $\therefore \bar{p}$
could be found in the reasoning of five-year-olds), there is every
likelihood that, given appropriate tasks, all structures could be
discovered in a child before he ever attends school. So, once
more, the educators' concern must be with contexts which elicit
operations, not with the presence of a 'structure d'ensemble'.

So in the assessment of the pupil prior to teaching, it seems
that the theory might offer a means of construing a level of
performance on a specific task but not a means of describing a
repertoire of similar behaviours, assuming that the criterion
problem can be solved. Having made that assessment, the teacher
would then be in a position to organize material for the next
stage in the child's development, given the theoretical assurance
that the hierarchical stages are invariable. The evidence to support this contention is, indeed, quite strong. Most studies,
including a great many cross-cultural ones, support the universality of the developmental sequence. Yet there are sufficient
irregularities to counsel caution (Dasen, 1971; de Lemos, 1966;
Bovet, 1974). The confident claim to an empirically established,
universal sequence made by Inhelder, Sinclair and Bovet (1974),
that 'studies undertaken in Geneva and by other researchers
in various countries confirmed this order' (p. 246), is open to
doubt.

An alternative explanation would be that the sequence is not
derived from observation of individuals, but is a logical necessity
of the tasks themselves. Piaget may have said this when he
wrote: 'to characterize the stages of cognitive development we
therefore need to integrate two necessary conditions without
introducing any contradictions. These conditions for stages
are (a) that they must be defined to generate a constant order
of succession. . . .' (Piaget, 1970, p. 710), in which case the
tasks are designed to meet the criterion, and there is no reason
to expect a universal sequence on other tasks. This may well
explain the cross-cultural inconsistencies. Other cultures may
simply construe the tasks in other ways, and in their versions
the sequence no longer applies.

Finally, the crux of any developmental theory must be the
mechanism of change. Without specification of this, a theory
of cognitive development is a collection of content 'milestones'
which support equally any theory, be it based on cognitive
processing, behaviourist conditioning, or exposure to cosmic
radiation.

In Genevan theory 'the logical structure is not the result of
physical experience. It cannot be obtained by external reinforcement. The logical structure is reached only through internal
equilibration, by "self-regulation"' (Piaget, 1954). So the
message to the teacher is to facilitate this internal equilibration
and active self-regulation. Procedures which attempt change
by external reinforcement will be doomed to produce only limited
and ungeneralizable advances in cognition. Procedures which
follow 'the natural' sequence of acquisition and which enable the

learner actively to create new understanding, on the other hand, produce lasting changes which generalize to other tasks.

As Brainerd (1977) has pointed out, this belief that 'mother nature knows best' is an act of faith. In fact, we know very little about the situations in which children make progress outside the experimental setup.

Furthermore, it is by no means clear what is meant by an 'active' learner. It is sometimes taken to mean 'physically engaging with task materials', and as such is linked with the activity methods of primary classroom practice. Yet this is almost certainly not what the Genevans mean (well most of the time, anyway). Inhelder tells us that 'being cognitively active does not mean that the child merely manipulates a given type of material; he can be mentally active without physical manipulation, just as he can be mentally passive while actively manipulating objects' (Inhelder et al., 1974).

Since we have no direct access to mental activity there is here a danger of a self-fulfilling prophecy. If the development occurs, then action took place; if not, it possibly did not. And is it not possible that external reinforcement may also cause internal action? Evidence from Kendler and Kendler (1975), Siegel (1978) and Vygotsky (1962) suggest that this is so. Fundamental changes appear to take place when children of certain ages take part in learning experiments involving reinforcement of correct responses. These changes may be related to their ability to verbalize, and the results give every indication that something very like active self-regulation may have occurred.

Engelmann (1971) asserts that it is possible to teach children and to obtain generalizable responses. Furthermore, he suggests that 'natural' experiences are often noisy instances of concepts, and that the skilled teacher can draw examples which emphasize salient characteristics of the task. In other words, mother nature may make a rather inefficient teacher in some circumstances. The literature contains many other examples of training studies which appear to have been successful in achieving relatively permanent changes of behaviour which have been generalizable to other situations (see Brainerd, 1977, and Zimmerman and Rosenthal, 1974).

Another important aspect of the mechanism of development is the question of whether different individuals take different routes from one stage to the next. If this is the case, it is an important aspect of the theory for the educator. It engages the problem of accounting for the mechanism of transition, and the possibility that knowing the level of knowledge a child possesses may not be sufficient to facilitate change.

The Piagetian view seems to be that there is one specific route. In the acquisition of conservation, for instance, Piaget (1976) argued that identical systems of compensations were to be seen in cross-cultural studies.

There is little evidence on this issue, but curiously, one study by Bovet (1974) seems to contradict the hypothesis.

Studying the route to conservation of continuous quantity with
Algerian children, she gave them first of all a traditional conservation task in order to classify them as conservers, non-
conservers or transitionals. Then followed a period of 'experience'
(observing quantities of liquids in vessels of various sizes),
after which the conservation tests were repeated. The results
showed some unusual features, with conservers becoming non-
conservers, and older children doing less well than younger
ones. Neither of these phenomena show, categorically, that
alternative routes may have been followed; but the divergence
from the predicted path makes it a possible explanation. Bovet's
justifications for ignoring the awkward data, i.e., that the
differences were only temporary and that the 'experience'
sessions brought them back into line, seem unconvincing.

A study by Greenfield (1966) suggested that children in
Senegal and the USA justified their non-conservation responses
in totally different ways. The former used a type of reasoning
that has been termed 'action magic', in which human intervention
is deemed to have effected magical transformations. The American
children, on the other hand, showed the more familiar perceptual
confusion. As a consequence of this difference, screening
procedures greatly assisted the American children, but not those
from Senegal. They were assisted by being permitted to pour
the liquids themselves. Greenfield concluded that 'different
modes of thought can lead to the same results'. If this interpretation is correct – and it has been contested – we are told nothing
about these routes.

To conclude, it does not seem that Piagetian theory is of direct
assistance in the psychology of education. The means by which
children's operations should be judged are not entirely clear.
Where prescription exists it seems to be at odds with the theory.
With respect to stages, the evidence that stage is a useful way
of characterizing a relatively uniform structure underlying a
wide range of cognitive acts is not convincing. The claim to an
invariant sequence of stages may be true within the context of
Piagetian tasks, but it may reflect the logical structure of the
tasks rather than some basic principle in the learner's cognitive
processing. In attempts to effect change, the exhortation that
the learner must be 'active' does not seem to be translatable
into practical terms, particularly if it is suspected that the
action may have to follow different paths for different learners.

It may be contended that none of these were Piaget's intentions, indeed it may be true that the theory is of competence,
not performance. If these are so, or if they are not, the answer
to the question, 'what does Piaget's theory contribute to the
psychology of education?' remains the same: a sensitivity to
detail, a desire to understand the child's 'mistake' rather than
dismiss it – but in specific classroom practice, not a great deal.

But, of course, a theory is a tool, not a statement of some
ultimate reality. So if the tool does the job, use it. But if it
becomes apparent that the job could be done better, then examine

the qualities of the tool and retain the helpful features, but redesign the others. The worthy successor to this influential and ingenious theory will be one which can capitalize upon the abstract descriptions of operations employed by the Genevans, and marry them with task variables, and possibly with organismic variables in the learner too. The neatness of structuralism has taken us too far from the real world of the classroom.

REFERENCES

Bovet, M. (1974) Cross-cultural Study of Conservation Concepts: Continuous Quantities and Length, in B. Inhelder et al. (1974), 'Learning and the Development of Cognition'. London: Routledge & Kegan Paul.

Brainerd, C.J. (1977) Cognitive Development and Concept Learning: An Interpretative Review, in 'Psychological Bulletin', 84, pp. 919-39.

Brown, G. and Desforges, C. (1979) 'Piaget's Theory: A Psychological Critique'. London: Routledge & Kegan Paul.

Dasen, P.R. (1971) Cross-cultural Piagetian Research: A Summary in 'Journal of Cross-cultural Psychology', 3, pp. 23-39.

de Lemos, M.M. (1966) The Development of the Concept of Conservation in Australian Aboriginal Children. Unpublished PhD thesis, Australian National University, Canberra.

Engelmann, S. (1971) Does the Piagetian Approach Imply Instruction? in D.R. Green, M.P. Ford and G.B. Flamer (eds), 'Measurement and Piaget'. New York: McGraw-Hill.

Ferreiro, E. (1971). 'Les Relations dans le langage de l'enfant'. Paris: Droz (cited by Karmiloff-Smith, 1979).

Flavell, J.H. (1971) Stage-related Properties of Cognitive Development, in 'Cognitive Psychology', 2, pp. 421-53.

Flavell, J.H. and Wohlwill, J.F. (1969) Formal and Functional Aspects of Cognitive Development, in D. Elkind and J.H. Flavell (eds), 'Studies in Cognitive Development: Essays in Honour of Jean Piaget'. New York: Oxford University Press.

Golding, E. (1981) The Effect of Past Experience on Problem Solving. Paper presented at the Annual Conference of the British Psychological Society, April 1981.

Greenfield, P.M. (1966) On Culture and Conservation, in D.R. Price-Williams (ed.) (1969), 'Cross-cultural Studies'. Harmondsworth: Penguin.

Hamel, B.R. (1974) 'Children from 5-7'. Rotterdam University Press.

Harris, P. (1975) Inference and Semantic Development, in 'Journal of Child Language', 2, pp. 143-52.

Inhelder, B. and Sinclair, H. (1969) Learning Cognitive Structures, in P. Mussen, J. Langer and J. Covington (eds), 'Trends and Issues in Developmental Psychology'. New York: Holt, Rinehart & Winston.

Inhelder, B., Sinclair, H. and Bovet, M. (1974). 'Learning and

the Development of Cognition'. London: Routledge & Kegan Paul.
Karmiloff-Smith, A. (1979) 'A Functional Approach to Child
Language'. Cambridge University Press.
Kendler, H.H. and Kendler, T.S. (1975) From Discrimination
Learning to Cognitive Development: Neobehaviouristic Odyssey,
in W.K. Estes (ed.), 'Handbook of Learning and Cognitive
Processes'. Willsdale, N.J. Lawrence Erlbaum.
Kuhn, T.S. (1970) 'The Structure of Scientific Revolutions'.
University of Chicago Press.
Lakatos, I. and Musgrave, A. (eds) (1970) 'Criticism and the
Growth of Scientific Knowledge'. Cambridge University Press.
Marx, M.H. and Goodson, F.E. (1976) 'Theories in Contemporary
Psychology'. New York: Macmillan.
Neimark, E.D. (1975) Longitudinal Development of Formal
Operations Thought, in 'Genetic Psychology Monograph', 91,
pp. 171-225.
Pascual-Leone, J. (1970) A Mathematical Model for the Transition
Role in Piaget's Developmental Stages, in 'Acta Psychologica',
32, pp. 301-45.
Piaget, J. (1954) 'The Origins of Intelligence'. New York: Basic
Books.
Piaget, J. (1970) Piaget's Theory, in J. Mussen (ed.),
'Carmichael's Manual of Child Psychology', 3rd ed. vol. 1.
New York: Wiley.
Piaget, J. (1976) Need and Significance of Cross-cultural Studies
in Genetic Psychology, in B. Inhelder and H.H. Chipman (eds),
'Piaget and his School'. New York: Springer Verlag.
Siegel, L.S. (1978) The Relationship of Language and Thought
in the Pre-Operational Child, in L.S. Siegel and C.J. Brainerd,
(eds), 'Alternatives to Piaget'. New York: Academic Press.
Siegel, L.S. and Brainerd, C.J. (eds) (1978) 'Alternatives to
Piaget: Critical Essays on the Theory'. New York: Academic
Press.
Sigel, I.E. and Hooper, F.H. (eds) (1968) 'Logical Thinking in
Children'. New York: Holt, Rinehart & Winston.
Smedslund, J. (1977) Piaget's Psychology in Practice, in 'British
Journal of Educational Psychology', 47, pp. 1-6.
Vygotsky, L.S. (1962) 'Thought and Language'. Cambridge, Mass.
MIT Press.
Wason, P.C. and Johnson-Laird, P.N. (1972) 'Psychology of
Reasoning: Structure and Content'. London: Batsford.
Zimmerman, B.J. and Rosenthal, T.L. (1974) Observing Learning
of Rule-governed Behaviour by Children, in 'Psychological
Bulletin', 81, pp. 29-42.

Part 6

Language

9 Language and communication: Piaget's influence

Peter Lloyd

What I have to say about Piaget's contribution to our understanding of language and communication will in no way amount to
a hymn of praise. Piaget's work in this field is too controversial
to allow unqualified acceptance, nor is it an area in which he
carried out extensive research. Nevertheless, he did produce
one major book in this field, 'The Language and Thought of
the Child' ('LTC'), and it is fitting in this tribute that I should
devote most of my attention to a work whose bones have by no
means been picked clean.

But to begin with I wish to refer briefly to two areas in which
Piaget's influence has been important, if indirect. I can afford
to be brief since there are a number of good sources for this
work already available.

THE ORIGINS OF LANGUAGE

When it became clear that an account of language development
would have to do more than write grammars of the verbal
output of fledgling speakers, a search began for the basis on
which language was built. Writers like MacNamara (1972) pointed
out that the infant had already constructed a world of meaning
before language began to be acquired, and it seemed sensible
to assume that the language system mapped on to these existing
meanings. Since there was a ready-made account of the growth
of meaning in the months before language, it is not surprising
that sensorimotor intelligence came to be used in the service of
theories of language development.

Piaget's theory appears to have been used in two ways. There
are those that adopt what Cromer (1974) has called the cognition
hypothesis, the leading exponent of whom is Sinclair. It was
she who first drew attention to the parallels between sensorimotor
and language structures. Others who have studied these
parallels include Edwards (1973) and Brown (1973) with a view
to 'increasing confidence in the linguistic analysis accorded to
the child's utterances' (Elliot, 1981, p. 51). The cognition

hypothesis basically asserts that linguistic structures are not acquired until the cognitive structures which underpin them are present. This is the strong Piagetian position of language reflecting existing cognitive structures.

A related approach to the problem, 'Where does language come from?' sought an answer in the preverbal patterns of communication between parent and child. Bates (1976), Greenfield and Smith (1976), Bruner (1975) and, in this country, Lock (1980) are leading exponents of the pragmatic approach. They also have found Piaget's theory helpful. Bates (1976), for instance, has traced linguistic precursors by observing the role of objects and gestures in communicative interactions with adults and has associated them with the fifth stage of the sensorimotor period. Golinkoff (1981) has noted that Piaget's description of the development of causality has an 'intimate link' with the shift from unintentional to intentional communication. Her chapter provides a good review of this area.

WORD MEANING

One of the industries that has been spawned by Piaget's massive theoretical system is that devoted to the manufacture of efficient verbal instructions. There has long been a suspicion that Piaget relied overmuch in his tests of reasoning on verbal terms, the meaning of which might have been ambiguous or at least indeterminate for young children. There are two ways round this problem. One is to abandon instructions and use non-verbal methods (e.g., Siegel, 1978); the other is to try to discover the meaning which the terms have for the child - words that crop up regularly in Piagetian tests such as 'same', 'more' and 'all'.

Some of the earliest investigations in this vein were done by Donaldson and Wales (1970) and their co-workers at the Edinburgh Cognition Project. Most of this work is available in print and so I want here only to offer one or two remarks. As Elliot points out in a succinct review of the area, 'the major concern is not whether the children understand the language used but whether they understand the properties of the objects and situations which are the topic of conversation' (Elliot, 1981, p. 129). But it is important to be sure that language is not getting in the way of this goal. Numerous studies have now shown that children's grasp of terms like 'more' and 'less', 'same' and 'different', and 'all' and 'some' is insecure. But it is no help, in my view, to label the strategies that children manifest in their handling of these terms as 'response biases', as is done by Richards (1979) in an otherwise valuable review of work generated by Clark's semantic features theory.

The danger of epithets like response bias is that it is to dismiss the factors that are going to help us account for the growth of word meaning as artefacts of poor experimental design. We know that language comprehension is affected by complex

interactions involving the materials used and the child's
familiarity with them, the type of response requested and various
pragmatic factors such as rules of discourse (Warden, 1981).
Early studies (Donaldson and Lloyd, 1974; Donaldson and
McGarrigle, 1974) pointed out the powerful influence that
features like fullness, size and amount could have on the interpretation of sentences. More recently we are seeing the
emergence of some superordinate organizing principles which
allow us to go beyond the stage of specifying particular contextual circumstances for the comprehension of each function
word. Canonicality would seem to be one such principle. This is
the notion that there are usual or canonical relations between
objects and events to be found in the world and that violation of
these conventions leads to errors in interpreting language
(Freeman, Lloyd and Sinha, 1980). Another set of principles
is contained in rules of discourse whether governing intention
(McGarrigle and Donaldson, 1975) or setting up the topic-
comment distinction (Freeman, Stedmon and Sinha, 1982).

COMMUNICATION BETWEEN CHILDREN

*The continuing appeal of 'The Language and Thought
of the Child'*
In the 1979 Citations Index 'LTC' was cited more than seventy
times, and that of course excludes citations that appeared in
books. What accounts for the popularity of Piaget's first book,
published originally in 1923 and translated in 1926? It seems to
me that there are a number of reasons why this work continues
to be cited and they are worth elucidating since they go some
way to explaining the nature of Piaget's influence on the field
of language and communication.
    To start with, 'LTC' was Piaget's first book. He refers to it
in the foreword to the third edition as 'merely a collection of
preliminary studies', but Claparède in his preface to the first
edition obviously considered it much more than that. He refers
repeatedly to the genius of Piaget, and it is apparent that he
recognized that in Piaget the Institut Rousseau had secured a
major talent who was providing 'a completely new version of the
child's mind'. (I doubt if even Claparède could have anticipated
that this new recruit would remain productive for well over
fifty years and produce sixty other books as well as countless
articles, and would truly revolutionize our understanding of
the child's mind.) The fact that a book is an author's first
gives it no special status in itself, but if it is at the same time
the first significant statement in a field of inquiry then it does
assume a special status. I will argue below that this is indeed
the case.
    A second reason for the book's surviving appeal is that it is
one of Piaget's most accessible works. To some extent this is
true of all the books of the early period before Piaget began

tackling the enterprise of genetic epistemology in earnest. The hallmark is there, however, in the form of theoretical discussion alongside subject protocols plus the attempt to fit the whole into the framework of a child logic. Despite the relative transparency of the work, it has not prevented its attracting considerable controversy, especially in relation to what Piaget did or did not mean by egocentrism, of which more anon.

A third reason for this book continuing to hold interest is that it is the only book that Piaget wrote on language. Anybody being attracted to Piaget's theory and also having an interest in language would want to read what he had to say on the subject. I doubt, however, that students of language in this position have drunk very deeply from this particular well. This is because 'LTC' is outside the tradition of language development and says virtually nothing about language acquisition. Nor, it must be said, does it have a great deal to say in the conventional sense about the relationship between language and thought. Those with an interest in these matters should read 'Play, Dreams and Imitation in Childhood' (1951).

What then is 'LTC' about? Piaget tells us in the very first sentence. The question he is attempting to answer is: 'What are the needs which a child tends to satisfy when he talks?' In other words, this is a functional approach which may seem surprising for a figure who is considered a structuralist. Claparède, in his preface, explains the contradiction by pointing out that Piaget is able to delineate structure only 'because . . . the questions he set himself in the first instance were questions of function' (Piaget, 1959, p. xvi).

This paradox is even more interesting when set against the historical context of the 1960s when, arguably, 'LTC' enjoyed a resurgence. At that time, in Chomsky's wake, structuralist approaches to language were in the ascendant. Those who felt that the essentially psychological aspects of language were being neglected searched around for an account that would focus on language as it is used, Skinner's theory having been discredited. And who should offer a way forward but the prince of structuralism himself, Piaget, with his account of how children in the preschool and early school years employed language.

I am not here proposing that Piaget through 'LTC' launched the reaction against formalism in psycholinguistics, so paving the way for pragmatics, speech act theory and other functionalist positions. (Clearly, linguists like Halliday, sociolinguists like Hymes and philosophers like Searle had not a little to do with it.) What I would suggest is that Piaget's was an important contribution and that re-reading the work reveals a number of lines of investigation that have surfaced in recent years as if they were quite new. Interestingly enough, another book to merit a revival at about the same time was a volume also published in the 1920s, de Laguna's 'Speech: Its Function and Development' (1927). Whereas de Laguna's book excited the interest of those concerned with the question of input, 'LTC' was an obvious starting point for those interested in what children who had acquired the basic structure of language could do with that system. This was the focus of studies in the late 1960s by Glucksberg and Krauss (1967) and Flavell et al. (1968).

A new dimension in that work – new at that time – was the attention given to communication between children, when the prevailing tide was represented by the corpora derived from very young children talking to adults. The research tradition of peer communication subsequently continued in naturalistic settings with pioneer studies by Garvey and Hogan (1973) and Mueller (1972). The link with 'LTC' remained but it became less an inspirational one and more one concerned with refuting some of the claims made about egocentric speech.

There are three more reasons which help to explain the central place that 'LTC' still enjoys. There is the powerful demonstration of a language deficit in the form of egocentric speech. This apparent inability to observe one of the basic rules of communication ranks alongside the object concept and conservation as a discovery. And the importance of the spectacular as well as the counter-intuitive should not be underestimated even in the scientific community. The fact that children said that the quantity of liquid changed merely through pouring it from one vessel into another of different proportions is a phenomenon that has played a large part in making Piaget's reputation. (What is the prophet without his miracles?)

But beyond this, Piaget's theory of egocentrism has been an influential construct in the whole field of social cognition. The debate with Vygotsky is well known, and doubtless students return to 'LTC' to discover precisely what Piaget did say. It is perhaps worth mentioning in passing that a clearer account can be found in Piaget's comments on Vygotsky's 'Thought and Language' (1962) in the hardback version of the MIT Press book.

Although 'LTC' is primarily remembered for what it has to say about egocentric speech, it also introduced an important methodology. Both observational and experimental methods were used, one to record the spontaneous conversations of children at play in the nursery and the other to examine the ability to pass on specific information. The former method revealed the extent of non-social speech among the children and the latter demonstrated a technique for measuring the degree of understanding between children. Both methods still flourish. Garvey and Hogan are in the tradition of naturalistic recording followed by linguistic analysis of the resulting data. Modern procedures of discourse analysis have sharpened the techniques, and subsequent research has allowed us to place different interpretations on some of the phenomena which Piaget first isolated. The experimental method was the forerunner of that used by Krauss and Glucksberg and those who work in referential communication. Here, it will be argued, contemporary approaches have neglected some of the features of Piaget's method that gave it its special strength.

The final reason I shall offer for the continuing popularity of 'LTC' is that it is a work to which one can keep returning with profit. Sinclair (1978), for instance, has looked again at the chapter on a child's questions and noted reference to the idea of presupposition which is currently exercising workers such as Bates (1979) and Greenfield and Zukow (1978). On re-reading the book for this occasion, I was struck by the references to what we now call 'speech-act theory', though Piaget traces them back to the psychoanalytic writers. As Sinclair says, it 'remains a very exciting work'.

Categories of egocentric speech
Having indicated why I believe 'LTC' is still often cited, I want to go on to explain what I think is still of value in the work and what should be treated more circumspectly. But first I should make it clear that this is not simply a rephrasing of what has gone before. What causes a work to be cited does not necessarily amount to its most valuable qualities. For example, the reason that 'LTC' appears in many reference lists is chiefly by way of a ritual genuflection to the original source. Hence my point about his being first in the field. There are undoubtedly a number of works that fall into this category in all branches of scholarship. Once one has gained a reputation as the first to say something authoritative, one is assured of being cited even if not read!

I shall begin with the distinctions that Piaget draws between the functions of language that he identified from his corpus of spontaneous speech. The main division is between egocentric speech, defined as speech where the child 'does not bother to know to whom he is speaking nor whether he is being listened to', and socialized speech, where communication is directed at another. It is worth briefly going through these categories, for they illustrate the changes that have taken place in our understanding as well as some of the confusion that has arisen.

The components of egocentric speech are repetition, monologue and collective monologue. Repetition is regarded as behaviour where the child repeats for the pleasure of talking with no thought of talking to anyone. Piaget is working here with six-year-olds, but interestingly he refers to the imitation of the young child who copies the syllables and sounds he hears. In both cases the phenomenon appears to hold little interest for Piaget, yet there is now evidence to show the important role played by repetition as a scheme for marking the given-new distinction (Keenan, 1977) and as a strategy for conserving information-processing capacity (Shatz, 1978). Wood (1981), working at Manchester, has examined the parts played by mothers and young children in maintaining a channel of communication and repairing breakdown when it occurs. The child's self-repeats, it appears, are an important aspect, but it is not Piaget's echolalia since there are frequently subtle changes of intonation or expansions and the child is clearly using the behaviour to influence the listener.

The other egocentric category is monologue, which comes in a simple and collective form. The only difference between monologue and collective monologue is that in the latter someone else is associated with the action but in both cases bystanders are 'expected neither to attend nor to understand' (Piaget, 1959, p. 9). But monologue does serve a function, and I think Piaget may have underestimated its significance. To make the point I need to quote at some length from 'LTC'. 'For the child,' Piaget says, 'words are much nearer action and movement than for us' (p. 13). And on the same page, 'words (are) so packed with concrete significance that the mere fact of uttering them, even without any reference to action, could be looked upon as the factor initiating the action in question' (p. 13). This seems to be very close to speech-act theory, which has become such a force in accounts of the growth of communicative competence some fifty years after Piaget wrote these words. But there is something more striking. Piaget writes of the child: 'Impelled, even when he is alone, to speak as he acts', and, further, 'the child will often talk with the sole aim of marking the rhythm of his action'.

Piaget gives an example of such a monologue which I cannot quote in full here, but one short extract will serve to illustrate. The child (Pie) is with his number book next to the counting frame. '(He goes to the frame to see what colour to choose for his number so that it should correspond to the ninth row in the frame). Pink chalk, it will have to be 9.' The significance of such sequences for Piaget is as follows: 'The whole of this monologue has no further aim than to accompany the action as it takes place' (p. 15).

By using a word like 'accompany', he seems to imply that speech is little more than a harmless appendage. Someone who takes a very different viewpoint is, of course, Vygotsky (1962, 1978) In 'Mind and Society' he claims that 'the most significant moment in the course of intellectual development occurs when speech and practical activity . . . converge' (1978, p. 24). And later, in reviewing results of a number of experiments, he says, 'A child's speech is as important as the role of action in attaining the goal. Children not only speak about what they are doing; their speech and action are part of *one and the same complex psychological function*, directed toward the solution of the problem at hand' (p. 25). This is surely what Pie is doing in the extract cited above.

In the celebrated debate between two of the giants of developmental psychology, I found myself leaning towards Vygotsky ever since an episode in the research I was carrying out at the Edinburgh Cognition Project. Two four-year-olds, a boy and a girl, were participating in a simple referential communication task in which the speaker had to select one of six pictures of a car and identify it for the listener with a verbal description. Essentially this required discriminating three features - the colour of the car, whether or not it was occupied,

and the pattern on the wheels. A number of trials had ensued
and it was the girl's turn to choose and describe a picture. As
she was about to start, the boy interrupted her with a remark
about the number of cars he had. The girl admonished him for
his interjection and bent to the task again saying quietly to
herself, but distinctly audible, 'colour first'. She then pro-
ceeded to give a description in which the colour of the car,
'blue' was spoken first. This reminded me of Vygotsky's claim
that egocentric speech in its regulatory function can be elicited,
brought to the surface, by using an interruption technique.

On its own my example is slender evidence, and I am aware
that replications of Vygotsky's and Luria's work on the regulatory function of speech have had mixed success (Wozniak,
1972). Nevertheless, the story that Vygotsky offers us in this
connection seems more convincing than that of Piaget, and
rereading 'LTC' has made me wonder if Piaget missed the force
of speech as an organizing factor in cognition (which is not the
same as saying a determinant of thought) through his desire
to deny speech a communicative role in such contexts; for
example, 'speech functions only as a stimulus, and in nowise
as a means of communication' (Piaget, 1959, p. 15). The striking thing to me is how aware Piaget is of the ubiquity of speech
in the child's interactions with his world and, what is more,
how he recognizes that it serves 'to accompany, to reinforce
and to supplement action' (p. 16). At points like this it seems
but a short step to the position of the Russian psychologist
but one that we know Piaget was resistant to taking.

Piaget and his supporters have for many years despaired of
critics who have attacked the notion of egocentrism without
understanding it. Although Piaget (1962) makes one of his
clearest statements in this regard in the reply to Vygotsky,
he must nevertheless shoulder much of the blame for the
confusion that continues. It is undeniable that not only does
he sometimes define egocentric speech as speech for oneself,
as I have indicated above, recent protestations to the contrary
notwithstanding (Inhelder and Karmiloff-Smith, 1978), but he
also makes radical claims about the all-pervasiveness of egocentric speech. And one does not have to delve back into
Piaget's first book to obtain evidence of this. It is sufficient
to examine the well-known textbook, 'The Psychology of the
Child', first published in 1966 and translated into English in
1969 (Piaget and Inhelder, 1969, p. 120):

> The fact is that the speech of subjects between four and six
> (observed in situations in which children work, play and
> speak freely) is not intended to provide information, ask
> questions, etc. (that is, it is not socialised language), but
> consists rather of monologues or 'collective monologues' in the
> course of which everyone talks to himself without listening to
> the others (that is, egocentric language).

This seems to be a ridiculous exaggeration, since there is abundant evidence from Piaget's own work that egocentric speech never coincided with speech as a whole. For instance, in the chapter appended to 'LTC' in 1959 it states that between the ages of three and six egocentric speech 'gradually decreases while at the same time it fluctuates between half and one-third of the total amount of speech' (p. 257).

Categories of social speech

It is time now to turn to the other side of a coin on which we have already seen egocentrism writ large. Socialized speech consists of adapted information, criticism, commands, requests and questions and answers. In his discussion of these categories Piaget makes some of his most telling observations, yet the work as a whole is remembered for what it has to say about egocentric speech.

Adapted information is that which 'makes the hearer listen and contrives to influence him, that is, to tell him something' (Piaget, 1959, p. 19). It accounts for about 30 per cent of spontaneous socialized speech and Piaget regarded it as the most advanced form of dialogue. In a fascinating passage which anticipates the work of Doise, Mugny and Perret-Clermont (1976) many years later, as well as my colleague James Russell, he says (Piaget, 1959, p. 20):

> The dialogue of children deserves to be made the object of a special and very searching investigation, for it is probably through the habit of arguing that . . . we first become conscious of the rules of logic, and the forms of deductive reasoning.

Yet Piaget also talks of those 'rare occasions when we can talk of arguments taking place between children'. Granting that Piaget means verbal dispute and not squabbles over possessions, recent research shows that the argument is by no means a rare phenomenon in child discourse. Genishi and di Paolo (in the press) found a total of 189 arguments in twenty hours of audiotape taken from a preschool classroom attended by seven children. Although the majority of these arguments were simple and repetitious, 28 per cent were defined as complex, consisting of three phases and involving topics like number, conduct, truth and role.

Adapted information is placed in a category apart from functions like 'criticism and derision', 'commands and requests' and 'question and answers'. The reasoning does not seem altogether sound. The justification hinges round the idea that only conversation which has ideas as its subject matter can be considered informative dialogue. The category 'criticism and derision', therefore, is 'not to convey thoughts but to satisfy non-intellectual instincts such as pugnacity, pride, emulation, etc.'. Leaving aside the question of whether such 'instincts' are devoid

of intellectual content, the examples which Piaget himself offers
hardly seem to support his position:

'I've got a much bigger pencil than you.'
'That's not like an owl. Look, Pie, what he's done.'
'We made that house, it isn't theirs.'

While none of these is an earth-shattering statement, they all
contain an exercise in comparison of classes, and all are communicating information. It would be unwise to exaggerate, but the
denigration of non-intellectual pursuits in 'LTC' sometimes
verges on the offensive. That which is subjective or emotive is
characterized as less worthy than pure reason. More remarkable
is the fact that commands and requests are regarded as language
that 'will only assist action', with the clear implication that
this is an inferior and not a truly social form. From a theorist
who gives action such a prominent role in his theory this is
surprising, all the more so since the examples quoted again seem
to involve the transmission of information. For example:

'Mustn't come in here without paying.'
'Give me the blue one.'

Questions and answers make up 50 per cent of socialized speech
and Piaget's analysis is an interesting one. But what is once
again apparent is that question and answer – the very stuff of
conversation – are relegated to something less than adapted
information. Answers are suspect because they 'do not belong
to the spontaneous speech of the child'. Since most of what one
says is contingent on what has been said, it is surprising that
anything fulfils the exalted criteria set for adapted information.
When we turn to questions, we get the familiar arguments
about the absence of intellectual intercourse among the children
on the subject of causality, and the absence of proof and logical
justifications in their discussions. On occasions like this one is
left wondering not merely whether Piaget ever had a conversation with the man on the Genevan equivalent of the Clapham
omnibus (of that we can be in no doubt), but whether he ever
stepped outside the confines of his own mind. An even more
staggering assertion is that 'there is no real social life between
children of less than 7 or 8 years' (Piaget, 1959, p. 40). Even
though one knows that Piaget is referring to the fact that the
child is unable to differentiate the individual from the social,
the statement is unpalatable to anyone who has observed the
everyday affairs of young friends.
Finally, then, Piaget's taxonomy for the functions of language
is inadequate, which is hardly surprising nearly sixty years
on. The dissatisfaction, however, is less with the discrete
categories themselves than with the pervading undercurrent
which wishes to equate 'socialized' with 'interchange of thought'
in a contemporary theoretical climate which, with good reason,

sees man as a creature inherently social from birth.

The current relevance of Piaget's views of communication
What, then, is the main value still to be derived from 'LTC'?
Apart from its enduring merit as a source of challenging ideas
(and I have tried to illustrate some of these), there are two
very important lessons. One concerns method and the other,
although a theoretical point, ultimately has its significance for
method also.

The functions of language that have been discussed were
derived from carefully documented spontaneous discourse. In
order to know what children understand of what they hear,
Piaget believed it was necessary to use an experimental method
in which one had control over the information to be communicated
and could measure the extent to which it had been successfully
assimilated.

The technique consisted of two types of task, one involving
recounting a story and the other explaining the workings of a
simple mechanical object like a tap with the use of diagrams.
The procedure was for an adult to tell a story (or explain how
a tap worked) to one child and then for that child to tell the
story in turn to a friend. The friend subsequently recounted
the story back to the adult. The accounts of both children
are noted.

The advantages of this method are that it allows comparison of
performance and pinpoints what aspects of a story or explanation
give difficulty, i.e., get omitted or distorted. One can also
compare the performance of adults and children as 'explainers'
on tasks of this nature. It is a paradigm, indeed, that has been
much favoured in research on referential communication
(Glucksberg, Krauss and Higgins, 1975; Asher, 1978; Lloyd and
Beveridge, 1981), although the majority of users have neglected
one of Piaget's basic tenets, that of reciprocity. It must also
be said that Piaget himself seems occasionally to have overlooked
this, one of the keystones of his theory. I will explain what I
mean.

We are all aware that communication is not only a social
phenomenon but a reciprocal one. It is an interaction that
demands exchange; participants take turns in contributing
passages of speech and react to the responses of others. If there
is no reciprocity we get monologue instead of conversation. It
is true that in certain situations, such as conferences and
political meetings, there may be long stretches where only one
individual is talking. But it would be misleading to think that
such contexts lack reciprocity any more than to assume that
they are not social. Even the least sensitive speakers take
account of their audience, so that they do not start until they
have been introduced and they wait until their audiences have
settled before starting their delivery. Should any part of the
speech produce laughter, applause or a hostile outburst, the
speaker will pause until the audience's contribution has ceased.

Thus I wish to make the unremarkable claim that communication takes place in social situations and that it is a reciprocal or interdependent activity in which one party's contribution determines, and is itself determined by, the contribution of the other party. Perhaps the only exception to this rule is the printed word and the broadcasting media in which the audience functions in a non-reciprocal manner, although, as all psychologists know, effective reading or listening is an active, rather than passive, affair.

Now, what has all this to do with Piaget's contribution to language and communication? I believe that one of Piaget's major contributions to developmental psychology is to have laid to rest for all time the notion of the child as a lump of clay to be moulded by agents of socialization. It has become what Bruner might call a psychological banality that the child plays an active role in the construction of his world. Be that as it may, these basic tenets seem often to have been abandoned in communication research. Thus much contemporary work uses situations which are distorted forms of interaction. One of the participants might be blindfolded or behind a screen or required to keep silent or to sit on his or her hands, yet the results are discussed as though they can be generalized to everyday contexts. What is more, measures are often taken from only one of the participants, either speaker or listener, as though the performance is unaffected by what the other does. Piaget himself seems to fall into the same trap by focusing only on what the explainer says and not examining the interaction that takes place between the two. If he had done the latter and used more appropriate tasks (see below), he might not have come to the conclusion he did (Piaget, 1959, p. 125):

> It is only from the age of 7 or 8 that there can be any talk of genuine understanding between children. Till then, the egocentric factors of verbal expression (elliptical style, indeterminate pronouns, etc.) and of understanding itself, as well as the derivative factors (such as lack of order in accounts given, juxtaposition, etc.) are all too important to allow of any genuine understanding between children.

Piaget would no doubt have argued that it is precisely because reciprocity is lacking that young children are such ineffective communicators, but the question is an empirical one and if one looks then one finds. Indeed, one finds many examples in Piaget's own work and in children below seven and eight. For example, this conversation between Hans three years, eight months) and Barbara (four years, one month) (Piaget, 1959, p. 247).

Barbara: I want to make a fire (goes near the stove).
Hans: No, Barbara, you mustn't make a fire because we have central heating.

Barbara: Yes, I will.
Hans: No, you musn't make a fire because it's already
          warm with the central heating.

and:

Hans: Yesterday, I had to have tea all alone.
Barbara: Why, all alone?
Hans: Because of you, you weren't there.

If, on average, this accounts for some 20 per cent of children's spontaneous conversation, why should it not be used at length in experimental situations which encourage it? The obvious answer is that Piaget did this and found the children's language 'saturated with egocentrism'. Piaget's tasks, however, were demanding, including twelve-point stories and nine-part explanations of the working of a mechanical object. Accordingly, we need to employ different formal task situations adapted to the capabilities of young children (e.g., Maratsos, 1973; Lloyd and Beveridge, 1981). Apart from the fact that Piaget's tasks are too demanding for preschool children, there is a methodological and theoretical preference for starting with the simplest situation and increasing the difficulty as necessary.

This brings me to the theoretical point made by Piaget which I believe should be adapted to his method. While considering what he calls the 'highest types of conversation between children', collaboration and argument, Piaget distinguishes two different cases: the acted case and the verbal case. The former, as its name implies, is connected with action; the collaboration or argument is said to be accompanied by gestures and hand movements. Piaget goes on to say, 'it matters little, therefore, whether the talk is intelligible or not, since the talkers have the object under their eyes' (Piaget, 1959, p. 77). Piaget's impression is that in acted conversation children of five and six years understand each other well but in the verbal case, involving abstraction, understanding comes only with the reduction of egocentrism between the ages of seven and eight.

Related classifications have been provided by Olson (1970) - sentences as descriptions and sentences as propositions - and Leushina (cited in Zaporozhets and Elkonin, 1971), who contrasts 'situational speech' (typical of pre-school children), which is heavily embedded in the ongoing situation, with 'contextual speech', where the meaning is contained in the sentence itself.

The point is therefore a simple one. If we wish to study the communication skills of young children, we should do so in situations which are appropriate to their cognitive capacities. Piaget's tasks are not a model in this respect, but in his terminology we should foster collaboration that involves action.

CONCLUSION

Piaget has done us a service in pointing out how far short of
communicative competence children are when they arrive in the
educational system. One of the important research areas now
opening up relates to how the transition from highly context-
dependent to relatively context-free language (and thought)
takes place and whether there are methods that can facilitate the
transition. This work is, and should be, done in both the field
and the laboratory. The laboratory, as I have argued elsewhere
(Lloyd and Beveridge, 1981), certainly has a role to play in
this effort because one can examine systematically the variables
that lead children to recognize the ambiguities and misunderstandings in what they say and hear. Furthermore, the laboratory is better able to simulate the classroom (where they are
going) than the home (where they have come from.)
   Piaget may well have had in mind what I have just been saying
when he wrote in his foreword to 'LTC' (1959, p. xix):

   I am convinced that the mark of theoretical fertility in a science
   is its capacity for practical application. This book is therefore
   addressed to teachers as much as to specialists in child
   psychology, and the writer will be only too pleased if the
   results he has accumulated are of service to the art of teaching. He is convinced in this connection that what he tries to
   prove in this work concerning the egocentrism of child thought
   and the part played by social life in the development of reason,
   must admit of pedagogic application.

At the beginning of this paper I said that I would not be
providing a paean to Piaget, and readers may now regard this
as an understatement. But my intention has been to demonstrate
that Piaget's only large-scale study of language is still a work to
be reckoned with. In doing this it has been difficult to ignore
shortcomings, and to have done so would have been to insult the
reader. Indeed, it would have been alarming if the advances in
knowledge and techniques that have taken place in the nearly
sixty years since the work was published had not made some of
the research obsolete.
   The remarkable thing is how little we can afford totally to
write off. With an increasing concern for ecological validity
levels of analysis in language and cognition have moved steadily
upwards so that investigations are directed towards text,
narrative and discourse rather than word, sentence or utterance. Those with an interest in these fields will find a fund of
ideas in 'Language and Thought of the Child'. The fact that so
little of this fund was actually cashed in by Piaget is our loss,
but the ideas remain for us to pursue, none the less.

REFERENCES

Asher, S.R. (1978) Referential Communication, in G.J. White-
hurst and B.J. Zimmerman (eds), 'The Functions of Language
and Cognition'. New York: Academic Press.
Bates, E. (1976) 'Language and Context: The Acquisition of
Pragmatics'. New York: Academic Press.
Bates, E. (1979) 'The Emergence of Symbols'. New York: Academic
Press.
Brown, R. (1973) 'A First Language: The Early Stages'.
Cambridge, Mass.: Harvard University Press.
Bruner, J.S. (1975) The Ontogenesis of Speech Acts, in
'Journal of Child Language', 2, pp. 1-19.
Cromer, R. (1974) The Development of Language and Cognition:
The Cognition Hypothesis, in B. Foss (ed.), 'New Perspectives
in Child Development'. Harmondsworth: Penguin.
De Laguna, G.A. (1927) 'Speech: Its Function and Develop-
ment'. New Haven, Conn.: Yale University Press.
Doise, W., Mugny, G., and Perret-Clermont, A.N. (1976)
Social Interaction and Cognitive Development: Further Evidence,
in 'European Journal of Social Psychology', pp. 245-7.
Donaldson, M. and Lloyd, P. (1974) Sentences and Situations:
Children's Judgments of Match and Mismatch, in F. Bresson
(ed.), 'Current Problems in Psycholinguistics'. Paris: CNRS.
Donaldson, M. and McGarrigle, J. (1974) Some Clues to the
Nature of Semantic Development, in 'Journal of Child Language',
1, pp. 185-94.
Donaldson, M. and Wales, R. (1970) On the Acquisition of Some
Relational Terms, in J.R. Hayes (ed.), 'Cognition and the
Development of Language'. New York: Wiley.
Edwards, D. (1973) Sensory Motor Intelligence and Semantic
Relations in Early Child Grammar, in 'Cognition', 2, pp. 395-434.
Elliot, A.J. (1981) 'Child Language'. London: Cambridge
University Press.
Flavell, J., Botkin, P., Fry, C., Wright, J., and Jarvis, P.
(1968) 'The Development of Role-Taking and Communication
Skills in Children'. New York: Wiley.
Freeman, N.H., Lloyd, S., and Sinha, C.G. (1980) Infant
Search Tasks Reveal Early Concepts of Containment and
Economical Usage of Objects, in 'Cognition', 8, pp. 243-62.
Freeman, N.H., Stedmon, J.A., and Sinha, C.G. (1982) All
the Cars - Which Cars? From Word-meaning to Discourse
Analysis, in M. Beveridge (ed.), 'Children Thinking Through
Language'. London: Edward Arnold.
Garvey, C. and Hogan, R. (1973) Social Speech and Social
Interaction: Egocentrism Revisited, in 'Child Development',
44, pp. 562-8.
Genishi, C. and di Paolo, M. (in the press) Learning through
Argument in a Pre-school, in L.C. Wilkinson (ed.), 'Communi-
cating in the Classroom'. New York: Academic Press.
Glucksberg, S. and Krauss, R. (1967) What Do People Say After

They Have Learned to Talk? Studies of the Development of
Referential Communication, in 'Merrill-Palmer Quarterly',
13, pp. 309-16.

Glucksberg, S., Krauss, R.M. and Higgins, E.T. (1975) The
Development of Referential Communication Skills, in F.D.
Horowitz (ed.), 'Review of Child Development Research',
vol. 4. University of Chicago Press.

Golinkoff, R.M. (1981) The Influence of Piagetian Theory on
the Study of the Development of Communication, in I. Sigel,
D. Brodzinski and R.M. Golinkoff (eds), 'Piagetian Theory
and Research: New Directions and Applications'. Hillsdale,
NJ: Lawrence Erlbaum Associates.

Greenfield, P.M. and Smith, J. (1976) 'The Structure of
Communication in Early Language Development'. New York:
Academic Press.

Greenfield, P.M. and Zukow, P. (1978) Why Do Children Say
What They Say When They Say It? An Experimental Approach
to the Psychogenesis of Presupposition, in K. Nelson (ed.),
'Children's Language', vol. 1. New York: Gardner Press.

Inhelder, B. and Karmiloff-Smith, A. (1978) Thought and
Language, in B. Presseisen, D. Goldstein and M. Appel (eds),
'Topics in Cognitive Development', vol. 2. New York:
Plenum Press.

Keenan, E.O. (1977) Making it Last: Repetition in Children's
Discourse, in S. Ervin-Tripp and C. Mitchell-Kerman (eds),
'Child Discourse'. New York: Academic Press.

Lloyd, P. and Beveridge, M. (1981) 'Information and Meaning
in Child Communication'. London: Academic Press.

Lock, A. (1980) 'The Guided Re-Invention of Language'.
London: Academic Press.

MacNamara, J. (1972) Cognitive Basis of Language Learning in
Infants, in 'Psychological Review', 79, pp. 1-13.

Maratsos, M.P. (1973) Non-egocentric Communication Abilities
in Pre-school Children, in 'Child Development', 44, pp.
697-700.

McGarrigle, J. and Donaldson, M. (1975) Conservation Accidents,
in 'Cognition', 3, pp. 341-50.

Mueller, E. (1972) The Maintenance of Verbal Exchanges between
Young Children, in 'Child Development', 43, pp. 930-8.

Olson, D. (1970) Language and Thought: Aspects of a Cognitive
Theory of Semantics, in 'Psychological Review', 77 (4), pp.
257-73.

Piaget, J. (1951) 'Play, Dreams and Imitation in Childhood'.
London: Routledge & Kegan Paul.

Piaget, J. (1959) 'Language and Thought of the Child', 3rd
ed. London: Routledge & Kegan Paul.

Piaget, J. (1962) Comments on Vygotsky's Critical Remarks,
in L.S. Vygotsky, 'Thought and Language'. Cambridge, Mass.:
MIT Press.

Piaget, J. and Inhelder, B. (1969) 'The Psychology of the Child'.
London: Routledge & Kegan Paul.

Richards, M.M. (1979) Sorting Out What's in a Word from What's Not: Evaluating Clark's Semantic Features Acquisition Theory, in 'Journal of Experimental Child Psychology', 27, pp. 1-47.

Shatz, M. (1978) The Relationship between Cognitive Processes and the Development of Communication Skills, in B. Keasey (ed.), 'Nebraska Symposium on Motivation, 1977'. Lincoln, Nebraska: University of Nebraska Press.

Siegel, L. (1978) The Relationship of Language and Thought in the Pre-operational Child: A Reconsideration of Non-verbal Alternatives to Piagetian Tasks, in L.S. Siegel and C.J. Brainerd (eds), 'Alternatives to Piaget'. New York: Academic Press.

Sinclair, H.J. (1978) The Relevance of Piaget's Early Work for a Semantic Approach to Language Acquisition, in B. Presscisen, D. Goldstein and M. Appel (eds), 'Topics in Cognitive Development', vol. 2. New York: Plenum Press.

Vygotsky, L.S. (1962) 'Thought and Language'. Cambridge, Mass.: MIT Press.

Vygotsky, L.S. (1978) 'Mind in Society'. Cambridge, Mass.: Harvard University Press.

Warden, D. (1981) Experimenting with Children's Language, in 'British Journal of Psychology', 72, pp. 217-22.

Wood, T. (1981) The Maintenance and Repair of Communications between Young Children and their Mothers. Unpublished PhD thesis, University of Manchester.

Wozniak, R.H. (1972) Verbal Regulation of Motor Behaviour - Soviet Research and Non-Soviet Replications, in 'Human Development', 15, pp. 13-57.

Zaporozhets, A.V. and Elkonin, D.B. (eds) (1971) 'The Psychology of Pre-school Children'. Cambridge, Mass.: MIT Press.

10 Cognitive structures and verbalized beliefs

James Russell

I shall begin by contrasting two views about the role of language in cognitive development. The three tenets set out on the left of Table 10.1 are more or less Piagetian; and those on the right represent some divergent claims that I want to develop in this chapter. The two sets do not represent opposing theories - indeed, there is a level of generality on which they do not conflict at all - but they do lead in different directions towards different kinds of research programme. Having described the significance of the tenets I will discuss the area of empirical divergence which they foreshadow.

Table 10.1

1(a) Language reflects operational structures.	2(a) Language expresses beliefs.
1(b) Interpretation of verbal judgments 'reveals' the state of these structures.	2(b) Experimentation can demonstrate how the child's beliefs system diverges from our own and how it is related to perceptual/informational capacities.
1(c) A state of knowledge is a stage in the continuous interaction between subject and object.	2(c) Conceptual knowledge is (justified) true belief.

1(a) means for Piaget that the judgments children make can be treated as indices of the degree to which conceptual intelligence has progressed in its construction (more accurately: reconstruction) of an equilibrated model of the world. The assimilation of data to a verbal concept must be matched by appropriate accommodation of the verbal concept. Thus, early language is flawed by an imbalance between construing the generality of the verbal concept and the particularity of the datum (cf. the

famous 'slug' example); which is essentially a repetition of the
infant's incompetence at balancing the generality of his action
schemes with the particularity of the concrete object. At a later
period the child's verbal judgments reflect another kind of disequilibrium: thought becomes stuck or 'centrated' on uni-
dimensional, perceptual attributes of arrays. But later still, in
the so-called concrete operational period, verbal judgments and
their justifications reflect 'grouped' structures which Piaget has
described by his well-known logico-mathematical competence
models.

As well as the deadeningly familiar I am also stating here the
way in which linguistic judgments are treated as grist to the
Piagetian mill: as evidence for the state of the operational
'machinery' that lies 'beneath'. But it is a rather more obvious
and positive function of language that is being described in
2(a): that language use expresses beliefs. Indeed, this is so
obvious that some would regard it as pointless. But in the context of Piagetian received wisdom it is far from being pointless.
Early holophrastic and telegraphic speech may lack grammatical
and conceptual elaboration, but it does allow us to ascribe
beliefs to the child; indeed, this is one construal of what
theorists such as Bloom, Schlesinger and Greenfield were about
in their so-called 'deep interpretation' of one- and two-word
utterances. As the functionalist critics of Chomsky were quick
to point out, the early utterances of children invariably *mean*;
and you cannot have meaning in language without belief.

But, it may be objected, this belief ascription to the child
who makes utterances about the world is simply verbal replication
of that allowed to us in our observations of infant action. That
is, if the two-year-old says 'Daddy ball', and we ascribe to him
the belief, given the context, that [Father has the ball], is this
not exactly parallel to our ascription of the belief that [ball is
behind the cushion] to the eight-month-old who is able to
retrieve a completely occluded object? But, in fact, this kind of
example illustrates precisely why belief ascription on the basis
of early language is highly problematic and therefore significant.
When the eight-month-old retrieves an occluded object, the
belief this action expresses is a very long way from the belief
that such an action might express in the child, of, say, six
years of age: Piaget's observation of later preservation errors
and inability to handle invisible displacements prove this if they
prove nothing else. Analogously, the utterance 'Daddy ball' -
we can be pretty sure, though we know lamentably little about
this - does not express a belief about a father and a ball that
is equivalent to the belief which an older child or adult evinces
when he makes a similar utterance in a similar context.

Perhaps my point will become clearer when we consider belief
ascription to children who are answering questions that we put
to them - or, more particularly, that Piaget has put to them.
In this case the child has not only to express a 'view of reality',
he has to ascribe beliefs to others regarding the significance of

the question and about the adequacy conditions for his answer. For example, we may ask the child to tell us how the clouds move. The answer from the child (see Piaget, 1930) may be that as people walk along on the ground they pull the clouds with them. When faced with an answer of this kind Piaget ascribed to the child a phenomenalistic conception of causality, a repetition of the 'magico-phenomenalism' found in infant actions. But, does not such a 'structuralist' interpretation assume an equivalence of status between the statement 'people make clouds move by walking' as said by a four-year-old and as said by an adult? More accurately, it assumes some equivalence between the kind of belief which the two statements express. Let us say that when an adult says this it expresses the belief [people make clouds move by walking]: but when a child says such a thing, although we can be fairly safe interpreting 'people' and 'clouds', there must be deep problems with 'make move'. For the child's usage in that context may express the belief that walking people correlate with cloud movements, or that as people walk they may see clouds move in the opposite direction, just like other objects. Or the child's use of language here may be metaphorical: it is 'as if' people pull clouds along, in which case it is the child's linguistic style which is phenomenalistic, not his 'concept of causality'. Again, the child's answer may be highly pragmatic, in the spirit of 'well, will this do as an answer?' Now of course we cannot say what beliefs or kind of beliefs are expressed by such a statement without further experimentation, but we do not have to assume that the child's utterance means [people make clouds move] - indeed, given the kind of creatures that young children are, this is a very odd assumption. And if we cannot make such an assumption, then we have no warrant for ascribing pre-logical conception of causation to the child.

The transition to 1(b) is an easy one to make: I am indicating here Piaget's 'clinical method'. The child is carefully questioned about his initial judgment and on the basis of this questioning is assigned to a stage and substage - Ib, IIIa, etc. - with the stage being equivalent to Piaget's a priori 'level' of cognitive equilibrium. The fact that Piaget places such confidence in this technique further illustrates his easy assumption that the relation between the child's language and the child's beliefs is not radically problematic. Indeed, two analogies spring to mind. The first is with Bertrand Russell's rejection of what he regarded as morbid self-consciousness about language usage in the philosophies of the later Wittgenstein, Ryle and Austin. Russell said that he had always regarded language as 'transparent': so, I believe, did Piaget. The second analogy is more direct. As is well known, Piaget was encouraged to adopt his clinical method through his acquaintance with psychoanalytical techniques. Freud too, in a sense, regarded language as transparent; and it is this assumption of transparency, this equation between word and referent, which recent psychoanalytical writers such as Lacan have been criticizing in classical psychoanalysis.

Turning to 2(b) in Table 10.1, we find the word 'experimentation' where 'interpretation' was in 1(b). Despite the fact that work by neo-Piagetian researchers such as Furth, Youniss and Sinclair is in the mainstream of experimental child psychology, the classical Genevan research programme is not experimental in the sense that different groups of children receive different treatments, tasks and instructions are systematically varied against other conditions, and so on. In the classic studies as well as in the more recent (e.g. Piaget, 1977, 1978), tasks are used as test cases, not as tests. But ironically, the empirical example I wish to take here by way of illustrating 2(b) comes from the work of someone who sees herself as researching within the Genevan framework - Annette Karmiloff-Smith. The techniques she employed in her studies of children's interpretation of articles and quantifiers (Karmiloff-Smith, 1979) were midway between the Genevan and the 'experimental', but her results unambiguously reinforce the scepticism about belief ascription through language sketched above. Let us take Karmiloff-Smith's own example of the classic conversation between Piaget and Jacqueline about the slug. Piaget concludes from the fact that his daughter will claim both that two separate appearances of slug are 'the same' slug and 'different' slugs that the child cannot equilibrate generality and particularity of reference and therefore lacks true verbal concepts. But as Karmiloff-Smith points out, her results show that the child's use of 'la' is deictic, not anaphoric; therefore 'la' in 'encore la limace' does not refer to one and the same item come round again, but is a verbal gesture towards an item. Moreover, her results also show that 'same' for the young child frequently does not mean 'one and the same' but 'of the same kind'. So if we take her answer to her father's question about sameness as expressing the belief [affirmative: it is the same kind of animal], then her answer is correct. The outcome of this exercise is that the basis for denying that 'encore la limace' expresses the belief [there is another slug] has dissolved.

Other experiments have also revealed that the young child's interpretation of size and shape judgment is phenomenalistic (Braine and Shanks, 1965a, 1965b); that the child's interpretation of quantifiers is indissociable from a particular perceptual context (see Donaldson, 1978); that quantity statements are interpreted uni-dimensionally or by reference to shape alone (Lumsden and Kling, 1968; Russell, 1975); and so on. In general, experimentation should have made sceptics of us all about the transparency of language, in a way that the technique of clinical interviewing plus interpretation, however brilliant and creative the studies, never could.

In the second part of 2(b) in Table 10.1 I mention something to which, within the scope of this paper, I can only give lip service: the capacity of the child's brain for processing information, in a wholly non-epistemic sense. It is a very difficult matter indeed to state clearly how this capacity is distinguishable

from the child's epistemic capacities with which Piaget and this
paper are concerned, because, of course, we must assume a
mutual dependence between them. Some 'process' theorists such
as T. Trabasso or D. Klahr would reject such a distinction out-
right; while other theorists, such as Robin Campbell (1979),
would argue that such a dualism is justified. Now although Piaget
has made a very significant contribution to our understanding of
the perceptual-mechanistic aspects of development in his work on
perception (Piaget, 1969), I think it is fair to say that, by
making clinical interpretation his core methodology, he created
a climate in which it was difficult to give factors such as
memory, pattern recognition, attention span – and all the other
chapter headings in cognitive psychology textbooks – their
full due. But in the context of 2(b) all I wish to say is that the
'belief approach', in contrast to the cognitive structuralist
approach, is more likely to consider questions about the relation
between verbal-epistemic processes and the theoretical neuro-
physiology of mechanistic cognitive theses as a major aspect of
the problem of development itself. Piaget does, of course, refer
to the relationship between neural and operational structures:
he mentions the 'isomorphism' between adolescents' propositional
judgments and the Boolean neural structures discovered by
McCulloch and Pitts (Piaget, 1971, pp. 221-3), and he speculates
that cognitive structures may be isomorphic to neural structures
in general (Piaget, 1954). But it is not within the Piagetian
compass empirically to study the relevance of process-modelling
within cognitive psychology to epistemic processes: Piaget's
cognitive structuralism, for reasons too complex to consider
here, precludes it.

In Table 10.1, 1(c) is represented the best I can do about a
one-sentence precis of Piaget's conception of knowledge. As
philosophers such as Hamlyn (1978) and Kitchener (1980) – also
see Russell (1978) – have pointed out, human knowledge is, for
Piaget, essentially a non-normative matter. Of course Piaget
attends to the fact that knowledge is normative (see Kitchener,
1980, p. 265).

But the normative aspects do relatively little to determine the
process of knowledge acquisition. Rather, the individual's state
of knowledge is a slice of the process of interaction between the
active organism and the datum, with a stage in the process being
represented in terms of the constructions to which these
interactions have given rise. Now the bold statement in 2(c)
does not preclude the consideration that what an individual knows
is in part the result of how his interactions with the world have
enabled him to construct a system of representations, nor does
it deny the role of re-afference in brain development (see
Russell, 1981a). It is at once a fairly standard thesis about
knowledge, to be found throughout the philosophical literature,
and a sloganized way of saying that the kind of knowledge with
which Piaget is concerned in his child psychology (the making of
judgments about physical and logico-mathematical reality) is

ineluctably normative. All verbal judgments evince beliefs, and the important difference between the true and false beliefs, in the sense discussed here, is that the former are appropriate to the regnant conventions of the conceptual system and the latter are not.

I am afraid that this may sound like the dewy-eyed relativism which proclaims that the child's view of reality is an alternative to our own, rather than inferior to it. But if it is physical and logico-mathematical knowledge which is at issue, such a view must be a mistaken one for the simple reason that the regnant conceptual system is superior to that of the child, by virtue of its greater coherence, parsimony, integration, objectivity . . . (Werner's quartet of stable, flexible, discrete and arti-culated is useful here) - in short, it is a better adapted conceptual 'organism'. But the false beliefs which children evince are false within the adult conceptual system, not false because they are less coherent . . . etc.: they are normatively false; whether they are biologically less well adapted or inferior on some 'transcendental' analysis is another matter.

It has been the Piagetian tradition that has largely determined the way developmental psychologists have asked questions of human nature, and we would not be here today if it had not brought major dividends. But, in addition to its empirical and theoretical dividends, this tradition has nurtured a motley collection of pseudo-issues, conceptual confusions, pessimism about children's capacities and the habitual covering of ignor-ance in the elastic cloak of terminology.

In 'The Language and Thought of the Child', which Peter Lloyd discusses in Chapter 9, Piaget made some sweeping claims about the egocentric nature of children's thinking. I would take the view that, by and large, recent research has shown the claims to be essentially unfounded. Now, of course, no one has a right to complain that Piaget was wrong, in some cases, about the facts of the case - these were early days. But what I think we are justified in saying is that the application of the interpre-tive schema of 'egocentricity' was a function of the three meta-theoretical assumptions we have just been discussing far more than it was a function of his data. Given Piaget's views that (1) incompetent or inappropriate language use entails disequili-brated cognitive structuring; (2) the interpretation of divergent language will reveal the symptoms of such disequilibrium, that is, egocentricity; and (3) it is the stage of cognitive structuring at which the child is located which determines linguistic failure, not vice versa, then his 'discovery' of the egocentric nature of childish thought was almost inevitable. There was, in effect, too much assimilation to metatheory and insufficient accommoda-tion to data on Piaget's part.

All along I have been suggesting that Piaget did not regard the relation between what may be loosely called 'thought' and 'language' as a sufficiently problematic relation. But what conceptual weapons may we use to tame such problems? I will start to answer this question by introducing the phrase 'propositional attitudes' into the discussion. This is a technical term in philosophy meaning the mental attitudes which makers of propositions have towards these propositions, attitudes such as 'belief', 'hope', 'expectation' and the like. These are strongly analogous to the relation between the intention and the movement in the sphere of action. Indeed, there is the associated term 'intensionality', which is used to refer to a feature shared by verbs such as hoping, fearing, knowing, etc.: that the truth values of sentences which contain propositions governed by intensional verbs are determined by the propositions' actual linguistic characterization not by their denotation or reference. Changing the way in which the denotation is achieved changes the truth value of the sentence. The classic example is one of Bertrand Russell's: 'George IV believed that [Scott was the author of *Waverley*].' Now the individual referenced by the phrase 'the author of *Waverley*' is of course Scott; but we cannot paraphrase this in the form that 'George IV believed that [Scott was Scott]'. Denotationally the King did believe this, but this was not his mental attitude, and mental attitudes as well as achieving reference determine the truth value of statements. Similarly, Jones may believe that his colleague Smith is planning to thwart his proposals for curriculum development at the next staff meeting. But he does not believe that a man with an uncle in Budleigh Salterton is going to do this; even if Jones does know this fact about Smith's uncle, this is still not what he believes.

There are two main lessons to be drawn from this. First, as the philosopher Donald Davidson (1975) has pointed out, this feature of the linguistic system shows us the mutual dependence of thought and language; it is an argument for holism, as against the alternative Chomskian (1980) viewpoint that language and thinking are separate 'organs'. The second lesson involves developing the argument about the dependency of achieved denotation upon a specific mental attitude in a somewhat different direction. The problem of 'intensionality' tells us that reference does not determine the meaning of a sentence which is the object of a propositional attitude, and this is illustrated by the replacement of one denoting phrase in the sentence by another. But what if, instead of replacing the denoting phrase, we replaced the speaker? What if we replaced an adult speaker of a proposition by a young child? The words and grammar in the propositions may be the same, but are the propositional attitudes the same? The fact is we cannot know the answer to this last question without doing some research.

In setting this final problem I am really harking back to the material covered before under 2(b) in Table 10.1. But in both places I think I am doing something of more consequence than dressing up the classic anti-Piagetian plaint that 'the child may be misinterpreting the instructions' with some philosophical jargon. This way of presenting the problem is supposed to bring

home the fact that the 'misinterpretation' of adults' language by
the child and the child's by adults is not a methodological
problem in the field of cognitive development: it is one of the
problems which constitute this field. For if we claim (lesson one)
that mode of language use characterizes mental attitudes, not
just mental content (i.e., the 'things in mind'), together with
the fact that children think differently from adults, then the
notion of children as thinking differently from ourselves and
yet using language more or less in the same way is profoundly
contradictory. My contention is that the Piagetian tradition of
inquiry, despite the dividends it has paid, has made it inevitable that such a way of theorizing should become submerged.

Obviously, this will all be beside the point unless it can be
given some empirical 'cash value' - and I wish I could flesh out
my conceptual points about early language use expressing
beliefs, with different degrees of concord and discord with
adults' beliefs, with some new, interesting data. However, what
I can do is describe some of the work that we have been under
taking at Liverpool on the development of logico-mathematical
concepts in middle childhood, because this has been motivated
by the suspicion that, beyond the problem of coming to express
beliefs in the appropriate language and ascribing the correct
beliefs to others, the child must come to believe certain propositions in the 'appropriate way'. In one domain the child's task
would appear to be the discovery of which kinds of propositions
have to be believed and contended in which ways.

But before illuminating this problem we must consider the neo-
Piagetian theory with which it will be explicitly contrasted. This
is the proposal of Willem Doise (see Doise, 1978 for a review)
and his colleagues (see, e.g. Perret-Clermont, 1980, for a
review) that 'socio-cognitive conflict' between children can
bring about cognitive performance at a higher level than either
child could produce when performing alone. This really is a true
offspring of the Piagetian tradition because it rests on the
assumption that inappropriate verbal judgments and responses
to instructions represent disequilibrated cognitive structures -
a uni-dimensional, centrated form of thought usually encompassed
by the term 'egocentricity'.

Now we must say what the neo-Piagetian hypothesis has to be.
Piaget clearly states (Piaget, 1950, chapter 6) that social life is
constituted by interchanges between people on an exact analogy
with cognitive interchanges between an individual's cognitive
centrations. Thus, in liquid conservation, for example, if the
centrated judgment 'it is more because the level is higher' is co-
ordinated with the centration 'it is less because the beaker is
thinner', then we have, by Grouping VII, the principle of
covariance and thence conservation - or at least (pace Acredolo
and Acredolo, 1979, and others) one necessary condition for it.
So, if individual dyad members are representatives of these
incomplete centrations, the 'dyad' as a social unit should represent the co-ordinated judgment - 'two wrongs' should make a

'right'. The general prediction from the hypothesis is this: if we ensure that two pre-operationally responding children inter-act around a display such that this perspectival conflict of mutually incompatible judgments is guaranteed, then co-operative co-ordination of judgments should produce a correct answer in the child who is in a state of assimilatory 'readiness' to construct the correct answer for himself.

How does the topic of belief and the adoption of 'styles' of propositional attitudes become relevant here? It becomes relevant by virtue of the fact that, for such 'socio-cognitive conflict' between symmetrically opposing perspectives to happen at all, the dyad members should regard the conflicting judgments as conflicting. To regard this mismatch as an actual conflict, the child must regard his own judgment ('it's more now') as true and his partner's ('it's less now') as false. However, if the child were merely stating his belief as a matter of subjective opinion ('it's more as far as I'm concerned but I'm prepared to accept that it's not for you') or phenomenally ('it looks like more from where I'm sitting'), then the children would be little more likely to 'conflict' than would two adults who are discussing whether they enjoyed a play, where one adult says he liked it and the other says that he did not.

Perhaps it is now evident why the structuralist and 'belief' approaches (for want of better terms) diverge so fundamentally around this issue. For the Piagetian, each child in the dyad represents a partial and irreversible structuring of a logical situation, and all partial structurings must - by the machinery of Piagetian theory - conflict. Because cognitive development is the process of integrating partial, irreversible centrations, social experience facilitates cognitive development to the extent that conflictual interactions are negotiated around to equilibrated judgments. However, the prediction from the 'belief' approach is quite different: there will be such conflicts only if the pro-positional attitude which each child adopts to his judgment is objective and necessary rather than subjective and phenomenal as described above. The nature of the belief is primary.

Having said that, let me mention in passing that Genevans have expanded the Piagetian thesis about the conditions for dyadic facilitation almost to the point that it no longer makes empirical predictions of any import. The term 'socio-cognitive conflict' is interpreted by the Genevan group (see for example Mugny and Doise, 1978; and Perret-Clermont, 1980, passim) as meaning not the 'logical mismatch of opposing perspectives' (as above) but any interaction between children who have shown different levels of performance on a pretest. In a sense such an expan-sion is justified from Piaget's writings because they are rather too open to interpretation. But I believe that, whether or not such an expansion is justified - and this is a matter for Piagetian scholars of whom I am not one - it is counter-productive.

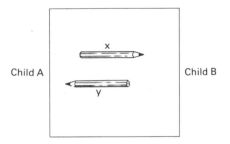

Child A   Child B

Figure 10.1

I will now illustrate the discussion by reference to a task which we have employed in our research on dyadic interaction and conservation attainment (see Russell, 1982b). Figure 10.1 shows the post-transformation display in a length conservation task. Pencils x and y are equal and have been transformed from a situation of perceptual equality by the experimenter. If they have been positioned thus on a table with a non-conserving child at each side of the table, as in the figure, then almost inevitably child A should say that x is the longer and child B should say that y is the longer. What will be the outcome of this interaction? According to the Piagetians, children should experience a conflict and - given, as always, a certain degree of assimilatory readiness - should co-ordinate between themselves the correct equality judgment. However, any prediction from the 'belief' account must be predicated upon an assumption about the propositional attitude that non-conservers have to their judgment. What do we know about these propositional attitudes? When I reviewed the evidence relevant to this question in a previous paper (Russell, 1981b), I concluded that the propositional attitude could be characterized as phenomenalistic/labile/pragmatic/ subjective/private/perceptual; and in videotaping the interactions between non-conserving children on such a task (see Russell, 1982b, for details) we found evidence to support this construal. First, the adoption of the answer was determined by (separately assessed) social dominance but was not associated with giving counters to the partner's answer. Inspection of the protocols explained this paradox, for we frequently witnessed interactions of the following kind: Child A says initially 'That one's bigger', and Child B says 'OK, let's shout ready'. That is, it was not a question of one child winning by being more insistent, but of the other child losing by complying without demur. Additionally, the non-conservers, relative to conservers, did not tend to support their answers by logical justification in those rare cases where they justified the answer at all, but pragmatically by statements such as 'my brother's good at these puzzles and he told me . . .'. And, as many other workers have also discovered (e.g., Silverman and Stone, 1972; Miller and

Brownwell, 1975), the non-conserver typically complied with
a paired conserver in the same situation. Indeed, the subjectivity
and pragmatism of the non-conserver's behaviour comes into
clearest focus when contrasted with the behaviour of conservers
in this situation. Typically, the conservers justified their
answers logically (e.g., by the reversibility principle) and
countered the answers of their non-conserving partners.

This brings me to the obvious question: why do non-conservers
typically comply with the conserver's answer? Our data suggest
that exposure to justification was not the crucial factor in either
compliance or post-test gain: exposure to the correct answer
alone was sufficient. Indeed, this question becomes more urgent
in the light of our recent data on dyadic interaction patterns in
other concrete operational tasks. For we have found that the
distinctive trend in dyadic studies of class inclusion (Russell,
1981d), transitive reasoning (Russell, 1981c), and spatial
perspective-taking (Russell, 1981e) is for the incorrect or less
competent child to comply with the judgment of the correct or
more competent child. Moreover, the data of Genevan workers
also demonstrates most unequivocally the power of the correct
judgment to outweigh the pre-operational judgment. Perret-
Clermont's (1980) findings, that non-conservers exposed to the
conservation judgments and justifications of a pair of children
not only improve substantially on a post-test but actually
generate new justifications that they had not heard before, are
handsome evidence for what I am calling here the 'compliance
phenomenon', rather than socio-cognitive conflict. Unfortunately,
the term 'compliance' as applied to data in this area does carry
a flavour of superficial, pragmatic submission; but the evidence
is strong that the child appears to recognize, at one period in
his development, correctness when he sees it, and to assimilate
it. Perret-Clermont's data show that the child complies because
he genuinely has assimilated the judgment to his cognitive
system.

But how does this marry with our account sketched out above
in terms of propositional attitudes? In fact, data and theory can
be related, though at a rather speculative level.

An initial assumption we shall have to make is that cognitive
structuring at an epistemic but non-verbal level does not alter
with the acquisition of basic verbal concepts relevant to conservation, class inclusion and the like. For instance, we would
have to assume, and have evidence for, the proposal (Miller,
1979; Russell, 1979; Weldall and Poborca, 1980) that competence
in conservation is present before such a judgment can be given
in answer to a question. This is not a safe assumption, but it
is a testable one; in any case I will make it for the sake of the
argument.

Second, we can hypothesize that what motivates the change
from pre-operational to concrete operational thinking is a change
in the child's belief system, of the following kind. The child
eventually appreciates that there are different kinds of truth

towards which certain propositional attitudes are appropriate
and certain are not. He becomes aware that certain of his judgments are held subjectively rather than objectively, contingently
rather than necessarily, as being true of a particular situation
rather than reflecting a general logical principle, as relative to
a perspective rather than as an absolute fact, and as dependent
upon personal decisions about how a situation should be characterized rather than upon causal laws of the behaviour of
matter. Our evidence for this proposal comes from studies we
have carried out of the child's ability to discriminate between
types of verbal judgment out of context – specifically, to discriminate between sentences which are necessarily rather than
contingently true, objective rather than subjective, absolute
rather than relative, general rather than particular, and causal
rather than intentional. Although this is something of a cari-
cature of the data, essentially we found that children within the
transitional age range between the so-called pre-operational and
concrete operational periods (five to eight years) are able to
make these distinctions, sometimes actively but invariably with
the aid of an experimenter's characterization of them (Russell,
1982a; Russell, in preparation). Given all this, I would suggest
that in a dyadic interaction of the kind described above, the
pre-operational responder who has some awareness of the fundamental distinction of which these four distinctions are facets,
will be made aware that it is possible to make necessary/objec-
tive/causal/absolute/judgments in this part of the logico-
mathematical domain.

But in order to claim further that this recognition generates
cognitive change, we have to make a third assumption: that
such a child 'prefers' the objective, etc., judgment to his own
subjective, etc., judgment; that he believes the true beliefs
which constitute logico-mathematical knowledge should have
these qualities. At present we have no evidence that such general
preferences exist.

Of course many will regard all that has gone before as highly
unsatisfactory. I begin with a few conceptual homilies dressed
up as a fundamental distinction between epistemologies of human
development, and end up with some vague, speculative gestures.
Maybe. But I hope that along the way some arguments shine
through, illuminating how Piaget's cognitive structuralism is
leaving something important out of account, and that beliefs,
propositional attitudes, mental orientations – however we wish
to name them – can be nailed down by determinate terminology
and researched by techniques which do not give an interpretive
carte blanche.

But perhaps one final caveat is in order. This alternative
approach implies nothing resembling a wholesale rejection of
Piagetian theory. Indeed, I hope I have done something to peel
away what many workers find unacceptable in the Genevan
account of verbal judgment to reveal Piaget's great thesis in
starker relief. This is the thesis that the child's early inter-

actions with the concrete world build, at a non-conscious level, the foundations upon which later conceptual-linguistic structures are established. Whether we regard these structures as really active constructions, with Piaget, or as elaborations of innate schemes is less important than the general acceptance of their existence. Nothing I have said denies their existence; indeed, this paper may be seen as an attempt to sketch out how these structures might come to be elaborated into consciousness.

REFERENCES

Acredolo, C. and Acredolo, L.P. (1979) Identity, Compensation, and Conservation, in 'Child Development', 50, pp. 203-17.

Braine, M.D.S. and Shanks, B.L. (1965a) The Conservation of Shape Property and a Proposal about the Origin of Conservation, in 'Canadian Journal of Psychology', 194, pp. 197-207.

Braine, M.D.S. and Shanks, B.L. (1965b) The Development of the Conservation of Size, in 'Journal of Verbal Learning and Verbal Behaviour', 4, pp. 277-42.

Campbell, R.N. (1979) Cognitive Development and Child Language, in P. Fletcher and M. Garman (eds), 'Language Acquisition'. London: Cambridge University Press.

Chomsky, N. (1980) Rules and Representations, in 'The Behavioural and Brain Sciences', 3, pp. 1-61.

Davidson, D. (1975) Thought and Talk, in S. Guttenplan (ed.), 'Mind and Language'. Oxford: Clarendon Press.

Doise, W. (1978) 'Groups and Individuals'. London: Cambridge University Press.

Donaldson, M. (1978) 'Children's Minds'. Glasgow: Fontana.

Hamlyn, D.W. (1978) 'Experience and the Growth of Understanding'. London: Routledge & Kegan Paul.

Karmiloff-Smith, A. (1979) 'A Functional Approach to Child Language'. London: Cambridge University Press.

Kitchener, R.F. (1980) Genetic Epistemology, Normative Epistemology and Psychologism, in 'Synthese', 45, pp. 257-80.

Lumsden, E.A. and Kling, J.K. (1968) The Relevance of an Adequate Concept of 'Bigger' for Investigations of Size Conservation: A Methodological Critique, in 'Journal of Experimental Child Psychology', 8, pp. 82-91.

Miller, S.A. (1979) Candy is Dandy and Also Quicker: A Further Non-verbal Study of the Conservation of Number, in 'Journal of Genetic Psychology', 134, pp. 15-21.

Miller, S.A. and Brownwell, C.A. (1975) Peers, Persuasion and Piaget: Dyadic Interaction between Conservers and Non-conservers, in 'Child Development', 46, pp. 992-7.

Mugny, G. and Doise, W. (1978) Socio-cognitive Conflict and the Structure of Individual and Collective Performances, in 'European Journal of Social Psychology', 8, pp. 181-92.

Perret-Clermont, A.-N. (1980) 'Social Interaction and Cognitive Development in Children'. London: Academic Press.

Piaget, J. (1930) 'The Child's Conception of Physical Causality'. London: Routledge & Kegan Paul.

Piaget, J. (1950) 'The Psychology of Intelligence'. London: Routledge & Kegan Paul.

Piaget, J. (1954) The Problem of Consciousness in Child Psychology, in 'Conference on the Problems of Consciousness'. New York: Jocara Macy Foundation.

Piaget, J. (1969) 'The Mechanisms of Perception'. London: Routledge & Kegan Paul.

Piaget, J. (1971) 'Biology and Knowledge'. Edinburgh University Press.

Piaget, J. (1977) 'The Grasp of Consciousness'. London: Routledge & Kegan Paul.

Piaget, J. (1978) 'Success and Understanding'. London: Routledge & Kegan Paul.

Russell, J. (1975) The Interpretation of Conservation Instructions by Five-year-old Children, in 'Journal of Child Psychology and Child Psychiatry', 16, pp. 233-44.

Russell, J. (1978) 'The Acquisition of Knowledge'. London: Macmillan.

Russell, J. (1979) Non-verbal and Verbal Judgments of Length Invariance, in 'British Journal of Psychology', 70, pp. 313-17.

Russell, J. (1981a) Piaget's Theory of Sensorimotor Development: Outlines, Assumption and Problems. in G. Butterworth (ed.), 'Infancy and Epistemology'. Brighton: Harvester Press.

Russell, J. (1981b) Propositional Attitudes, in M. Beveridge (ed.), 'Children's Thinking through Language'. London: Edward Arnold.

Russell, J. (1981c) Children's Memory for the Premises in a Transitive Measurement Task Assessed by Elicited and Spontaneous Justifications, in 'Journal of Experimental Child Psychology', 31, pp. 300-9.

Russell, J. (1981d) Dyadic Interaction in a Logical Reasoning Problem Requiring Inclusion Ability, in 'Child Development', 52, pp. 1322-5.

Russell, J. (1981e) Why 'Socio-cognitive Conflict' May Be Impossible: The Status of Egocentric Errors in the Dyadic Performance of a Spatial Task, in 'Educational Psychology', 1, pp. 159-69.

Russell, J. (1982a) The Child's Appreciation of the Necessary Truth and the Necessary Falseness of Propositions, in 'British Journal of Psychology', 73, pp. 253-66.

Russell, J. (in preparation) Children's Ability to Discriminate Between Types of Proposition, Manuscript submitted for publication, 1982.

Russell, J. (1982b) Cognitive Conflict, Transmission and Justification: Conservation Attainment through Dyadic Interaction, in 'Journal of Genetic Psychology', 140, pp. 283-97.

Silverman, I.W. and Stone, J.M. (1972) Modifying Cognitive Functioning through Participation in a Problem-solving Group, in 'Journal of Educational Psychology', 63, pp. 603-8.

Weldall, K. and Poborca, B. (1980) Conservation without Conversation? An Alternative Nonverbal Paradigm for Assessing Conservation of Liquid, in 'British Journal of Psychology', 71, pp. 117-35.

Part 7

Moral development

11 Approaches to moral development: Piagetian influences

Nicholas Emler

INTRODUCTION

Piaget made but one substantial contribution to the study of
moral development, in a series of investigations conducted fifty
years ago and published as 'The Moral Judgment of the Child'
in 1932. It was a subject in which he never seriously involved
himself again thereafter. One is in the habit of saying 'only
one contribution' because on other topics his investigations and
writings were much more substantial. Yet it is perhaps unfair
to judge him only in terms of his own prodigious standards;
by anyone else's, this book represents no mean piece of work.
It contains, depending on how you count them, reports of seven
or eight studies of children's moral judgments, beliefs and
behaviour. But that is not all: it is also an account of some
pioneering methods in the study of children's moral development.
And it presents an original theory of moral development, though
not all commentators are agreed on precisely what this theory
states.

I shall argue that in the intervening years Piaget's influence
on the study of moral development has been considerable, but
also that, significantly, it has not been confined to this book;
that quite possibly much of this influence is not what Piaget
himself foresaw or intended; and finally that Piaget's contribution remains, even after fifty years, the most valuable we
have, not entirely because it is essentially correct in all details,
but because no better alternative has emerged.

The very scale of Piaget's influence makes any reviewer's task
difficult. The number of studies stimulated directly by Piaget's
book prompted one reviewer to remark that for a change further
research was *not* needed (Lickona, 1976). I shall certainly not
try to present a comprehensive review here (see instead Lickona,
1976; Modgil and Modgil, 1976). Instead, I shall develop my
argument through some selective illustrations. Thus I touch only
in passing on the originality and importance of Piaget's contributions to methods of study. Likewise, there will not be the
space to do justice to the general heritage of a cognitive approach

to moral development; I note only that we owe largely to Piaget the conviction that moral development is not just a matter of internalizing cultural values, that it does not consist solely in acquiring desirable habits, guilty feelings or strong anxieties about doing wrong; it is also a matter of intellectual growth and developing insight into the bases of social arrangements.

I shall consider very briefly, because it is ground well-worked, what Piaget reported and said; in a little more detail what others have found who have tried to replicate and evaluate his findings; then, again briefly, the more ambitious 'stage' theories of moral development proposed by Kohlberg and others; and shall finally return to consider the current potential of Piaget's contribution as a theory of moral development. This order has the advantage of a rough fit with the chronology of things.

'The Moral Judgment of the Child'

In this book Piaget describes studies of various aspects of children's moral judgments, in particular judgments regarding rules (the rules of children's games), guilt or culpability, and justice. In each case he describes two - and sometimes three - types of judgment, one more characteristic of younger children and another more often found in the words and actions of older children. The youngest children included in the more systematic studies were five-year-olds, the oldest fourteen. In the final part of the book he develops the idea that these different types of judgment reflect two different moralities, two different types of respect for rules. These are described respectively as heteronomous morality, or a morality of constraint, and autonomous morality, or a morality of co-operation.

The former reflects the styles of judgment that are more characteristic of the younger subjects and which Piaget described as instances of moral realism. These include beliefs such as that rules are sacred and untouchable, that a person's wickedness and the overt consequences of what they do are directly correlative, that punishment for naughtiness is immanent in nature, that punishment should properly be severe, and that it is always wrong to disregard parents' instructions. The latter type of morality is characterized by judgments which appeal to the intentions of actors or the purpose of social arrangements, e.g., the purpose of rules, the intention behind punishments or the intentions of individuals as determinants of their guilt, and by judgments that equal consideration be given to the opinions and claims of different individuals, whether in agreeing how a game should be played, or burdens be distributed, or resources be allocated.

REPLICATIONS AND EVALUATIONS

For some reason the attention of subsequent investigators has been grossly unequally divided in favour of just one or two of these aspects of moral judgment. As a result we know a great deal about immanent justice (young children's belief in the conspiracy between parents and nature), and an immense amount about the decline in consequence-based judgments of guilt and the growth of intention-based judgments (more than a hundred studies worth). We know relatively little about other aspects of justice and even less concerning ideas about rules. None the less, there is enough all round to draw some conclusions about Piaget's findings as a whole.

These findings, except for a few details, probably do not reflect just peculiarities of French-speaking Swiss culture in the early 1930s. The observations regarding children's views about rules of games have been replicated in at least two North American studies (Bobroff, 1960; Brooks-Walsh and Sullivan, 1973); younger children regard rules of games as unalterable but have little idea of their purpose, whereas older children regard them as changeable by mutual consent and grasp their purpose in regulating and constituting the game. A sex difference reported by Piaget has also been replicated (Lever, 1978); boys are more interested than girls in games with complex rules. In addition, Piaget's speculation that what children understand about the rules of games they play among themselves will not immediately be applied to all other kinds of rules has also received some confirmation (cf. Epstein in Lickona, 1976). Research on political socialization has shown that awareness of the possibility of legal reform comes much later in development (e.g., Adelson, 1971; Emler and Hogan, 1981).

Much of the research on the objective versus subjective bases for judgments of guilt seems to have been concerned with proving or disputing a claim that Piaget was in fact unwilling to make: namely, that this distinction represents an invariant, universal, irreversible, 'stage-like' developmental change. I believe that on balance Piaget's caution was justified. No instance has been found of this shift of emphasis occurring under normal circumstances in anything but the direction Piaget reported. But this apparently simple distinction and the developmental processes underlying it have proved to possess a considerable complexity.

It is clear, for instance, that the judgments children make depend in part on a variety of task characteristics; the same child may judge by intentions in one case and consequences in another. But except in terms of a very simplistic model of cognitive development, this should cause no surprise; it is precisely what has also been found in studies of logic and conservation. It is also emerging that there is not one single change but possibly several (e.g., Berndt and Berndt, 1975; Gutkin, 1972; Emler, 1978). In one of our studies conducted in

Dundee we found that sensitivity in moral judgments to the fact of intention is developmentally distinct from sensitivity to the quality of intentions (Emler, 1978). It is apparent, too, that the factors that children at a particular age can process in making moral judgments represent more complex considerations than they can articulate. For instance, though they may articulate only one consideration - e.g., consequences - their judgments will be influenced in varying weights by both consequences and intentions, and possibly by several other factors as well (e.g., Weiner and Peter, 1973).

One unfortunate aspect of the studies concentrated on this one aspect of Piaget's research is the lack of exploration of alternative aspects of children's moral judgments of culpability or responsibility. In everyday life the distinction between the deliberate and the accidental is probably of less consequence than questions of mitigation, negligence and foreseeable harm which are likely to occupy rather more of our time as moral judges. Of what the child knows or comes to believe about these matters we know very little.

If we turn to the development of ideas about justice we are again hampered by a lack of relevant research. The exception is belief in immanent justice which numerous investigations show declines everywhere with age - in Europe, Scotland, West Africa, the Lebanon - everywhere, in fact, except certain parts of North America (Havighurst and Neugarten, 1955; Curdin in Lickona, 1976). But this is perhaps of less direct interest for moral development than for what it tells us about the child's developing ability to disentangle natural cause and moral purpose.

With respect to retributive justice between children, Piaget reported a very marked sex difference which suggests that girls may be more sensitized to maintaining good relations with others whereas boys are more sensitized to considerations of relative status. Boys believed in giving at least blow for blow whereas girls infrequently believed in going even this far. Sadly, there has been no published attempt to explore this finding further. With respect to distributive justice, recent research has begun to indicate a more complex picture of alternative types of judgment than Piaget reported (e.g., Damon, 1975; Moessinger, 1975). There is though only one detail of Piaget's findings that seems to be directly contradicted here. Damon (1977) reports that young children show little inclination to equate fairness with whatever authority figures choose to impose; instead, they assert that what is fair is what they want.

CRITICISMS OF PIAGET'S FINDINGS

There is also now sufficient evidence to comment upon some of the principal criticisms that have been raised against Piaget's research. One of the earlier criticisms was that the age-related changes in moral judgment that Piaget reported were not reflec-

tions of intellectual change, but simply shifts in verbal habits
that could just as easily be reversed through modelling (e.g.,
Bandura and McDonald, 1963). Not only has the modelling interpretation been refuted, but a number of investigations have
revealed clear relations between specific aspects of moral judgment and skills in other specific areas of cognitive functioning
(e.g., Stuart, 1967; Whiteman, 1976; Damon, 1975; Kurdek,
1978). It does not, however, follow that other intellectual processes are somehow more basic, and that moral reasoning is but
an application of these to the moral domain (Emler and Heather,
1980).

Another criticism was that Piaget's studies dealt only with
children's moral reasoning and that moral reasoning tells us
very little about conduct, about how people will actually behave.
The first criticism is only partly true. Recall that Piaget examined
the ways in which children practise rules and not just what they
think about rules. The second can be confronted more adequately
if we can first dispose of the over-simplified terms in which it
is often cast.

It is unreasonable, I would submit, to insist on a simple
dichotomy between thought and action, especially in so far as
Piaget's work is concerned. This particular distinction is quite
antithetical to the spirit of Piaget's theory of knowledge, a theory
which emphasizes knowledge as a relationship between subject
and object; things are known only through actions upon them,
and conversely knowledge is expressed through these actions.
On the other hand, Piaget was well aware that many of his
investigations of moral judgment were indirect, relying on
children's reactions to hypothetical situations and moreover
upon what they could consciously articulate about these judgments, their conscious realization of the principles they applied.
Piaget suggested that this conscious realization would lag
behind application, and there are clear confirmations of this
(e.g., Breznitz and Kugelmas, 1967; Solomon et al., 1972). A
straightforward correlation between theoretical moral judgments
and conduct will therefore not necessarily be found.

One could also protest that what has been interpreted as
moral conduct - resisting temptation, doing what you are told,
not cheating, not injuring people, showing generosity, sharing
- is not necessarily all that one would wish to explain in moral
development. Also relevant are processes such as prediction,
interpretation and making sense of others' actions, processes
which necessarily determine how we react to them. Thus far
there has been little research on the development of such processes, but what there is suggests that children increasingly
come to see others as reacting on the basis of the same moral
norms as they apply in their own judgments of others' behaviour
(Emler, 1974; Berndt, 1977).

It is also a mistake to partition 'mere talk' and behaviour. A
great deal of social behaviour consists of talk (a fact which
much social psychology seems perversely to ignore, perhaps

for fear that the territory would be lost to linguists or philosophers). What is particularly significant in this for moral development is that what people say about what they do is as of much
and sometimes of more consequence than what they actually do
(cf. Blumstein, 1974). In these terms children's ability to
generate moral arguments and provide moral reasons for what
they do is in itself an important social skill. It also turns out to
be largely the same skill that was apparent in the judgments
Piaget studied (e.g., Ugurel-Semin, 1952; Dreman and Greenbaum, 1973; Gerson and Damon, 1978).

But if all these provisos are set aside and the evidence which
is supposed to support the second criticism is examined, it turns
out to be far more equivocal than the critics have implied. Two
studies report no relation between moral judgment and resistance
to temptation (Grinder, 1964; Medinnus, 1966). Considering the
very doubtful value of resistance to temptation measures, this
is not very compelling evidence. On the other hand, at least four
studies have indicated a relation between moral judgment and
activities characterized by sharing or generosity (e.g., Dreman,
1976; Dlugokinski and Firestone, 1973; Emler and Rushton, 1974;
Rubin and Schneider, 1973). Perhaps most impressive in this
context, however, is the accumulating evidence regarding
children's allocation behaviour (Hook and Cook, 1979). This
indicates a developmental sequence in the application of principles
of distributive justice which corresponds very closely to that for
the theoretical judgments Piaget reported. There is so far one
important exception to this happy picture which I will mention
below.

Another major criticism is less easily dismissed. It is that the
collections of moral beliefs Piaget described respectively as moral
realism and moral autonomy do not constitute distinct general
stages of development (e.g., MacRae, 1954; Johnson, 1962;
Harris, 1970). Although the elements taken separately do
change with age and do relate to intellectual growth, they do
not, taken collectively, exhibit the characteristics of 'structures
d'ensemble'; they are not parts of functionally and structurally
unified systems of thought.

STAGE THEORIES OF MORAL DEVELOPMENT

Lawrence Kohlberg, one of the principal critics of Piaget's moral
judgment research on these grounds, argues that the changes
reported fail to meet the criteria for developmental stages that
Piaget identified in his work on the development of logico-
mathematical thinking. Kohlberg's own work has set out to do
for moral reasoning what Piaget has done for logico-mathematical
thought, that is, to specify a set of generalized stages of
development (e.g., Kohlberg, 1963; 1969; 1971). But more than
that, Kohlberg has taken the development of operational thinking,
that is of logical thought, to be the basis of moral development.

He has argued that moral reasoning develops directly as a function of intellectual development and that moral reasoning reflects the application of logical principles, developed in the intellectual domain, to moral problems. The theory of development that Kohlberg has advanced, based on an interpretation of Piaget's theory of cognitive development and particularly his concept of equilibration, characterizes it as a process in which both the direction and the dynamics of change are located within the individual. Moral development is a self-generating process which springs from the internal logic of thought.

Kohlberg's theory thus represents a major influence of Piaget upon the study of moral development, but an influence which derives from his work on cognitive rather than moral development. Other researchers have advanced other 'stage' theories of aspects of moral development which have in common the idea that developmental changes have a cognitive-structural form, that these changes can be described in terms of a sequence of qualitatively distinct stages which represent an invariant sequence of increasing adequacy, and that one can account for both the content and the fact of change in constructivist terms; i.e., these stages represent the successive attempts of the growing child to make sense of its social world (e.g. Turiel, 1975; Selman, 1976).

I have written at length elsewhere about the shortcomings of Kohlberg's theory (e.g., Hogan and Emler, 1978; Emler, in the press), and I will make only the following points here. First, I do not accept that Kohlberg's theory, as some commentators have proposed, renders Piaget's redundant, that it is a more complete and inclusive account of moral development. The fact is that Kohlberg's approach does not work very well with children between the ages of four and ten (see, e.g., Damon, 1977, p. 74). Adolescents (and adults) make better moral philosophers, and this is essentially what Kohlberg's method of inquiry demands of its subjects. In this respect Kohlberg was undoubtedly correct; there are developmental changes in moral thinking that occur beyond the range Piaget studied. But under ten years Piaget's methods and the results they provide give a more effective and differentiated picture of moral development.

Second, that Piaget's findings do not provide evidence for general stages of development is not a problem. Indeed, the criticism can be turned in the other direction; it is odd to embark as Kohlberg has done upon the enterprise of defining general stages of development just when doubts have arisen about their existence in the development of operational thought. In particular, cross-cultural research indicates that children acquire specific logical and infra-logical operations separately and not as elements in the development of integrated structural wholes. The picture provided by Piagetian moral judgment replication studies of a set of separate developments in moral concepts is consistent with this. And despite the research resources that have been expended on Kohlberg's theory, there is still as yet no published evidence that the separate aspects of moral reasoning he describes do make up general stages.

Finally, the constructivist approaches, and in particular Kohlberg's, are too rationalist and too individualist; too much is assumed of the solitary thinker and the power of his own thought, while at the same time his thought is left too isolated from his actions and his social existence. For Piaget, moral judgment was the reflection of forms of social relationship. And if moral judgments also reflect the maturation of thought, this is only because thought itself is socialized through these relationships. This brings us back to Piaget's theory, but first a quick glance at the remainder of the opposition.

ALTERNATIVE THEORIES OF MORAL DEVELOPMENT

I suggested at the beginning of this paper that Piaget's account of moral development remains the most adequate we have, a claim that, it may be felt, requires a little justification. After all, a considerable body of literature exists on this topic which owes little to Piaget's influence. There are two main lines of non-cognitive theory and research that have attracted serious attention in the past. The first of these has been reflected in naturalistic research on the effects of child-rearing practices, and specifically the effects of styles of discipline upon the child's moral development. This research seems to have been influenced by Freudian theory and to a lesser extent by learning theory, the guiding assumption being that some styles of discipline or control will foster the development of moral controls more effectively than others. This might be described as a 'frown, grunt and bash' theory of socialization, for it appears to have been assumed that styles of discipline are in all important respects nonverbal. A popular hypothesis was that bashing would be less effective than withdrawing one's loving affection. Decades of research seemed to add up to the conclusion that this was the wrong contrast (Hoffman, 1970).

What is for me more surprising than this is that for so long so little consideration was given to the possibility that there might be a relation between two of the species' most distinctive features – the capacity of humans for speech, and their tendency to regulate social life according to moral codes. Significantly, it has transpired that parents have a greater effect on their children's moral development if their discipline relies more on explaining why something is wrong and less on nonverbal and object-oriented forms of control (Hoffman, 1977).

The second line of research, sometimes described as the social learning approach, has relied almost entirely upon experimental analogues of what might happen between parents and children, and unfortunately the method necessarily excludes what is probably the most crucial element in the parents' impact upon the child: a relationship. The major thesis in this approach has

been that children learn by observation of the behaviour of
others. Interaction is not considered particularly important;
talk is reduced to the status of verbal reinforcement – and
presumably grunts, frowns or smiles would do as well; language
is at best useful for encoding observed behaviour in memory.
Research devoted to this thesis has demonstrated only how
children can learn, and not particularly how they do in fact
learn, or indeed what they do learn, by imitation or observation. Moreover, those who still hold to some form of behavioural
social learning theory have none the less begun to acknowledge
the role of cognitive change in socialization (e.g., Mischel and
Mischel, 1976).

MORAL JUDGMENTS AND SOCIAL RELATIONSHIPS: PIAGET'S THEORY

Piaget's also is a social learning theory in the sense that he
assumed children's moral development involved learning from
others, but his emphasis is distinctly different. First, what
children learn and how they learn it depends on who the others
are that they interact with and what relationship they have with
these others. Second, the relevant interactions with these
others are conducted substantially through the medium of
language.
  Piaget proposed that forms of moral judgment reflect types
of social relationship (and I think we must assume he did mean
'relationship' here and resist the temptation to reduce it to
social interaction). The two moralities, heteronomous and autonomous, he suggested were the reflections of two basic types of
such relationship, relations respectively of unilateral respect
as between parent and child and of equality as between children
of a similar age. The argument he returns to throughout the
book is that the different kinds of moral judgment he observed
reflect and emerge within these different forms of social relationship. The objective of the empirical investigations was to confirm
this thesis and show that moral relations with parents would be
characterized by constraint, those with other children by
co-operation.
  Thus he supposed that moral judgments reflecting co-operation
would arise most readily in areas of life in which children must
deal with one another as equals and largely without the intervention of adults, hence his studies of children's games. Conversely, moral notions reflecting constraint would be most
apparent with respect to matters involving relations with
parents, hence studies of judgments about guilt and punishment.
  Moral ideas change with age because the nature of children's
relationships change with age. The earliest significant social
relationships are with parents; relationships with other children
come later. And as children grow older they also grow; relations
with parents are modified by this fact if nothing else.

This aspect of Piaget's theory has proved difficult to test, and such evidence as has emerged has prompted some critics to claim that it does not hold up. One difficulty is a lack of clarity about what it implies concerning the conditions of moral development. One interpretation is that more interaction with peers will lead to more rapid development, and conversely more interaction with parents will slow it down. In a review of the available evidence in 1976, Lickona concludes that it gave no support to the importance of increased independence from adult constraint, and mixed but generally positive support regarding the contribution of peer experience.

So where does this leave us? I think first we should consider some qualifications to this thesis made by Piaget. Constraint and co-operation are idealizations; relations with parents are not exclusively relations of constraint and relations with peers are never purely co-operative. Second, we have been inclined to suppose that Piaget believed relations of constraint to be a malign and negative influence on moral development. Some interpretations imply that heteronomous morality is the starting point and the objective of development is escape from this condition into autonomy. On the contrary, Piaget argued that both forms of social relationship are important sources of moral socialization, both contribute something essential to the moral development of the child.

With respect to constraint, Piaget noted that 'it is of great practical value for it is in this way that there is formed an elementary sense of duty and the first normative control of which the child is capable' (Piaget, 1932, p. 390). As Piaget also observed, the young child is saturated in adult rules, and we cannot suppose that its accommodation to this state of affairs is not a significant aspect of its socialization. The sheer extent of this saturation is evident from observational studies of mother-child interaction (e.g., Minton, Kagan and Levine, 1971), which indicate that, for instance, in the years from two to four children are typically subject to some kind of order at the rate of one every three to four minutes of the day. It is also significant that the medium of control is speech; overwhelmingly, parents rely on telling their children what to do or not to do, and not on shoves, frowns, grunts or blows. Furthermore, for the most part children do comply, and their willing compliance seems to reflect the security of their attachment that characterizes their relationship with their mothers (cf. Stayton, Hogan and Ainsworth, 1971). This has led some writers to identify a significant convergence between Piaget's thesis and research on attachment, concluding that the quality of this first relationship, albeit of constraint, is fundamental to acquisition of a sense of moral obligation (e.g., Wright, in the press; Youniss, 1978).

A particularly helpful interpretation of Piaget's theory has recently been provided by James Youniss (e.g. Youniss, 1975, 1978; Youniss and Volpe, 1978). Youniss proposes that the underlying thesis should be thought of not as being particularly concerned with types of moral judgment, but as being concerned with the child's adaptation to society through discovery of the principles by which social relationships are ordered. The child is born into a network of social relationships in which he or she comes to participate. These relationships take different forms and each form is characterized by particular principles of operation or 'methods' of interacting. The child's moral knowledge is knowledge about forms of social relationship, constructed in particular social relationships by the child and the other participants; this knowledge is thus a collective achievement of the participants, not an individual and private discovery. It consists of what Moscovici (1980) has called 'social representations'.

The two types of social relationship Piaget describes are in effect two methods of interacting; the method of constraint and the method of co-operation. What the child learns in each is not just different forms of moral judgment but the rules for interacting in each of these types of social relationship. In relations of constraint the child learns that the parent has the right to impose tasks and make demands but not vice versa. There is an irreducible inequality which gives the adult the initiative in the relationship. In relation to equality between children there is no ready-made script which is imposed. In their relations with their friends children must work out between themselves some means for ordering their interactions. In effect, they must co-operate in agreeing upon rules, submitting suggestions for mutual inspection. We may note that here again the important medium of interaction is speech. Co-operation requires discussion, argument, debate.

So what does this imply for future research? Youniss (1978; Youniss and Volpe, 1978) has already begun, through a study of children's views of friendship, to show that children recognize that the principles applying to interactions with friends are different from those applying to other relationships (cf. also Lerner, 1977). Work is also needed on children's relations with parents and others in authority over them, and a start in this direction has been made by Damon (1977) in an investigation of children's notions of authority.

Another important area will be the study of the processes by which moral knowledge is generated in social interaction, and one could point to recent Genevan studies as a possible model here (e.g., Doise, Mugny and Perret-Clermont, 1975; Mugny and Doise, 1978; Doise and Mugny, 1979).

Then there is the question of other forms of social relationship. Max Weber (1922) emphasized the distinctiveness of what he called legal-rational relationships in industrial societies. Not only does this form of social relationship entail its own distinctive rules of interaction - impersonal, based on formal role requirements, with formally specified jurisdictions, and entitlements - but it might be supposed that the ways in which children accommodate to the requirements of this form of social relationship

will constitute significant aspects of their moral development
(Emler and Hogan, 1981). It might also help to explain variations
in the one major area of moral conduct which has not yet been
explained in terms of socio-cognitive variables: delinquency
(cf. Emler, Heather and Winton, 1978).

REFERENCES

Adelson, J. (1971) The Political Imagination of the Young Ado-
lescent, in 'Daedalus', 100, pp. 1013-50.
Bandura, A. and McDonald, F.J. (1963) The Influence of Social
Reinforcement and the Behavior of Models in Shaping Children's
Moral Judgments, in 'Journal of Abnormal and Social Psy-
chology', 67, pp. 274-81.
Berndt, T.J. (1977) The Effect of Reciprocity Norms on Moral
Judgment and Causal Attribution, in 'Child Development', 48,
pp. 1322-3.
Berndt, T.J. and Berndt, E.G. (1975) Children's Use of Motives
and Intentionality in Person Perception and Moral Judgment,
in 'Child Development', 46, pp. 904-12.
Blumstein, P.W. (1974) The Honouring of Accounts, in 'American
Sociological Review', 39, pp. 551-6.
Bobroff, A. (1960) The Stages of Maturation in Socialized Think-
ing and in the Ego Development of Two Groups of Children, in
'Child Development', 31, pp. 321-38.
Breznitz, S. and Kugelmas, S. (1967) Intentionality in Moral
Judgment: Developmental Stages, in 'Child Development', 38,
pp. 469-79.
Brooks-Walsh, I. and Sullivan, E. (1973) Moral Judgment, Causal
and General Reasoning, in 'Journal of Moral Education', 2,
pp. 131-6.
Damon, W. (1975) Early Conceptions of Positive Justice as
Related to the Development of Logical Operations, in 'Child
Development', 46, pp. 301-12.
Damon, W. (1977) 'The Social World of the Child'. San Francisco:
Jossey Bass.
Dlugokinski, E. and Firestone, I.J. (1973) Congruence Among
Four Methods of Measuring Other-centredness, in 'Child Devel-
opment', 46, pp. 301-12.
Doise, W. and Mugny, G. (1979) Individual and Collective Con-
flicts of Centrations in Cognitive Development, in 'European
Journal of Social Psychology', 9, pp. 105-8.
Doise, W., Mugny, G. and Perret-Clermont, A.-N. (1975) Social
Interaction and the Development of Cognitive Operations, in
'European Journal of Social Psychology', 5, pp. 367-83.
Dreman, S.B. (1976) Sharing Behavior in Israeli Schoolchildren:
Cognitive and Social Learning Factors, in 'Child Development',
47, pp. 186-94.
Dreman, S.B. and Greenbaum, C.W. (1973) Altruism or Reci-
procity: Sharing Behavior in Israeli Kindergarten Children,

in 'Child Development', 44, pp. 61-8.

Emler, N.P. (1974) The Child's Understanding of Social Behaviour: Development of Psychological and Normative Explanations. Paper presented at Scottish branch meeting of British Psychological Society, Dundee, 1974.

Emler, N.P. (1978) Children's Development and Use of Inferences about Intentions and Motives in Moral Judgments, in 'British Journal of Educational Psychology', 48, pp. 201-9.

Emler, N.P. (in the press) Morality and Politics: The Ideological Dimension of Moral Development, in H. Weinreich-Haste and D. Locke (eds)', 'From Thought to Action: Essays on Moral and Social Development'. New York: Wiley.

Emler, N.P. and Heather, N. (1980) Intelligence: The Ideological Bias of Contemporary Psychology, in P. Salmon (ed.), 'Coming to Know'. London: Routledge & Kegan Paul.

Emler, N.P. Heather, N. and Winton, M. (1978) Delinquency and the Development of Moral Reasoning, in 'British Journal of Social and Clinical Psychology', 17, pp. 325-31.

Emler, N.P. and Hogan, R. (1981) Developing Attitudes to Law and Justice, in S.S. Brehm, S.M. Kassin and F.X. Gibbons (eds), 'Developmental Social Psychology', New York: Oxford University Press.

Emler, N.P. and Rushton, J.P. (1974) Cognitive Developmental Factors in Children's Generosity, in 'British Journal of Social and Clinical Psychology', 13, pp. 277-81.

Gerson, R. and Damon, W. (1978) Moral Understanding and Children's Conduct, in W. Damon (ed.), 'Moral Development'. San Francisco: Jossey-Bass.

Grinder, R.E. (1964) Relations between Behavioral and Cognitive Dimensions of Conscience in Middle Childhood, in 'Child Development', 35, pp. 881-91.

Gutkin, D.C. (1972) The Effect of Systematic Story Changes on Intentionality in Children's Moral Judgments, in 'Child Development', 43, pp. 187-95.

Harris, H. (1970) Development of Moral Attitudes in White and Negro Boys, in 'Developmental Psychology', 2, pp. 376-83.

Havighurst, R.J. and Neugarten, B.L. (1955) 'American Indian and White Children'. University of Chicago Press.

Hoffman, M.L. (1970) Moral Development, in P.H. Mussen (ed.), 'Carmichael's Manual of Child Psychology, vol. 2, New York: Wiley.

Hoffman, M.L. (1977) Moral Internalization: Current Theory and Research, in L. Berkowitz (ed.), 'Advances in Experimental Social Psychology', vol. 10. New York: Academic Press.

Hogan, R. and Emler, N.P. (1978) The Biases in Contemporary Social Psychology, in 'Social Research', 45, pp. 478-534.

Hook, J. and Cook, T. (1979) Equity Theory and the Cognitive Ability of Children, in 'Psychological Bulletin', 86, pp. 429-45.

Johnson, R.C. (1962) A Study of Children's Moral Judgments, in Child Development', 33, pp. 327-54.

Kohlberg, L. (1963) The Development of Children's Orientations

toward a Moral Order, I: Sequence in the Development of Moral
Thought, in 'Vita Humana', 6, pp. 11-33.
Kohlberg, L. (1969) Stage and Sequence: The Cognitive Develop-
mental Approach to Socialization, in D. Goslin (ed.), 'Hand-
book of Socialization Theory and Research'. Chicago: Rand
McNally.
Kohlberg, L. (1971) From Is to Ought: How to Commit the
Naturalistic Fallacy and Get Away With It in the Study of Moral
Development, in T. Mischel (ed.), 'Cognitive Development and
Epistemology'. New York: Academic Press.
Kurdek, L.A. (1978) Perspective Taking as the Cognitive Basis
of Children's Moral Development: A Review of the Literature,
in 'Merrill-Palmer Quarterly', 24, pp. 3-28.
Lerner, M. (1977) The Justice Motive: Some Hypotheses As To
its Origins and Forms, in 'Journal of Personality', 45, pp. 1-52.
Lever, J. (1978) Sex Differences in Complexity of Children's
Play, in 'American Sociological Review', 43, pp. 471-83.
Lickona, T. (1976) Research on Piaget's Theory of Moral Develop-
ment, in T. Lickona (ed.), 'Moral Development and Behaviour:
Theory, Research and Social Issues'. New York: Holt,
Rinehart & Winston.
MacRae, D. (1954) A Test of Piaget's Theory of Moral Develop-
ment, in 'Journal of Abnormal and Social Psychology', 49,
pp. 14-19.
Medinnus, G.R. (1966) Behavioral and Cognitive Measures of
Conscience Development, in 'Journal of Genetic Psychology',
109, pp. 147-50.
Minton, C., Kagan, J. and Levine, J. (1971) Maternal Control
and Obedience in the Two-Year-Old, in 'Child Development',
42, pp. 1873-94.
Mischel, W. and Mischel, H.N. (1976) A Cognitive Social-learning
Approach to Morality and Self-regulation, in T. Lickona (ed.),
'Moral Development and Behavior; Theory, Research and Social
Issues'. New York: Holt, Rinehart & Winston.
Modgil, S. and Modgil, C. (1976) 'Piagetian Research: Compil-
ation and Commentary'. Vol. 6: 'The Cognitive Developmental
Approach to Morality'. Slough: National Federation of Edu-
cational Research.
Moessinger, P. (1975) Developmental Study of Fair Division of
Property, in 'European Journal of Social Psychology', 5(3),
pp. 385-94.
Moscovici, S. (1980) Representations Sociales. Paper presented
at Colloquium on Social Representation, Maison des Sciences
de l'Homme, Paris, January 1980.
Mugny, G. and Doise, W. (1978) Socio-cognitive Conflict and
the Structuration of Individual and Collective Performances,
in 'European Journal of Social Psychology', 8, pp. 181-92.
Piaget, J. (1932) 'The Moral Judgment of the Child'. London:
Routledge & Kegan Paul.
Rubin, K.H. and Schneider, F.W. (1973) The Relation between
Moral Judgment, Egocentrism and Altruistic Behavior, in

'Child Development', 44, pp. 661-5.

Selman, R.L. (1976) A Structural-developmental Analysis of Interpersonal Conceptions: Peer Relations Conceptions in Poorly Adjusted and Well Adjusted Preadolescents, in A. Pick (ed.), 'Minnesota Symposium on Child Development', vol. 10. Minneapolis: University of Minnesota Press.

Solomon, D., Ali, F.A., Kfir, D., Houlihan, K.A. and Yaeger, J. (1972) The Development of Democratic Values and Behavior among Mexican-American Children, in 'Child Development', 43, pp. 2625-38.

Stayton, D., Hogan R. and Ainsworth, M. (1971) Infant Obedience and Maternal Behavior: The Origins of Socialization Reconsidered, in 'Child Development', 42, 1057-69.

Stuart, R.B. (1967) Decentration in the Development of Children's Concepts of Moral and Causal Judgments, in 'Journal of Genetic Psychology', 111, pp. 59-68.

Turiel, E. (1975) The Development of Social Concepts, in D.J. DePalma and J.M. Foley (eds), 'Moral Development: Current Theory and Research'. Hillsdale, NJ: Lawrence Erlbaum Associates.

Ugurel-Semin, R. (1952) Moral Behaviour and Moral Judgment of Children, in 'Journal of Abnormal and Social Psychology', 47, pp. 463-74.

Weber, M. (1922) The Social Psychology of the World Religions; reproduced in H.H. Gerth and C.W. Mills (1946), 'From Max Weber: Essays in Sociology'. New York: Oxford University Press.

Weiner, B. and Peter, N. (1973) A Cognitive-developmental Analysis of Achievement and Moral Judgments, in 'Developmental Psychology', 9, pp. 290-309.

Whiteman, M. (1976) Children's Conceptions of Psychological Causality as Related to Subjective Responsibility, Conservation and Language, in 'Journal of Genetic Psychology', 120, pp. 128-226.

Wright, D. (in the press) The Moral Judgment of the Child Revisited, in H. Weinreich-Haste and D. Locke (eds), 'From Thought to Action: Essays on Moral and Social Development'. New York: Wiley.

Youniss, J. (1975) Another Perspective on Social Cognition, in A. Pick (ed.), 'Minnesota Symposium on Child Psychology', vol. 9. Minneapolis: University of Minnesota Press.

Youniss, J. (1978) A Conceptual Discussion of Cognition, in H. McGurk (ed.), 'Issues in Childhood Social Development'. London: Methuen.

Youniss, J. and Volpe, J. (1978) A Relational Analysis of Children's Friendship, in W. Damon (ed.), 'Social Cognition'. San Francisco: Jossey Bass.

12 Piagetian psychology of moral development: some persisting issues

Peter Tomlinson

This paper's status as part of a tribute to Piaget is in no way lessened by the fact that the structure of this collection involves my taking a 'con' rather than a 'pro' side in the debating structure chosen here. Paradoxically, perhaps the most basic grounds of one's admiration for the Piagetian contribution lies in the fact that without it we would probably not yet have got round to the sorts of issues that are now current. It will also become apparent that much of what I say implicitly accepts, even derives from, Piagetian notions. Nevertheless, I shall also hope to pay Piagetian psychology the respect of raising some rather important issues that persist with respect to its contribution to our understanding of moral development.

By 'the Piagetian contribution' to this area I refer both to Piaget's own pioneering study, 'The Moral Judgment of the Child' (1932), which is typical of his early phase, and to the massively influential work of Lawrence Kohlberg (e.g., 1971, 1976), whose work in some ways continued where Piaget left off, but which also increasingly sought to apply the stage-structural ideas of Piaget's later, more systematic, phase to produce what can quite fairly be termed a 'grand theory' of morals and moral development. This naturally also implies that there are a great many aspects on which such an approach might be challenged. There have also been a variety of critiques and counter-defences (for example Kurtines and Grief, 1974; Simpson, 1974; Broughton, 1978; Liebert, 1979) with which people may be familiar. I do not intend simply to review these here; rather, my purpose is to indicate a selection of, to me, important issues that persist with respect to the Piagetian contribution to the study of moral development. It will be clear that these issues vary both in nature and implications and that, while distinct, they relate to aspects of the one grand approach and are, therefore, interrelated in various ways.

A first issue concerns the extent to which the Piagetian contribution has 'asked the right questions' concerning moral development or at least, having seen particular problems, has actually pursued them successfully. This issue potentially

154

embroils large areas of moral philosophy and social science, to put it mildly. But it must be pointed out that in their various ways, both Piaget and Kohlberg bring a strongly Kantian defini- tion of morality to their empirical studies, which then has them dealing with judgments and reasoning involving moral rules and principles. This concern with moral cognition then assimilates the basic issues of moral motivation emphasized by the Humean tradition and its psychological counterpart, neo-behaviourist social learning theory. Similar slippages between Piaget's initially posed problems and offered treatments have recently been analysed in some detail by Helen Weinreich-Haste (1981). Now, as both she and I (Tomlinson, 1980) have pointed out, it is easy to mount a critique simply by adopting an alternative definitional perspective or explanatory paradigm. But we do not need to do this to become aware of the fact that the Piagetian approach has tended to ignore certain basic issues. For instance, a Kantian subjectivism in the form of, say, Richard Hare's prescriptivist meta-ethics soon brings us back to that most basic and perennial question which is so often confronted by any reflecting person: why be moral at all? When one does try to investigate this particular issue, as Ted Trainer (personal communication) has recently been doing in Australia, one finds very little evidence of extensive reasoning behind the value stances people adopt: 'taken-for-grantedness' seems more the order of the day, as I have also been finding in recent research to which I shall return later. Of course, no one approach should be expected to tell us everything about as complex a domain as morals, but when the empire-building tendencies that Kuhn (1970) attributed to all paradigms can call on the sorts of resources available to the Piagetian grand theory, close criticality is called for.

A second, somewhat connected, issue concerns what Brunswick would have termed the 'ecological validity' of Piagetian findings; that is, the extent to which they are generalizable across the domain of situations and topics that might be designated 'moral'. Clearly, Kohlberg, with his use of artificial dilemmas in a specific interview or paper-and-pencil situation, is more at risk here than the marble-playing Piaget. Even so, students of psycho- logical stress and its cognitive effects, such as Daniel Berlyne, Joseph McVicker Hunt or George Mandler, would doubtless agree that a positively motivated game situation is likely to pro- vide optimal conditions for cognitive processing, certainly compared with the much heavier stresses and anxieties that can be expected to characterize many 'moral task' situations. Doubtless it is preferable initially to investigate cognitive processes under optimal motivational conditions, rather than to risk building merely a model of pathology; but the personal significance of moral decision-making certainly means that its content and situation must never be lost sight of. Note that this point includes the more traditional accusation that Piagetian psychology has neglected affective and motivational consider-

ations to a degree detrimental to a number of its possible applications. I will return to this point later.

A third issue, highly related to both of the previous two, concerns what I have termed the 'phenomenological validity' of the
Piagetian approach, particularly that of Kohlberg's ideas. By
this I mean the extent to which the content and structure of his
stage descriptions actually characterize the moral thinking of
people in their everyday lives. The assumption, and it seems to
be no more than this, appears to be that these notions do in fact
adequately cover people's everyday outlooks, but there has been
little attempt to check on this systematically. I suspect, for
instance, that for many readers this point is implicitly covered
by the claims that 50 per cent of a person's moral reasoning
tends to be at their dominant stage, with the remainder spread
across the adjacent stages. However, this does not directly
confront the point. What might we expect in theory? We have
just seen that Kohlberg clearly plumps for a particular meta-
ethical position, namely the Kantian/Rawlsian stance, which
defines morals in terms of rights and justice. Moreover,
Kohlberg's stages originated, on his own account, as Weberian
ideal-types, and even though he has emphasized their structure, which he has interpreted in terms of the more abstract
features of Piaget's developmental logics, Kohlberg's structures
must be considered more specific than the latter. Even in
theory, therefore, we should hardly expect them to do justice
to all aspects of everyone's moral thinking across all situations.
Yet we have insufficient evidence on this issue: at an informal
level, I am sure that, like me, many who have attempted to
apply the Kohlberg manuals even to material derived from the
purpose-designed Kohlberg dilemmas will have found themselves
having a hard time forcing some responses into the Kohlberg
measuring chamber. When one attempts to follow the individual
into his or her construals of decisions in their everyday life-
world, then the little formal evidence we do have suggests that
things look rather different from the Kohlbergian picture. In
one of the finest studies in the area, Carol Gilligan (1977)
found that her abortion counsellees saw things in terms very
different from those of Kohlberg, and she was inclined to interpret this in terms of sex differences and of Kohlbergian bias
originating from and sustained by the use of an exclusively
male sample. However, work by Norma Haan (1977, 1978) and
Steven Yussen (1977) in America and by Tom Kitwood (1980)
in this country suggests that the discrepancies from Kohlberg
are not solely a function of sex differences, but have probably
more to do with an over-constructive (not to say projective)
Kohlbergian interpretation of responses to what is in any case a
tailor-made Kohlbergian instrument. So we still seem to be in
need of some direct evidence on the extent to which the Kohlbergian phenomenology covers everyday social and moral reasoning.
(I might mention that I am currently attempting to investigate
this question using the open-ended methodology devised by

Tom Kitwood, as part of a longitudinal research project funded
by the Social Science Research Council, whose results should
become available shortly.)

The last three points are perhaps not the most typical of
those raised by developmentalists concerning the Piagetian
contribution to the moral domain. In fact, we might say that
they require some sort of reflection on the paradigm itself as
opposed to being issues generated within the Piagetian approach.
For my next point I want to turn to an issue that is typically
raised regarding developmental theories, and rightly so. This
is the issue of longitudinal evidence. I think it is fair to say
that, when one compares the massive influence that the work of
Kohlberg in particular has had, its longitudinal data base is
singularly restricted. As is well known, the only longitudinal
data bridging any appreciable time-span that Kohlberg can call
upon are the data from his own original all-male Chicago
sample. The length of the time-span across which data have
been collected on this group is indeed impressive, and there do
exist other forms of data which support the Kohlbergian position,
such as cross-sectional data and the evidence on stage comprehension and preference from the work of James Rest and Elliot
Turiel. Nevertheless, it is indisputable that a developmental
theory sooner or later requires sound longitudinal evidence.
Now, apart from the usual resource problems associated with
gathering such evidence, it may well be that in Kohlberg's case
there are a variety of other constraints which have deterred
would-be longitudinal investigators. First, we can note with
Deanna Kuhn (1976) that, given that Kohlberg's central contention is only that his stages form an irreversibly invariant,
step-wise sequence, pinning down the required sort of evidence
can be no mean achievement. For as Kuhn points out, if we
follow people over a period of years and find no change, this
is not necessarily disconfirming evidence, since no particular
rate of change is hypothesized. Nor would the step-wise
postulate be necessarily refuted by a finding that one's subjects
jumped a stage from one data gathering point to another: the
reply could simply be that they must have passed through the
intervening stage during the interval between testings. It
would appear that the only disconfirming pattern would be one
involving regression to a lower stage. This brings us to a second
deterrent to our intrepid Kohlbergian prober, who will doubtless
remember that, when Kohlberg and Kramer (1969) found such
regressions in their college sample, their initial response was to
discount the findings in terms of mere functional as opposed to
structural change (whatever a backward structural change might
mean!). The more considered, longer-term, reaction has been
to revise the definition of certain of the stages so as, as Kohlberg
and his group explicitly tell us in their 1977 manual, 'to yield a
classification system meeting the invariant sequence postulate of
stage theory'. On the one hand, therefore, one has this and
other pieces of evidence that Kohlberg is an honest and flexible

investigator willing to follow the truth where the empirical
findings seem to lead, while on the other hand one has the nasty
suspicion that some sort of developmental sequence is 'going to be
found' at whatever cost. A third form of deterrent is the frequent
assertion that, not only do Kohlberg stages form an invariant
sequence, but this is logically necessary. The seductive fascin-
ation of this particular line is all the more enhanced by Kohlberg's
attempts to specify a common strand in the stage sequence.
Earlier versions spoke of an evolving set of justice structures.
And the later line has emphasized changes in socio-moral perspective (see Kohlberg, 1976). To this connotative approach
there even correspond certain reinterpretations of Kohlbergian
development in denotative terms. I am thinking here of the
suggestions by people such as Ian Vine in this country and
Robert Carter in Canada, that we might see the Kohlberg stage
sequence as involving a progressive expansion of the 'moral
community' to which one extends rights and considerations of
justice and equity.

However, the Kohlbergian approach itself also offers certain
positive reasons for gathering the longitudinal evidence that
an independent critic would in any case consider essential.
These reasons include the fact that, if one gets past the
unitary ideology to which I just referred and looks at the
actual nature of stage descriptions, preferably by attempting
to score a large amount of real data, then I think it will become
very clear that the different stages do show very different
emphases and that likewise their differentiation and resemblances
constitute very much a family of similarities and differences as
opposed to an exclusive and unitary set of gains along any
single, unequivocal dimension. Thus, although Joachim Wohlwill
(1973) has disputed it, Kohlberg's claim that his stages constitute structured wholes as required by Piagetian theory implies
that they must be complex and contain a number of aspects or
elements. If this is so, then it's clearly possible that progression
might take place on the basis of development on any of the
multiple aspects involved in any given pair of stages, adjacent
or otherwise. Furthermore, just as some reinterpretations of
Kohlberg have deterred the conception of alternative possible
sequences and the associated need for longitudinal data to decide
among them, so have there been other reformulations which
point to specific possibilities by way of alternative sequences,
even if still in terms of Kohlbergian stages. For instance, one
of Kohlberg's closest associates, John Gibbs (1977), suggests
among other things that Stage 5 may be seen as the explicit
formalization of Stage 2, and, likewise, Stage 6 as the formalization of Stage 3. On this account one might surely expect the
possibility of direct jumps between Stages 2 and 5 and 3 and 6.
More recently, a German research group under Lutz Eckensberger
at the University of Saarbrücken have attempted to 'clean up'
Kohlbergian stage formulation by expressing it in terms of a
systematic conception of the nature of human action, deriving

from the work of Goldman. According to the highly complex portrayal of the Kohlbergian stages that emerges from this new exegesis, certain stages show an identity of structure and elements and differ only in the generality with which they are applied. Thus, Stage 4 is considered to be a generalization of Stage 1, Stage 4½ a generalization of Stage 2 and Stage 5 a generalization of Stage 3. Here, then, we have another basis for investigating the possibility of alternative sequences, though once again within the Kohlbergian perspective. Furthermore, as a counter to the difficulties Deanna Kuhn alludes to in pinning down evidence for or against a step-wise invariant sequence, it is only fair to Kohlberg to point out that his own longitudinal data do provide some sort of baseline for rate of development, which can, in turn, provide a criterion for what would count as an adequate frequency of time sampling in a longitudinal study. If we go on Kohlberg and Elfenbein's (1975) results, in which the maximum speed of stage transition was roughly one stage every three years, then frequency of sampling should pose few problems. On the other hand, the total time-span across which one would need to follow subjects in order to be likely to discover any appreciable progress through the stages would be correspondingly long. I might add that the study of mine which I mentioned earlier has been carried out over a period of six years, and my current impression of the rate of development in the teenage school pupils it involved is very much in line with the slow rate one would expect from Kohlberg's own results.

Having focused somewhat on Kohlberg for the last point, for my final critical reflection I return to an issue which concerns both Piaget and Kohlberg, namely the role of conscious thought in moral action and development. Here, it seems to me, we have a question which is, on the one hand, crucial and problematic in the psychology of thought and its development and application and, on the other hand, for which there exist some very interesting and promising strands in the corpus of Piagetian ideas. There is, indeed, a very strong contrast between the accounts given by Piaget on the one hand and Kohlberg on the other of the role of conscious thought with respect to action and development. Kohlberg's position is in some senses more straightforward, in that it reflects the rationalism associated with simpler forms of commonsense versions of mind-body dualism. In other words, first we think, then we do; we guide our actions by our conscious thoughts. The same domination of conscious processing is held to underlie the development of moral thinking. There are a number of indications that Kohlberg believes that stage transition is due at base to a conscious reworking of one's socio-moral outlook. Leaving aside the problems that might arise when this view is faced with the length of time it seems to take to get from one stage to another, we can point out that Piaget's conception of the nature of development through what he then referred to as the phases of moral judgment outlook was very different indeed. For Piaget this development was characterized by a type of process to whose study he returned in the last decade of his life, namely conscious realization. For Piaget, what comes first is the capacity for systematic action and what follows it, typically at an appreciable time-lag, is the conscious realization, conscious formulation, or conscious grasp of what has been going on, starting with an awareness of what he calls the peripheral aspects, the initiating intentional aspects and the outcomes. This conscious realization is said to be not merely a passive reflecting at the conscious level of what has gone on at the action level, but, like any other form of cognition, to involve a reconstruction using whatever one has available for the purpose. Piaget also holds that there are always unconscious aspects of processing, including cognitive or conceptual processing no less than sensorimotor or skilled action processing. From this we can see that Piaget certainly does not share Kohlberg's rationalism regarding the relationship between conscious thought and systematic action. But, perhaps more subtly, nor does he share Kohlberg's rationalism with respect to cognitive developmental progress. While I believe that there are a number of reasons why we will need to look more closely at what Piaget is hypothesizing in this area, the implications for moral development and certainly for attempts at moral education are potentially very serious. In a paper to be published shortly in a book edited by Weinreich-Haste and Locke, Derek Wright (1982) points out that applying the notion of conscious realization to the area of morals means that what gets consciously grasped is a set of reasons for acting in relation to others, and that this can be a bridge between the individual's development and the nature of his social interaction, which Piaget and others have held to be so important. So we have this interesting rediscovery not only of the social dimension of Piaget's ideas about morals, but also of possible ways in which its effects on the individual participant might come about.

So Kohlberg and Piaget would seem to be saying very different sorts of things. They seem to have very different psychologies of action, including whatever actions are involved in the cognitive progress from one stage outlook to another. Space limits comment on this very important set of ideas to my saying that it seems to me that there is no need to construe these sets of ideas of Kohlberg and Piaget as alternatives which shall do battle to see which is the universally true account; rather, it seems to me quite possible that there may be occasions when either or both may apply. A 'nothing-but' type of controversy would seem to be all too reminiscent of the earlier stages of an analogous debate with which we are all too familiar, namely the one concerning 'the' relationships between language and thought in intellectual development.

So I come to the end of my list of selected problematic issues in the Piagetian psychology of moral development, issues which I think it fair to say have immense theoretical and practical importance. I should certainly add that I think that Piagetian

psychology itself does contain some as yet underdeveloped conceptual tools for grappling with these issues, and the renewed
concern with conscious realization is perhaps the best example
in this context. However, it also seems to me that, when one
turns to a level of analysis as molar and complex as the social-
developmental-psychological one we have been considering
here, one needs all the conceptual resources one can lay one's
mind on. I therefore strongly welcome the renewed emphasis
on the social nature of moral outlooks and the likely role of
social interaction in their development. It also seems to me very
healthy that various writers in the Piagetian tradition should be
reflecting critically on the nature of the paradigm they are
seeking to employ to understand this area of moral development
and behaviour. Here I am thinking particularly of work by
Charles Levine (1979a, 1979b) and Deanna Kuhn (1978). I
would very strongly welcome Levine's emphasis on the interaction of persons and situations in understanding variations in
levels of moral judgment stage usage, and I very much share
Deanna Kuhn's contention that there is more to moral development and behaviour than can be understood by either of the two
major approaches, the organismic and mechanistic paradigms
which Overton and Reese have described as characterizing the
psychology of development. However, I will finish by repeating
a point which I have made often before, and that is to express
surprise that in this area of developmental concern no one
seems as yet to have turned towards the neo-Piagetian notions
that have developed over the last decade or so, or to the
associated ideas from the cognitive psychology of skill and skill
acquisition pioneered mainly in this country (see Tomlinson,
1981). Yet the correspondence between certain aspects of that
paradigm and the recently resurrected Piagetian work on conscious realization are singularly striking. If Piaget is indeed
right about the function of negative feedback as a trigger for
conscious reconstruction, then hopefully my pointing to this set
of persisting problem issues may stimulate the use of these
wider conceptual resources in our own attempts at conscious
grasp of the processes in moral development.

REFERENCES

Berlyne, D. (1960) 'Conflict, Arousal and Curiosity'. New York:
    McGraw-Hill.
Broughton, J.M. (1978) The Cognitive-developmental Approach
    to Morality: A Reply to Kurtines and Grief, in 'Journal of
    Moral Education', 7, pp. 81-96.
Carter, R. (1980) What is Lawrence Kohlberg Doing? in 'Journal
    of Moral Education', pp. 88-102.
Eckensberger, L.H. and Reinshagen, H. (1980) Kohlberg's
    Stufentheorie der Entwicklung des moralischen Urteils: Ein
    Versuch ihrer Reinterpretation im Bezugsrahmen handlungs-

theoretischer Konzepte, in L.H. Eckensberger and R.K.
Silbereisen (eds), 'Entwicklung sozialer Kognitionen: Modelle,
Theorien, Methoden, Anwendung'. Stuttgart: Klett-Cotta,
pp. 65-131.

Gibbs, J.C. (1977) Kohlberg's Stages of Moral Judgment: A
Constructive Critique, in 'Harvard Educational Review', 47,
pp. 42-61.

Gilligan, C. (1977) In a Different Voice: Women's Conceptions
of Self and of Morality, in 'Harvard Educational Review', 47,
pp. 481-517.

Haan, N. (1977) 'Coping and Defending: Processes of Self-
environment Organization'. New York: Academic Press.

Haan, N. (1978) Two Moralities in Action Context: Relationships
to Thought, Ego Regulation and Development, in 'Journal of
Personality and Social Psychology', 36, pp. 286-305.

Hunt, J.M. (1971) Toward a History of Intrinsic Motivation, in
H.I. Day, D.E. Berlyne and D.E. Hunt (eds), 'Intrinsic
Motivation: A New Direction in Education'. Toronto: Holt,
Rinehart & Winston.

Kitwood, T. (1978) The Morality of Inter-personal Values: An
Aspect of Values in Adolescent Life, in 'Journal of Moral
Education', 7, pp. 189-98.

Kitwood, T. (1980) 'Disclosures to a Stranger: Adolescent Values
in an Advanced Industrial Society'. London: Routledge &
Kegan Paul.

Kohlberg, L. (1971) From Is to Ought: How To Commit the
Naturalistic Fallacy and Get Away With It in the Study of
Moral Development, in T. Mischel (ed.), 'Cognitive Development and Epistemology'. New York: Academic Press, pp. 151-
236.

Kohlberg, L. (1976) Moral Stages and Moralization: The Cogni-
tive-developmental Approach, in T. Lickona (ed.), 'Moral
Development and Behaviour: Theory, Research and Social
Issues'. New York: Holt, Rinehart & Winston, pp. 31-53.

Kohlberg, L. and Elfenbein, D. (1975) The Development of
Moral Judgments Concerning Capital Punishment, in 'American
Journal of Orthopsychiatry', 45.

Kohlberg, L.A. and Kramer, R. (1969) Continuities and Dis-
continuities in Childhood and Adult Moral Development, in
'Human Development', 12, pp. 93-120.

Kuhn, D. (1976) Short-term Longitudinal Evidence for the
Sequentiality of Kohlberg's Early Stages of Moral Judgment,
in 'Developmental Psychology', 12 (2), pp. 162-6.

Kuhn, D. (1978) Mechanisms of Cognitive and Social Development: One Psychology or Two? in 'Human Development', 21,
pp. 92-118.

Kuhn, T.S. (1970) 'The Structure of Scientific Revolutions',
2nd ed. enlarged. University of Chicago Press.

Kurtines, W. and Greif, E.B. (1974) The Development of Moral
Thought: Review and Evaluation of Kohlberg's Approach, in
'Psychological Bulletin', 81, pp. 453-70.

Levine, C.G. (1979a) Stage Acquisition and Stage Use: An Appraisal of Stage Displacement Explanations of Variation in Moral Reasoning, in 'Human Development', 22, pp. 145-64.
Levine, C.G. (1979b) The Form-content Distinction in Moral Development Research, in 'Human Development', 22, pp. 225-34.
Liebert, R.M. (1979) Moral Development: A Theoretical and Empirical Analysis, in G.J. Whitehurst and B.J. Zimmerman, (eds), 'The Functions of Language and Cognition'. New York: Academic Press, pp. 229-65.
Mandler, G. (1975) 'Mind and Emotion'. New York: John Wiley.
Overton, W. and Reese, H. (1973) Models of Development: Methodological Implications, in J.R. Nesselroade and H. Reese, 'Life-span Developmental Psychology: Methodological Issues'. New York: Academic Press.
Piaget, J. (1932) 'The Moral Judgment of the Child'. London: Routledge & Kegan Paul.
Rest, J.R. (1975) Longitudinal Study of the Defining Issues Test of Moral Judgment, in 'Developmental Psychology', 11, pp. 738-48.
Scharf, P. (ed.) (1978) 'Readings in Moral Education'. Minneapolis: Winston Press, ch. 1.
Simpson, E.L. (1974) Moral Development Research: A Case Study of Scientific Cultural Bias, in 'Human Development', 17, pp. 81-106.
Tomlinson, P.D. (1980) Moral Judgment and Moral Psychology: Piaget, Kohlberg and Beyond, in S. Modgil and C. Modgil (eds), 'Toward a Theory of Psychological Development'. Windsor: National Foundation for Educational Research.
Tomlinson, P.D. (1981) 'Understanding Teaching: Interactive Educational Psychology'. London: McGraw-Hill.
Turiel, E. (1974) Conflict and Transition in Adolescent Moral Development, in 'Child Development', 45, pp. 14-29.
Vine, I. (1982) The Nature of Moral Commitments, in H. Weinreich-Haste and D. Locke (eds), 'Morality in the Making: Thought, Action and the Social Context'. Chichester: Wiley.
Weinreich-Haste, H. (1981) Piaget's Moral Judgment of the Child - A Critical Perspective, in S. Modgil and C. Modgil (eds), 'The Taming of Piaget'. Windsor: National Foundation for Educational Research.
Wohlwill, J.F. (1973) 'The Study of Behavioural Development'. New York: Academic Press.
Wright, D. (1982) 'The Moral Judgment of the Child' Revisited, in H. Weinreich-Haste and D. Locke (eds), 'Morality in the Making: Thought, Action and the Social Context'. Chichester: Wiley.
Yussen, S.R. (1977) Characteristics of Moral Dilemmas Written by Adolescents, in 'Developmental Psychology', 13 (2), pp. 162-3.

Part 8

Philosophy

13 Reflections on 'The Growth of Logical Thinking'

Wolfe Mays

INTRODUCTION

Piagetian criticism has been warmly pursued by some Anglo-Saxon psychologists and philosophers in the manner of a blood sport, almost as exciting as 'The Hunting of the Snark', immortalized by Lewis Carroll. You remember the lines:

> They sought it with thimbles, they sought it with care;
> They pursued it with forks and hope;
> They threatened its life with a railway-share;
> They charmed it with smiles and soap.

I doubt whether Piaget would have been charmed with smiles and soap, but I agree that his writings are far from being a model of clarity and that at times his ideas are loosely and obscurely expressed - so much so that one requires more than 'forks and hope' to get to grips with them. However, the translators of his work are sometimes to blame for this. They do not always convey the meaning he wishes to convey, and this may easily lead to misunderstanding.

There is another reason why English-speaking readers have difficulty in understanding Piaget's writings. Most psychologists and philosophers in this country and the USA look at his work through the astigmatic lenses of English empiricism. Piaget's thought, on the other hand, is rooted in the continental rationalist tradition. When English-speaking readers try to understand his writings, they often do so in terms of an epistemology which is foreign to Piaget's own. His ideas then appear out of focus and consequently blurred. Because of this Piaget is a writer whom it is very easy to criticize but more difficult to understand. I myself believe that he is an important thinker and that it is worth making the effort to understand him, even if this does mean learning a little about continental philosophy.

In what follows I will examine perhaps one of the most influential criticisms of Piaget's work: Jerome Bruner's 1959 review of Inhelder and Piaget's 'The Growth of Logical Thinking: From

Childhood to Adolescence'.[1] This review has passed into the psychological literature as an authentic critique of the theoretical conceptions used by Piaget in his account of the development of logical thought. It has been said of Bruner's review that it has considerable merit, since he tries to deflate and clarify some of Piaget's more confused ideas. What I shall do in this paper is to look a little more closely at Bruner's criticisms and see how far they can be sustained.

BRUNER'S CRITICISM OF THE NOTION OF EQUILIBRIUM

I will begin by examining Bruner's criticism of Piaget's use of the notion of equilibrium. Bruner asserts that by this notion Piaget does not wish to say more than 'each stage of operational thinking develops its own internal consistency, its own compensatory reversibility, and predictability by virtue of being based on a set of rules of operation and that these rules can be described as logical structures'.[2] Little is added, Bruner thinks, 'save some confusing imagery - by insisting on re-summarizing the definition of concrete operations and labelling the summary "equilibrium"'.[3]

One can certainly find passages in Piaget's writings where the notion of equilibrium occurs, which at first sight seem singularly unilluminating. But with a certain amount of patience one can usually make clear their meaning. Piaget uses the notion of equilibrium in a fairly general sense, as Bruner himself recognizes. Not only does it cover the way in which the child develops logical operations, but it is also descriptive of the way biological and social processes achieve a certain stability. Although Piaget tells us, 'the special equilibrium of logical structures is one of the finest achievements of living morphogenesis',[4] it is only one kind of psychological activity described by him in terms of this notion.

Bruner, however, has little sympathy with the notion of equilibrium and regards it as a kind of surplus baggage, which, as he puts it, perhaps 'gives Piaget a comforting sense of continuity with his early biological apprenticeship'.[5] But there seems no intrinsic reason why one should not use biological categories in the interpretation of psychological phenomena. After all, human beings have something in common with other members of the animal kingdom in the way they adapt themselves to their environment.

Bruner does not adequately bring out the connection between Piaget's notion of equilibrium and the related notions of assimilation and accommodation. The latter notions are descriptive of the way the child adapts his behaviour so as to cope with environmental change. Such adaptive behaviour is of two sorts: (1) lower level adaptations - the way in which a child's needs achieve their satisfaction by means of directed trial and error activities; and (2) higher level ones - the way, for example, the child's concrete logico-classificatory activities develop into abstract propositional ones.

Most accounts of the child's adaptive behaviour start off by postulating instincts of some sort. A good example of this is Freud's libido, which during development becomes fixed on to different persons and objects. Kurt Lewin has claimed that the concept of instinct as thus used is simply a classificatory label referring to descriptions of the kinds of behaviour which the instinct is presumed to explain and is hence tautological. In a similar way the effects of opium were once explained by saying that it sent you to sleep because of its dormative powers. Lewin went on to argue that, for example, an emotion like anger is not simply the result of some inherent psychological tendency, but is a function of the total field of which the subject forms part.

When Bruner refers to Piaget's notion of equilibrium as surplus baggage, he would seem to assimilate Piaget's position to this sort of instinct psychology. But Piaget, like Lewin, wishes to study the child's behaviour in the context of the specific concrete situation in which it arises. Hence he regards the child's adaptive behaviour as an attempt to achieve a balance (or equilibrium) between the way it acts on his social and physical environment and the way that the environment acts on him. It may be that Piaget is wrong or misguided in attempting to give what is in effect a Galilean account of adaptive behaviour. There may perhaps be no alternative but to fall back on Aristotelian final causes. But he ought not to be accused of what he is patently trying not to do.

Bruner goes on to tell us, 'The main difficulty of all such self-regulatory balances is not so much that they explain too little, but rather that they explain so much as to be useless.'[6] Bruner seems to be saying here that, owing to the generality of this sort of notion, it has little value as an explanation. But Piaget's application of the notion of equilibrium to adaptive behaviour would seem to be largely descriptive. Further, general laws of a descriptive nature are not to be despised, as they may have considerable scientific value. A good example of this is to be seen in the second law of thermodynamics. Bruner would seem to assume that the main function of a scientific theory is to explain. There is, nevertheless, a strong tradition in science which takes the function of theories to be essentially descriptive.

Piaget contends that conceptual knowledge is not to be found a priori in the child's mind, but arises through genetic development. He is then faced with showing how the relatively static logical structures develop out of our directed trial and error activities. The difference between the older view, that logical ideas were in some way innate in our mind, and Piaget's view is analogous to the difference between the physics of Aristotle and that of Galileo: whereas Aristotle takes rest as fundamental and has to explain how motion arises, Galileo instead takes motion as fundamental and has to explain how rest arises. In a similar way, Piaget regards our directed behavioural activities as fundamental, and endeavours to show how our synchronic logical structures are derived from them.

In 'The Growth of Logical Thinking', the notion of equilibrium as used by Piaget is taken as descriptive of the process whereby logical operations develop so that they form systems having certain formal properties. But this notion is not simply a short-hand expression for a 'set of rules of operation', as Bruner assumes. Piaget is rather concerned to show how these rules arise from our structured thought processes through a series of interchanges between the individual and his social and physical milieu. When such interchanges become stabilized (or achieve equilibrium), they give rise, he claims, to the operational rules of logic. Hence Piaget is not, as Bruner suggests, concerned with basing thought operations on these rules, since for Piaget the rules themselves arise through such operations.

It is usually overlooked that Piaget's account of the way the child's logical operations develop through his handling of objects is a simplified model of what actually occurs. This model regards the child as a closed system only entering into exchanges with his physical environment. If we renounce this artifice, Piaget asserts, it will be seen that, if logic consists of an organization of operations, the child does not arrive at such an organization himself. To account for this development we also need to take note of his relationships to other individuals. Logical progress, he concludes - and here he is primarily referring to rational thought processes - goes hand in hand with the socialization of the individual.[7]

Piaget contends that rational discourse arises as a result of an interchange of ideas or propositions between individuals. This interchange can be described in terms of what sociologists nowadays call social exchange theory. But this scheme of social exchange has for Piaget applications to other forms of mental activity. He would claim that feelings like sympathy and love, as well as moral and legal judgments, arise through such an interchange. Thus the feelings we experience and the normative judgments we make are to be described in terms of transactions between ourselves and others.[8]

DEMANDS, NEEDS AND EQUILIBRIUM

Bruner states that, as far as the child is concerned, 'It is not equilibrium that keeps him back in the concrete operational stage and not a new equilibrium that brings him forward. It is the vicissitude of coping with demands - internal and external'.[9] But the point Bruner is making here is not so very different from that made by Piaget in his earlier work, 'The Origins of Intelligence in Children'.[10] Where Bruner talks of demands Piaget talks of needs, but for Piaget one can talk of needs only in relation to the object or state of affairs which satisfies that need.

Needs for Piaget exist not in the abstract, but always in relation to some particular end or object sought after or desired. Thus, he says,

> there is need when something either outside ourselves or within us (physically or mentally) is changed and behavior has to be adjusted as a function of this change. For example, hunger or fatigue will provoke a search for nourishment or rest: encountering an external object will lead to a need to play . . . or it leads to a question or a theoretical problem. . . .

On the other hand, he goes on, action ends when a need is satisfied. Equilibrium is then re-established 'between the new factor which has provoked the need and the mental organization that existed prior to the introduction of this factor'.[11]

Piaget's theory of needs also has a sociological dimension, and here it resembles Sartre's account in his 'Critique',[12] where the latter identifies need with the conscious awareness of a 'lack', which arises from scarcity. This leads to alienation and hence social conflict. Piaget describes the same sort of sociological phenomenon in terms of his disequilibrium/equilibrium model. He makes the point that in Marx's sociological theory, through the existence of social conflict and continual opposition, history comes to be conceived as a succession of class struggles (or disequilibria) which eventually lead to the advent of socialism.[13] The final state of equilibrium then would seem to play the same role as 'synthesis' does in the Marxian dialectic.

In the light of the somewhat pained if not hostile reception that Piaget's use of the notion of equilibrium has met with in Anglo-Saxon academic circles, it is worth looking at its methodological status. As Piaget uses it in his account of adaptive behaviour, it would seem to have the status of a descriptive hypothesis or model. Stebbing points out that such hypotheses are not put forward as generalizations from experience; 'they are descriptions that serve the function of models enabling the scientist to understand the mode of connexion between the facts for which he is trying to account'.[14] This sort of hypothesis is to be distinguished from an explanatory one, where we might attempt to explain, say, anti-social behaviour in terms of such unobservables as instincts or motives.

But it must be recognized that Piaget, in common with other French writers, also uses the word 'équilibre' as a descriptive term to denote well balanced behaviour or a well balanced state of mind, which is defined as 'Harmonie entre les tendences psychique, que se traduit par une activité, une adaptation normale'.[15] I give some dictionary examples illustrating this: 'C'est un homme très intelligent, mais il manque d'équilibre. On craint pour son équilibre mental.' 'L'amour durable est celui qui tient toujours les forces de deux êtres en équilibre' (Hugo).[16]

The Académie Française would not seem to be unduly perturbed by the use of the world 'équilibre' in such contexts. And if Piaget uses this term in his description of the interpersonal character of emotions like love, he is in the good company of novelists like Victor Hugo. Of course, it might be said that if a little Anglo-Saxon linguistic analysis had rubbed off on the French they might have known better. However, the word 'equilibrium' was at one time also used in English to indicate a well balanced mental state, or one in which there was a neutrality of judgment. I give some examples from the New English Dictionary:

(1608) 'Salomon a man in perfit aequilibrium and stablest state of his age.'
(1625) 'Simple Atheism consists of an equilibration of the mind.'
(1750) 'Drowsy equilibrations of undetermined counsel'. (Dr Johnson)
(1875) 'It is best to preserve our minds in a state of equilibrium.'

THE DEVELOPMENT OF INTELLECTUAL OPERATIONS

Bruner remarks that it is plain that[17]

the adolescent differs from the child not simply in that he uses a propositional calculus . . . but rather that he is *forced* to deal with possibility by the nature of the tasks he undertakes and by the nature of the unfolding and developing of his drives and the social connexions required for filling them. . . . So the concretely operational child need not manipulate the world of potentiality (save on the fantasy level) until pressure is put on him, at which point propositionalism begins to mark his thinking.

Logical structures then develop to support the new forms of commerce with the world.

Bruner's criticism here with its implication that Piaget neglects the role of social factors in intellectual development resembles some of the early criticisms made by Susan Isaacs of Piaget's work. She criticized Piaget for believing that social experience becomes effective at the age of seven to nine years only as a result of some inner ripening. She went on to argue that Piaget thereby overlooked the whole of the child's direct and cumulative interaction with the world in favour of the inner history of structural development. Susan Isaacs's criticism is presumably aimed at Piaget's stage theory of development, which, however, is not as inflexible as some critics have made it out to be.

Piaget has been openly critical of the view that social factors à la Durkheim play the major role in determining intellectual development, and here he would seem to be answering Bruner's critique. He tells us:[18]

> Very rarely have I been able in America to expound any aspect
> of my stage theory without being asked 'How can you speed
> up the development?' And that eminent psychologist J. Bruner
> has gone so far as to state that you can teach anything to any
> child at any stage if you only set about it the right way.

But, Piaget asks, would it ever be possible to make the theory
of relativity or even the simple handling of propositional or
hypothetico-deductive operations comprehensible to a four-year
old?[19]

Piaget is probably overstating Bruner's position when he
suggests that for Bruner social factors are paramount in intellectual development. Bruner does, after all, refer to the part
played by the child's drives and the way they are filled out by
social connections during development. Further, Piaget's comments need qualification, since he is talking about normal
Western educated children as we know them today. It is, of course,
possible that 'Wunderkinder' might yet at some future date be
grown in glass containers in the best Brave New World manner.
Such children, with a sufficiently stimulating social and physical
environment, might come to understand the theory of relativity
as well as 'Principia Mathematica' by the age of four. But even
then it would seem unlikely that they would be able to reason
abstractly before they could perform concrete operations - that
is, if they had to learn or understand logic and mathematics,
rather than having such knowledge programmed into them at
birth. I assume that science fiction, unlike magic, has to exhibit
some form of internal consistency.

In any case Piaget does not deny that social and intellectual
pressures play an important part in the development of the
child's logical functions. He believes that the passage from the
concrete logico-mathematical stage to the more formal stage of
logical thought can be accelerated or retarded by favourable or
unfavourable social conditions as well as by internal conditions
of an emotional or volitional sort. He remarks, 'As for the role
of culture in the education of the individual one would have to
be very naive not to take it into consideration.'[20] In addition,
he would also wish to take into account the maturation of the
child's intellectual capacities.

As far as this goes, there seems little significant difference
between Piaget's views and those of Bruner. Where they would
seem to differ is in the greater degree in which Bruner believes
that concept formation can be accelerated by external pressures.
That there are limits to the extent to which this is possible can
be seen in the case of severely mentally handicapped children,
who may be unable to learn to use propositional operations, or
even the concepts of substance, weight and volume. As a consequence of their disability, they are not even able to form the

concrete classificatory concepts upon which Piaget assumes the later propositional stages of thought are based.

PROBLEM-SOLVING, STRATEGIES AND LOGICAL OPERATIONS

Bruner assumes that Piaget in his studies is largely interested in the nature of problem-solving. It is true that, in the book under review, Piaget discusses the application of hypothetico-deductive reasoning to simple problem-situations in natural science. However, he is concerned primarily with describing the structure of the child's intellectual activities rather than that of the problem-situation. Thus, for example, he uses his logical formulae to describe the intellectual categories in terms of which the child organizes his experiences. He believes that the child's conception of the world is not identical with that of the adult. He would hold that the 'Weltanschauung' of the Western adult is much more complex and includes the findings of Galilean physics.

On the other hand, Bruner, accepting as he does an uncom-plicated Anglo-Saxon empiricist view of things, takes the world as a going concern directly given as such in perception. He therefore emphasizes the problem-situation as the motor of our intellectual development. The problem-situation would seem to exist for Bruner in itself without any process of interpretation entering in on the part of the subject. On the other hand, Piaget is not simply interested in showing how the child uses logical models to solve some particular problem. He is also concerned, in keeping with his more sophisticated philosophical approach, with the question of how the child comes to build up the funda-mental categories - namely, those of space, time, quantity, number, etc. - on which our thought about the world is based. Once these categories have been constructed, the problem-situation can then be specified in terms of them. Further, it is only in such works as 'The Growth of Logical Thinking' that hypothetico-deductive reasoning, which for Piaget is an essential factor in problem-solving, becomes the main topic under dis-cussion.

Bruner criticizes Inhelder and Piaget for 'talking about their tactics of thought without sufficient regard for the fact that tactics derive direction from the strategies of which they are a part'.[21] He considers Piaget's operations to be sub-species of broader programmes or strategies, and tells us 'that they grow in terms of the changing objectives of such strategies and are responses to the vicissitudes through which the person is going in pursuit of his objectives'.[22] These strategies are therefore linked with broader motivational changes. Bruner senses 'that some of the reluctance to take this step from tactics to strategy comes from Piaget's reluctance to make messy the beauty of the logical structures that conform to the cognitive structures that seem to underlie the child's and adolescent's problem-solving'.[23]

Bruner then urges Piaget to extend his theory of tactics into a
broader theory of strategy 'that takes into account the objectives
towards which thought is forced to move in order to cope with
the goal-striving necessary for the maintenance of a going life'.[24]

When Bruner urges Piaget to adopt a broader theory of strategy
he again assumes that Piaget's work is concerned largely with
the question of problem-solving. Bruner's approach, which has
overtones of Morgernstern and Von Neumann's 'Theory of Games',
overlooks that, when Piaget refers to logical operations, he is
not talking about tactics or even strategies of thought. Logical
operations are not therefore for him a sub-species of broader
programmes or strategies: they are rather general principles
which any such strategy must follow. Further, Bruner's
criticism of the notion of equilibrium as 'explaining so much as
to be useless' would seem applicable to his own use of the concept
of strategy as an explanatory device. I also doubt whether
Piaget would have attributed any aesthetic value to the elementary logical formulae he uses to describe the child's intellectual
operations.

Before strategies can be formulated, we need to have a logic
in terms of which they can be stated. Although such a logic is
at hand for us adults, it must not be assumed that it is also
present ready-made, as it were, for the child. Before the child
can deal with a large range of problem-situations, he has first
to construct the logical operations and rules in terms of which
any strategy employed by him must be formulated. Only when
this has been done will his response to the vicissitudes through
which he is going in pursuit of his objectives, be a reasonable
and adequate response. Even the 'Theory of Games' has to pre-
suppose the basic axioms and definitions of set theory before
it can get off the ground.

PRAGMATIC TESTS OF MODELS

Bruner believes that if we are to be successful in problem-
solving we need to employ good models or theories to aid us in
finding solutions. He therefore proceeds to state the conditions
which he thinks a good model or theory ought to satisfy. This,
he tells us, 'presupposes that the model will, by appropriate
manipulation, yield descriptions (or predictions) of how behaviour
will occur and will even suggest forms of behaviour to look for
that have not yet been observed - that are merely possible'.[25]
This 'model will simulate the behaviour resultants of any input-
output process, simulate not only correct moves in problem
solving but also the characteristic "errors" that are committed,
and show what brought them about'.[26]

Bruner would seem here to be doing once again what he chides
Piaget for allegedly doing: giving a very general account of our
goal-striving behaviour. In this case Bruner uses the mechanical
model of an input-output process. Good models, then, for Bruner

need at least to satisfy pragmatic tests; and this seems to be
what his statement that the model will enable us to simulate
correctly the observed results comes to. But the capacity to
make predictions is not the only or main criterion, as Bruner
himself would no doubt admit, of a good fit for a model. It is
possible for a model to simulate the resultants of a particular
process, without having the same structure as that process
itself. Usually when one speaks of a good model, for example
of a physical system, one assumes that the model and the system
share a common structure. It is doubtful whether we would
want to describe a model as good if its structure proved to be
radically different from that of the system it was meant to
model, even though it predicted successfully within a certain
range of phenomena.

Bruner goes on to raise the question of whether, on Piaget's
system, all errors (presumably in reasoning) are regressions
to earlier forms of logical operations.[27]

> What of the error whereby there is a mismatch between the
> logical model applied to a problem and the actual structure or
> requirements of that problem? . . . Piaget gives us no account
> of how they come about nor what is the process whereby we
> locate and correct errors involving the imposition of an
> inappropriate logical structure.

Once again, Bruner is observing the child from an adult perspective, putting him in the position of a scientist who tries to
find the solution of a problem by trying out different theories
and discovering that some fit and others do not, in which case
there is a mismatch. However, the child is not in this position
when he fails to solve problems involving theoretical reasoning.
He has not yet developed a system of propositional operations to
enable him to make use of such models. It is therefore pointless
in this context to talk, as Bruner does, of the location and correction of errors involving the imposition of an inappropriate
logical structure. To locate such errors the child would already
need to possess the logical operations whose development it
is Piaget's prime concern to study. Piaget's problem is to see
how children starting from the concrete classificatory stage
become able to solve problems involving theoretical reasoning.

Further, the sort of error Piaget was primarily concerned with
in his earlier work on the logical thought of the child arose
mainly from the child's logic being incompletely formed, as when
he is led to reason incorrectly as a result of being unable to
differentiate between part and whole relations. In this case there
can be no regression to earlier forms of logical operations, as
they have not yet been formed.

THE HARVARD STUDENT SYNDROME: THAT WE ARE ALWAYS
CONSCIOUS OF THE LOGICAL STRUCTURES WE USE

A common reaction to Piaget's work is that which Bruner
reports on when he quotes his research student's remark:
' "What puzzles me is why any good 14-year-old can't get right
up and give Phil 140" (Professor Quine's course in logic).'[28]
One might have expected a little more perspicuity from a Harvard
graduate student. His puzzlement seems self-inflicted. What he
is mistakenly assuming is that the fourteen-year-old has a
Cartesian clear and distinct idea of the logical structures he
uses when he sets about solving problems involving hypothetico-
deductive reasoning. Bruner, however, sees the error of his
student's ways. He agrees with Piaget that our thought activities
can manifest logical structures without our being fully cognizant
of them, although we can become conscious of them at a later
date. As every critic is not as clear as Bruner is on this point,
it would be worth while examining Piaget's position here more
closely. Piaget tells us that 'these structures exist in what the
children I study "do" and not only in the semiformalizations I
make of them'.[29]
Piaget further points out:[30]

> The adolescent is not conscious of the system of propositional
> operations. He undoubtedly uses these operations, but he does
> this without enumerating them, or reflecting on their relation-
> ships, and he only faintly suspects that they form such a
> system. He is unaware of this, in the same way that in singing
> or whistling he is unaware of the laws of harmony.

Similarly, the younger child, when he classifies and orders
objects, does not necessarily grasp on a conscious level the
formal structures implicit in these actions. Piaget quotes the
case of a young child who knew how to order three sticks, each
longer than the other, but who was unable to think this problem
out verbally, since he had not yet grasped the formal concept of
transitivity.
The fact that we are not always conscious of the formal operations we use in such problem-solving is a point Piaget repeatedly returns to, giving examples, among others, from the
development of scientific thought. Thus he notes that mathematicians throughout the ages have reasoned according to the
laws of certain fixed structures without being conscious of them.
The most important of these are the group laws, which are, for
example, implied in Euclid's 'Elements'. It was, he says, only at
the beginning of the nineteenth century that Galois formulated
these laws. Similarly, he goes on, by reflecting on the way he
and his contemporaries reasoned, Aristotle formulated certain
structures: the logic of classes and the syllogism. He was
unaware of a whole group of structures which he himself used;
namely, the logic of relations. This occurred only in the nine-

teenth century, as a result of the work of de Morgan and others.[31] It is clear that Aristotle himself would not have been able to stand up and give Professor Quine's Phil 140 course without first doing some homework.

I know that philosophers trained in the analytic tradition may find it hard to understand how one can use logical structures without having a clear understanding of their meaning, or as Frege puts it, of their sense. It seems to be a dubious argument by analogy to assign to the child the sort of mental experiences philosophers assume they have when they engage in epistemological discussions.

Even psychologists seem prone to this fallacy. Victoria Hazlitt, in 1930 when discussing Piaget's early work, held that children under the age of five could reason formally because they were able to give the correct answer to a problem involving generalization. She gave her subjects four plates on which she put respectively toy models of a dog and a bird, a dog and a pig, a dog and a sheep and a dog and a cow. The child had to discover the object which these four plates had in common. It will be seen, however, that the common object - the dog - occurs four times more frequently than each of the others. The child could give a correct answer by a simple perceptual apprehension, without any conscious ratiocination entering in, and even without having understood the exact meaning of the question asked. In this case, as in others of this type, the experimenter facilitate the task of the subject.[32]

Somewhat similar remarks might be made of attempts to show that children possess the concept of number even as early as three years. For the young child, however, number at first has the character of a perceptual Gestalt in which spatial extension and numerosity are not clearly distinguished. What such experiments seem to do is to constrain the experimental situation so that the child in his perceptual judgments of 'more than', 'equal to' and 'less than' is prevented from confusing the spatial extension of the perceptual Gestalt of, for example, a row of counters with their actual number. A source of ambiguity has thus been removed, at least for some children. But that these children can match rows of counters in certain situations rather than others proves only that they have not yet got the general concept of number, which is invariant in all situations. Care needs to be taken not to read into the subjects' replies the articulated conception of number which the experimenter himself possesses.

CONCLUSION

It seems to me that one of the reasons for Bruner's not adequately understanding Piaget's position is that he has not appreciated that it is based on a theory of social exchange. Piaget's theory has certain similarities to that put forward by Bruner's former

Harvard colleague, the sociologist George Homans. In 'The
Growth of Logical Thinking' Piaget spoke of formal structures
as being 'forms of equilibrium which gradually settle on the
systems of exchanges between individuals and the physical
milieu and on the systems of exchanges between individuals
themselves'.[33] But he adds that these two systems of exchanges
are really aspects of one and the same process. In less esoteric
language, he is pointing out that formal structures, as they
occur in our thought processes, are a function of our relationships to others and the way we adapt ourselves to the world
around us.

His position here is not radically different from that held in
his earlier writings. He told us there that 'conversation and
social intercourse unify the opinions of individuals, namely by
giving due weight to each, and extracting an average opinion
from the lot'.[34] The extraction of a common opinion could be
described as the achievement of a balance (or equilibrium)
between individual opinions. Piaget was there trying to explain
how we come to accept propositions as true not simply in the
Cartesian sense of an ego contemplating isolated propositions,
but through an interchange of ideas with other individuals.

In fairness to Bruner, I should add that near the end of his
review he says: 'Let me make it clear that what is said above is
not in the spirit of criticism of what Piaget has already done, but
rather in the form of a suggestion of what, in my opinion, he
must do before his approach to cognition is complete.'[35] Unfortunately or fortunately, depending on where your sympathies
lie, Piaget does not seem to have heeded Bruner's advice, and
cannot do so now. But on one matter at least I can agree with
Bruner, and that is when he says, 'One final point has to do
with a matter that Piaget's teacher Claparède used to refer to as
prise de conscience, the rendering conscious and manipulable of
assumptions in terms of which one works.'[36] Bruner makes this
point rightly to show the limitations of his student's question
relating to why the average fourteen-year-old cannot give Phil
140.

I think that Claparède's notion of 'prise de conscience' has
also another application in what might be termed 'the hermeneutic
of Piagetian criticism'; namely, the attempt to bring to the light
of day the epistemological presuppositions accepted tacitly by
some Anglo-Saxon critics of Piaget. That such presuppositions
are related to a difference in cultural outlook can easily be seen
from Piaget's remark at one symposium: 'As for Premack, I was
greatly impressed by his beautiful presentation. In contrast to
Toulmin and so many Anglo-Saxon authors, he understands what
I mean by "structures".'[37] You can detect the note of exasper-
ation here.

In view of the enormous literature, critical and uncritical, now
available on Piaget's work, we have in 'the hermeneutics of
Piagetian criticism' a rich vein of gold, which could be reward-
ingly mined by successive generations of PhD students. It could

become a new academic industry, attracting researchers from the other side of the Atlantic and thus helping to augment our depleted dollar reserves.[38]

NOTES

1 Jerome S. Bruner, Inhelder and Piaget's 'The Growth of Logical Thinking': I. A Psychologist's Viewpoint, in 'British Journal of Psychology', November 1959 (hereafter referred to as B).
2 Ibid., p. 365.
3 Ibid.
4 J.M. Tanner and Barbel Inhelder (eds), 'Discussions in Child Development'. London: Tavistock Press, 1960, pp. 82-3.
5 B., p. 365.
6 Ibid., pp. 368-9.
7 Jean Piaget, 'Études sociologiques'. Paris: Droz, 1965, pp. 155-8.
8 Cf. ibid., especially chapter on Essai sur la théorie des valeurs qualitatives en sociologie statique ('syncronique').
9 B., p. 369.
10 Jean Piaget, 'The Origins of Intelligence in Children'. New York: International University Press, 1952.
11 Jean Piaget, 'Six Psychological Studies' University of London Press, 1968, pp. 6-7.
12 J.-P. Sartre, 'Critique de la raison dialectique'. Paris: Gallimard, 1960.
13 Piaget, 'Etudes sociologiques', pp. 39, 48, 76-8.
14 L.S. Stebbing, 'A Modern Introduction to Logic'. London: Methuen, 1946, p. 308.
15 Le Petit Robert 1: 'Dictionnaire de la langue française', 1979.
16 Ibid.
17 B., p. 369.
18 Jean Piaget, 'Biologie et connaissance'. Paris: Gallimard, 1967, p. 30.
19 Ibid.
20 A. Massimo Piatelli-Palmarini (ed.), 'Language and Learning: The Debate between Jean Piaget and Noam Chomsky'. London: Routledge & Kegan Paul 1980, p. 282.
21 B., p. 370.
22 Ibid., p. 369.
23 Ibid., p. 370.
24 Ibid.
25 Ibid., p. 368.
26 Ibid., p. 368.
27 Ibid., p. 368.
28 Ibid., p. 370.
29 Massimo Piatelli-Palmarini, 'Language and Learning', p. 282.
30 Jean Piaget, 'Logic and Psychology'. Manchester University

Press, 1953, pp. 39–40.

31 Jean Piaget, Inconscient affectif et inconscient cognitif, in 'Problèmes de psychologie génétique'. Paris: Denoël/Gonthier, 1972, p. 39.

32 Victoria Hazlitt, Children's Thinking, in 'British Journal of Psychology', 1930, pp. 354–61. Her experiment is discussed by M. Laurendeau and A. Pinard, 'La Pensée causale chez l'enfant'. Paris: Presses Universitaires de France, 1962.

33 Barbel Inhelder and Jean Piaget, 'The Growth of Logical Thinking: From Childhood to Adolescence'. London: Routledge & Kegan Paul, 1958, p. 338.

34 Jean Piaget, 'Judgment and Reasoning in the Child'. NJ: Littlefield Adams, 1964, p. 204.

35 B., p. 370.

36 Ibid.

37 Massimo Piatelli-Palmarini, 'Language and Learning', p. 282.

38 After this paper was written, Dr J.-J. Ducret, Librarian of the Archives Jean Piaget at Geneva, drew my attention to the important role played by Herbert Spencer's philosophy in influencing French philosophical thought in the last quarter of the nineteenth century and the early part of this one, and in the formation of Piaget's thought. Piaget's concept of equilibrium would seem to be directly derived from the evolutionary philosophy of Herbert Spencer. This concept already appears in Piaget's philosophical novel 'Recherche' published in 1918. It is intriguing to learn that the writings of an English metaphysician had such an important influence on the thought of the young Piaget. If I had known this earlier, I would have rewritten parts of this paper to take account of this fact

14 Piaget: possible worlds or real worlds?

Michael Garfield

I am only too well aware that any criticism can be met with the
counterclaim that it is misdirected and mistaken because the
object of one's criticism never intended their work to be understood in the way claimed. The case is no different with Piaget.
Experimental findings which seem to disprove the results that
Piaget came to are not uncommonly said to miss the point of
his ideas or to be incidental to the main direction of his theory,
and philosophers have also seen their criticisms of Piaget
similarly countered.[1]

It is indeed always the case that in attacking an idea one has
failed to notice that the idea is not held or is not a vital con-
stituent of the theory; that in fact one is attacking a straw man.
But, then, that does seem to me to be the ongoing job of scholarship and criticism; not simply to find out what was meant (was
Piaget always clear about every detail of his own ideas?) but, in
a sense, to sharpen up on what can legitimately be said in the
area. If the much vaunted accolade of the good theory – that it
is rich and generates more research of itself – is merited, then
my own criticism of Piaget from a philosophical point of view
should be seen in this light. I am reminded of B. Barry's[2] comment on J. Rawls's book, 'A Theory of Justice', that, while in
the last analysis it may be shown to be mistaken, the diversity
of argument and the richness of the conceptual framework constructed can only lead to a fuller understanding of the problems
involved and an advance towards what is further required. We
are all the richer for a rich theory, and while Piaget may, in
the end, be seen to be fundamentally mistaken, it is in the
spirit of better understanding the process of cognitive development that the reader should locate the focus of my criticisms.

Initially and fundamentally there is a problem concerning the
role of the philosopher seen vis-à-vis the experimental scientist.
And here I am making a point which is not specific to Piaget but
applies generally to all scientific activity. The problem can be
put like this: is the philosopher to be seen as one who can
legislate a priori about the methods, claims, results of the
scientist, or must the philosopher and his ideas be guided, in

the reverse direction, by new discoveries in science? Is knowledge from the world possible, and if so how? As soon as one
puts the question like that, one can see that the sorts of issue
which arise for Piaget in his examination of the sources and
growth of knowledge in the child are reflected in his own activity
as a scientist/philosopher. The problem, of course, of the
source of our knowledge of the world – between rationalism and
empiricism, the problem of ontology, between the realist and
the idealist – is not a new one; it is as old as philosophy itself.
What I think makes it particularly important today is that the
very value and status of scientific activity is itself at stake. The
traditional view of science as the means whereby discoveries are
made about the world, whereby science is seen as broadly progressing towards true understanding via the neutral activity of
observation and testing, is seen by certain sections of the
philosophical community as radically misconceived. Science does
not scan a neutral eye over neutral data; rather, on the view
under consideration science through its theories determines the
data. From Kuhn to Feyerabend,[3] the view of the world of
scientific facts, as descriptions of reality discovered by man, is
translated, on the contrary, into terms of construction by man;
and the sort of construction intended is not that man has had to
spend many hours of his time experimenting, hypothesizing and
testing results before the laws could become known, but rather
that the constructing is a kind of making up, almost, if not
entirely, a matter of invention. This is one reason why one
always has to look with some care at claims such as Piaget's that
the child constructs his knowledge, since the danger is ever
present that construction implies something arbitrary and
invented. The point is made by I. Scheffler:[4]

> That the ideal of objectivity has been fundamental to science
> is beyond question. The philosopher's task is to assess and
> interpret this ideal; to ask how, if at all, this objectivity is
> possible. The task is especially urgent now, when received
> opinions as to the sources of objectivity in science are
> increasingly under attack. The notion of a fixed observational
> given, of a constant descriptive language, of a shared
> methodology of investigation, of a rational community advanc-
> ing its knowledge of the real world – all have been subjected
> to severe and mounting criticism from a variety of directions.
> The overall tendency of such criticism has been to call into
> question the very conception of scientific thought as a res-
> ponsible enterprise of reasonable men. The extreme alternative
> that threatens is the view that theory is not controlled by
> data, but that data are manufactured by theory; that rival
> hypotheses cannot be rationally evaluated, there being no
> neutral court of observational appeal, nor any shared stock
> of meanings; that scientific change is not a product of
> evidential appraisal and logical judgement but of intuition,
> persuasion and conversion; that reality does not constrain the

thought of the scientist but is rather itself a projection of
that thought.

In the same vein certain interpretations of the writings of the
later Wittgenstein, and the very explicit statements in his work
'On Certainty',[5] which develop the notion of truth as the social
product of our interpersonal agreements and forms of life, have
been extended by some in the direction of the relativization of
all knowledge. On this view of interpersonal agreements what is
important to note is that questions of truth are answered by
looking at the fundamental agreements in a form of life; things
are true because they are the fundamentals of what people agree
about, not the converse - that people agree interpersonally
because certain things are independently true. Truth is a
product, not a cause, of our agreeing. Such a view, untempered,
leads directly to a relativization of knowledge and truth; all
seeing involves knowledge; all perception is epistemic. And so
on this view science cannot escape from its epistemic net and
be neutral.

While Piaget finds the child - world - knowledge relationship
problematic, he does not appear to find his own methodology so.
If, as we are led to believe, Piaget undertook his psychological
research in the hope of solving epistemological problems, then
he seems to see science and the scientific method as some firm
anchor point from which to set off. But then his methodology, in
a sense, begs the question, since it assumes that which is in
part at least at issue and which it is trying to explain. The clear
danger is that, by treating his experiments with and observations of children as providing archimedean neutral points,
Piaget is failing to recognize the fact that his own observations
are not neutral but radically theory-laden. It is as if to accept
a naive realism which is taken as an a priori of his work. It
should be repeated that this is not specific to Piaget; if true it
would undermine the whole of science as a valid enterprise as
distinct from a game engaged in by consenting adults in private.
The world is the way our conceptual structure maps it, and the
idea that by examining the world we find out something about
it is mistaken; all we find out about is the map which we have
imposed upon it, in this instance a particular map of cognitive
development.

Piaget was obviously concerned with the traditional philosophical questions and cannot have been unaware of the problems
I have raised above, even if he did not have them before him
in quite that form. However, he did strongly uphold the view
that experimental science could assist the answer to those
philosophical questions. Indeed, he disparages the armchair
philosophers who a priori determine the bounds and limits of
the scientific enterprise and who lack any scientific training
themselves. But many philosophers would, as I have suggested,
claim a primary place for the philosopher, if only on the ground
that the world cannot be understood simply on a scientific base

with its implication of positivism and naive realism.[6] Piaget, when
looking for answers to his epistemological problems, refers us
back to his psychology and biology. His is indeed an enterprise
in experimental epistemology and philosophy. But such an appeal
is acceptable only if one has a justified view already of the
relationship between the philosophical issues and science which
does not beg the question by simply assuming that one half of the
problem is unproblematic and can itself provide an answer to
the question. This begging of the question becomes more acute
when one looks at what is at stake in terms of the dangers of
lapsing into idealist positions. How can Piaget be sure that all
his reliance on science is not a product simply of his own mind,
his own ideas? Piaget seems to have been happy with his own
response to that charge, which was that knowledge had a biological base. But then the circularity of justification becomes
apparent. Is that the force of the 'circle of the sciences'? If
one wants to talk about knowledge and objectivity, does one
not need to break out of such a circle? The answer to this can
only be a forceful yes.

The trouble is, of course, that Piaget's own view of the world
and the activity of the experimental scientist reflects also the
relationship as he sees it between the child and the world. I
should point out that my own sympathies are with the realist
side of Piaget here. In the end the relativism of science and
knowledge is perhaps incoherent; how could one come to know
anything about the world, even as a relativist, unless there
were certain fixed points for us to locate initially? Furthermore, the more extreme the version of relativism becomes, the
more one lapses into the possibility of idealism, in its more
recent forms of a conceptual and linguistic kind, and Piaget
would have been very much against that. But the warnings of
those who have sought to show that science itself is problematic
should act as a caveat when we see Piaget using a number of
biological analogies and referring us back to the biological
bases of knowledge. In defence of Piaget and scientific realism,
I believe one should be wary of moving from the position of
accepting in some sense the necessary theory-laden epistemic
nature of our observations to the view that the world is simply
the conventional way that we see it. Critiques of Piaget from
those on the political left, who would wish to expose the ideological nature of science itself by attacking the realist assumptions of science or who argue against Piaget in particular that
he fails to see the essential social determination of our concepts,
seem to me to fail to recognize that with such a wholesale
critique their own position could be radically undermined.[7] I am
reminded of a colleague who attended a conference recently on
social psychology and, when he asked of a particular theory
whether it had been shown to work or not, was greeted with
looks of disbelief that anyone could possibly ask such a positivistic question.

I have said already that the problem of science is not

essentially different from the task which Piaget sets himself in his examination of cognitive development. The question for both is how we construct our knowledge and where it comes from, and the accompanying questions of the nature of the objectivity and necessity involved. There have been two traditions in the history of philosophy which seek to offer answers to such questions and explain the source of our knowledge: empiricism and rationalism. Empiricism is the theory which says that knowledge comes from outside of ourselves through experience. The world outside of us is seen, on this view, as giving us bundles of more or less constructed reality; the mind is seen as an unexposed photographic plate, or as Locke put it a 'tabula rasa', on which experiences imprint themselves over time and exposure through the senses to the world outside it. Despite its prima facie simplicity and common-sense appeal, it was its inability to offer a full theory of how we come to know which led to the rejection of it. How could the relationship be so simple? Surely one needed some sort of prior capacity in the mind to make sense of experience at all, whether this be innate knowledge or some sort of mechanism. Additionally, the idea of necessity on the empiricist theory becomes at best little more than slightly more regular regularities. The answer of rationalism, therefore, was to start from the other end and require that there be structures independent of experience which account for the self-evidence of certain truths, e.g., logical ones, or provide the necessary framework to our experience to make them meaningful. The trouble with empiricism had been the naive realism that lay behind it. The trouble with rationalism is either that it has no need of a world at all, and so is but a short step to a fully fledged idealism, or, if it retains a claim as significant to the world, that the question of why our innate ideas conform to reality at all requires an independent conception of experience against which to check them.

The initial plausibility of each position ended up usurping territory which by a relentless logic it was forced to but never wished to adopt. Thus, at one end there is the reasonable-sounding claim that there is a world from which it is possible to derive knowledge about it. Indeed, the sense in which that claim is important is what one wants to hold on to, come what may, when one looks at the other end of the argument, in which the equally reasonable claim is made that before one can have experiences at all one needs some prior system with which to categorize or make sense of one's experience. What one needs to keep is the view of 'reality' making a difference to our knowledge, at the core of the reasonable empiricist claim, while avoiding the naive realism that often accompanies such a view, in such a way that one does not end up with the other extreme view that all experience is impossible without knowledge which carries with it the drift to idealism.

Essentially, what one wants, if both extremes are to be avoided, is a theory in which one can account for knowledge by some sort of interaction between the subject and the world in such a way that neither the innatism/a priorism of the subject nor the given experience of the world swamps the account. It certainly seems to me that it was in this spirit that Piaget was working, as is shown by his criticism of those who advocate structure without genesis (rationalism), or those who advocate genesis without structure (empiricism). What Piaget, on this view, is setting himself to do is to ask how the child, given a minimalist view of natural abilities of the child, is able to interact with the world and come to know certain things. The way I put that here is not meant to prejudge the issue of whether the child should properly be regarded as separate from the world, and so having the problem of coming to know it, or as part and parcel with the world, and so having the converse problem of having to separate itself out from its initial world.

Clearly, the attempt is Kantian in spirit in trying to provide a way between, or an analgam of, rationalism and empiricism, though clearly there is a more specific link to Hegel in the way that knowledge proceeds and develops dialectically. The important question here of course is about the status of the knowledge that the child comes to in the end; if it is objective and necessary, what makes it so? Piaget wanted to retain a sense of the logically necessary which had the force that all the a priorists had intended, and at the same time he was aware that empiricism was deficient in this respect and could not give a plausible account. But what about the sort of necessity governing the sequence of the stages? One important question about Piaget's exercise is whether, while thinking that he has told us something important about the child's coming to understand reality, all he has done is to have informed us about certain logical categories or formal concepts which he has mapped on to the world of the child. Piaget sees the stages and development of knowledge as noncontingent, as necessary in some sense, as natural, if you like, since they are invariant. Is this a reflection of truths in the world, a truth about logic, or are we witnessing a manifestation of truth about human development or simply a projection of some arbitrary theory on to otherwise determinable data? The sorts of answer that arise indicate that for Piaget the relationship is between the child, its active relationship with objects in the world backed up by social beings, parents and others. But then one wants to know where and what sort of necessity it is that comes in that makes development proceed in certain directions; is it because of the nature of the objects in the world, because of a priori principles of action and communication, or what?

There are occasions when one imagines that the biological terms 'assimilation', 'accommodation' and 'equilibration', along with the idea of initial dissonance, account substantially for such a developmental story. But my feeling is that, while useful in a biological model, these terms fail in acting in an explanatory way in anything more than a formal sense, and in the sense of telling us anything about the process of development. I am not

sure that at bottom they are explanatory at all. In the first
place, it is clear that the concepts of dissonance, assimilation,
accommodation and equilibration form a group of terms which
seek to explain why and how development proceeds. It is of
course true that for any change to take place initially there has
to be some felt need for the requirement of change; and, following the logic of the idea of learning, if what was there before
is different from the cognitive structure afterwards, then we
need concepts like assimilation and accommodation to describe
the features of such a change; and finally, if one has anything
like stable knowledge for a time, then one needs some sort of
idea like equilibration to explain why the process, if only
temporarily, comes to a halt. But since these are purely formal
concepts, they help us not at all in terms of substantive
content; why the child finds dissonance initially, a radically
crucial question for any developmental theory, why the child
has to assimilate and accommodate in particular ways, and finally,
why the end of that process finds equilibrium in terms of some
cognitive satisfaction with a particular structure. Is this because
the mind finds certain states inherently dissonant or dis-
equilibrious, or because of certain psychological mechanisms
in terms of emotional feel, or what? Is there a sixth sense of
human beings which senses when things are cognitively adrift
or misfitting? Why does the child not simply remain where she is?
Or do we have here a concealed appeal to the self-evidence of
the world to the child in that dissonance is started off by the
child's constantly recognizing the inadequacy of the equilibrated
schema? But if that is the case, then the construction of the
world that Piaget is thinking of by the child is more akin to
discovery of what is out there through activity than a genuine
construction, the view of the child as experimental scientist
chipping away at reality. The other horn of the dilemma, of
course, is that, if it is construction in a stronger sense, then
one is immediately required to show how the constructivist
approach avoids idealism. I have already indicated that in
Piaget's case the appeal to biology is not to answer or refute
that question but to beg it.

The second point I was raising in this context concerned
rather the explanatory import of terms like 'equilibration'; are
they really explanatory, or do they serve rather like logical
names for processes which are otherwise defined or known to
exist? For example, it is clear, given our conceptions of coming
to know and learning, that there are as a matter of fact states
of affairs where children do not know X and where at a subsequent date they do know X. We call this process, generally,
learning X. We therefore have a way of independently understanding such situations as 'learning' paradigms, that that is
what we mean by learning. Assimilation, etc., seek to explain
that movement from not knowing to a state of knowing; but it is
clear that they do no more than give a name to what we know
happens (and call 'learning') but cannot explain. My suggestion,

therefore, is that these terms parade as explanations when in fact they are simply descriptions in disguise. Like the child who, marvelling at the ability of pigeons to find their way home from great distances, asked his teacher how they could do it and was told that they find their way home because they have a homing instinct. Both teacher and child seemed to find the explanation satisfactory. But, of course, what one wants to know is something which approaches more the form of a genuine explanation and can be understood in such terms. In the final analysis even science has problems over such explanations / descriptions, and in the end explanations must come to an end simply in a description of what is. Otherwise explanations would never be complete. That objects fall because of gravity and that gravity just is a description of the general law governing the fall of objects does not worry us as a basic unexplained datum of the world. But there is a strong unsatisfactoriness with the level of explanation at which Piaget pulls in terms like 'assimilation' when they seem to be no more than names. One reason for this emptiness lies, I believe, in the fact that the terms have been taken out of their biological context, where they could be given substantive meaning and used in an area where radically different considerations apply.[8] There has been a different but related concern felt by some concerning the nature of the sequences of the stages which have been felt to be little more than tautologies or even redundant.[9] Hamlyn, for example, has suggested that the stages simply reflect the general necessity of seeing progression from the particular to the general – something we do not need experimental evidence for.

In my argument above on the emptiness of terms like 'equilibration' I have laid some stress both on the importance and possibility of substantive explanation. Indeed, such explanations seem to be part of our intellectuality and curiosity. We feel dissatisfied with explanations which do not really explain, we search for proper explanations, we accept that events require explanations, and so on. Explanations are part and parcel of our very thinking and acting. Wittgenstein warned us against two sorts of search for explanations. For example, on the nature of necessity and certainty there can in the end, so Wittgenstein seems to be saying, be only description. Why must certain things be so? Because that is the way things are in certain forms of life. Ultimately there is no explanation, only a description of what is taken as necessary by people. Second, Wittgenstein also warns against formula-type explanations in trying to explain how someone knows how to write, speak, tell jokes, etc. To look for some sort of mental formula would be for Wittgenstein a mistake.

In the end of course, as I argued above, all explanation must come down to description otherwise one is involved in an infinite regress. What science or explanation generally tries to do is to minimize the base 'unexplained' descriptions on which explan-

ations are based. My point in connection with Piaget was very
much that substantive explanation could go further before it
came to a 'it just is so' stop. Norman Malcolm takes up
Wittgenstein's argument to attack, as myth, any idea of employing processes, structures, schemas to explain our knowing. At
one level the claim quite plausibly reminds us that, when we
recognize a face or say we know 2 + 2 = 4, we are not engaged
in any process. (In some cases we might be, however - for
example, when we cannot remember where we have left the
cheque book and we actually go through a process of mentally
retracing our steps.) Normally we simply recognize, know and
remember. The redundancy of further explanation is pushed
home by Malcolm when he says that, since, in the end all
explanation must cease with a straight description, unexplained,
of what happens, why not accept that knowing, remembering
and so on simply happen and require no deeper explanation?
I am not sure whether psychology would continue to exist under
Malcolm; but in defence of Piaget and all psychologists who wish
to explain, there does seem to me to be an offence against
reason if, of two people with different cognitive abilities, say
a child and an adult, we simply say there is no deeper explanation of the difference than that is the way it is, and we do
not need to look any further than that the one can and the other
cannot perform cognitively in certain ways. In this sense, at
least, reason demands reasons why one is different from the
other; and that surely is what explanations are. A more general
point remains, however: why we should accept one level of
explanation/description as more satisfactory or more true than
another? The point is not academic and is crucial when one
turns it into the stronger question of how we know that the
description we offer of the child's activity is even accurate as
a description. In terms both of reference and meaning, what is
clear is that one must be able to decide on the transparency
or opacity of a particular description by the observer of the
child's activity and the way the child 'describes' his actions
before we can even start talking of explanation. One here enters
very central problems of meaning and translation which I cannot further enter into except to repeat that they are central to
Piagetian psychology and the Piagetian experimentalist.

But to return to my discussion of the nature of the development of knowledge and the nature of the necessity and objectivity
involved, the drift of my remarks has been enough to show my
difficulty in getting a clear understanding of what Piaget is
claiming here. There is undeniably a strong feel to his work
which suggests a straight empiricism, as the nature of the world
puts limits to and determines the objectivity and direction in
which cognitive development moves. The child's activity on
this view is seen as necessary to coming to grips with that
reality - in much the same way as scientists have to work in
their laboratories to discover the 'facts' of nature. On the other
hand, the notion of activity is often seen in a more internal

relation to the subsequent knowledge in such a way that the
knowledge is reducible to the sorts of activities engaged in and
so is a real construct of them.

The whole question of reductionism is fraught with difficulty,
and one needs to distinguish between positions which lead to
reductionism and those which more innocently point to conditions
of genesis or causal circumstances, though quite what the
distinction amounts to here is partly what is at issue. I suppose,
a priori, I can say that there must be an explanation of certain
states of affairs arising which is distinct from the state of affairs
itself. Thus I can address myself to the Cartesian question,
'do I know that I exist?' and be aware that I am aware of myself
– I am self-conscious. Now, there is a sense in which there must
be an explanation of how such self-consciousness is possible,
whether through neurology or God or something else. The sort
of explanation, however, would not reduce my 'being self-
consciously aware' any more than showing how pains or colours
become the object of my awareness changes what pains or colours
mean to me. In this sense, of course, one cannot be other than
sympathetic with Piaget's explanatory efforts. Showing how
something comes about on this view is to point to a 'mechanism',
a way of seeing coherently how X arises from Y; it does not
invalidate X (say, my idea of self-consciousness) to know that
this is caused by some physiochemical system in the brain.

It is, however, precisely where such explanations do invalidate
or change the meaning of what is so explained that reductionism
takes bite as a complaint. So the fact that belief in God is
explained by some as being the result of having a weak father
figure changes the meaning of believing in God by rendering it
invalid. Certainly, semantically, 'I believe in God' stays the
same in meaning, but if meaning in that sense were all that were
at issue there would be no problem. The question of reductionism is no longer the clear philosophical crime it used to be.
Even if meaning remains the same, the history of a concept may
make us reject it because its history has invalidated or made it
insignificant for us, and in a sense that is to change its meaning
for us.

So with Piaget one can say one of two things in response to his
claim that 'genetic epistemology attempts to explain knowledge
and in particular scientific knowledge on the basis of its history,
its sociogenesis and especially the psychological origins of the .
notions and operations on which it is based'.[10] One can say that
such explanations are not reductionist in that they do not change
the meaning of 'logical necessity' for example; they simply show
'how necessity which a priorist theories have always thought
necessary to point out at the outset . . . instead of being the
prior condition for learning, is its outcome'.[11] Whether such
explanations really do explain how there comes about what we
mean by logical necessity is a matter for further examination.
The truly reductionist way to look at what Piaget is doing (and
it should be remembered that he did not see himself as offering

reductionist explanations) is to say that he is reducing the
meaning of logical necessity to its historical or psychological
use. This does present difficulties, since proof of logical or
mathematical kind is seen normally as atemporal, ahistorical,
acontextual, and indeed that is what one means almost by the
sort of necessity involved.

But even if we suppose that full reductionism is Piaget's
position, it is no use crying 'sin of reductionism' and hoping
that that will do the trick, nor is it fruitful to fill out the sin
and say that epistemological terms cannot be translated into
psychological terms since that is to beg the issue, sympathetic
as I am to the spirit of the attack on reductionism.[12] Much
modern European philosophy criticizes Anglo-American philosophy
precisely because it is not concerned with the origin of its ideas,
and instead treats those ideas as autonomous, eternal verities.
And there is too much at stake here for anyone to say simply
that Piaget has made some category mistake when the issue is
whether at all, or in what sense, the category of the epistemological is rightly seen as autonomous and distinct from the
psychological or historical or political.[13] All one can really say
is that these are important questions which Piaget does not appear
to have systematically thought out in the sense of showing how
he has avoided the traditional problems associated with them.
And until one knows what is meant, one cannot know how to
treat notions like 'necessity' and 'objectivity' in Piaget.

The discussion of reductionism arose out of the sense in which
the child's activity could be seen as constructing knowledge. I
had further suggested a strong and a weak sense of construction
of roughly working away to discover truths or a more internal
relation of construction to the activity. The difficulty with
Piaget's account is that it is not clear how one can square these
two positions in such a way that one preserves a third way
between the rationalist and empiricist approaches. By talking of
structures Piaget is saved from crude empiricism, and the fact
that his theory is genetic shows that it is seen as developing
through some interaction with the environment, but we are no
clearer about the nature of what is involved. There are times
when Piaget is almost purely rationalist, while at others he
seems to be adopting the position that the ways of organizing
that knowledge gives us are but bundles of coherent possibilities.
This is where the danger of talking of the construction of
knowledge is most in danger of lapsing into idealism.

Indeed, it can reasonably be said that, far from giving us a
third way between a priorism and empiricism, Piaget simply
oscillates between the two in the attempt to avoid idealism. There
are occasions when Piaget seems to see the child, as I suggested
above, chipping away at the world in good empiricist fashion,
constrained by a recognizable reality beyond itself. But then
when talking of the child constructing knowledge one can almost
feel Piaget pull back from the idealist pit and invoke an a priori
necessity.

It has been suggested that in order to guarantee the possibility of objectivity one needs to import, where Piaget does not, the necessary social and interpersonal nature of knowledge and truth. Piaget's emphasis on the child and the child's developing structures through his activity with the world seem to make knowledge a very individualist activity – the biological model comes through strongly here. But, it is argued, the concepts of truth and knowledge are necessarily located between people giving and accepting correction, adopting criteria not given in perception; and the best that Piaget could give us is some sort of accidentalist version of why we do or do not agree with others in our world over truth. The coming to know that certain things are true or the object of our knowledge necessarily involves the child's growing up in a community of people who do know and who can direct knowledge. But it is here that Piaget again seems to want to suggest the relative unimportance of the social in the development of cognition; almost as if cognition were some self-regulating autonomous development requiring only an actor and something to be acted upon. If this model is behind development, then the interpersonal nature of knowledge goes. And in a strong sense, if we are to preserve knowledge and truth we need a way of showing how children come to recognize things as true, as false, as mistaken, etc., and it is not clear that Piaget's account does this.

The danger with taking Piaget as ignoring the social is that we are left simply with the person and the world, which leaves us in turn with the traditional problem that there is no way of knowing that what we are witnessing in the development of cognition has anything to do with knowledge and truth; it may simply be the working out of a particular structuring, coherent as it may well be. Following on from this is the consequent danger of idealism: that the world we construct is not a real world at all. As D.W. Hamlyn puts it succinctly, 'The idea of genesis with structure does not explain why it is that what develops in this way without being subject simply to the vagaries of experience is in fact knowledge.'[14]

One way of looking at the child's progression through his developing cognition is as a traveller through a series of possible worlds, possible ways of seeing the world. Here there is no conception of objectivity, of there being a proper, correct or right way of seeing things or of an incorrect way requiring modification; it is rather just that that is the way he or she does go. But possible worlds are not necessarily real worlds, possible states of affairs are not necessarily true states of affairs, and one wants to know the sorts of differences that Piaget would have in mind in distinguishing between them.

NOTES

1 See for example D.W. Hamlyn's criticism of Piaget that the necessary social dimension of knowledge is lacking in Piaget's account, and W. Mays's counter that this is to have misunderstood Piaget: D.W. Hamlyn, 'Experience and the Growth of Understanding', London, Routledge & Kegan Paul, 1978; W. Mays, in N. Bolton (ed.), 'Philosophical Problems in Psychology', London, Methuen, 1979.

2 B. Barry, 'Liberal Theory of Justice', Oxford, Clarendon Press, 1973.

3 T.S. Kuhn, 'The Structure of Scientific Revolutions', Chicago University Press, 1970; P.K. Feyerabend, 'Against Method', London, New Left Books, 1975.

4 I. Scheffler, 'Science and Objectivity', Indianapolis, Bobbs-Merrill, 1967; See also recent defences by R. Trigg, 'Reason and Commitment', London, Cambridge University Press, 1973; R. Trigg, 'Reality at Risk', Brighton, Harvester, 1980: R. Bhaskar, 'A Realist Theory of Science', Brighton, Harvester, 1978.

5 L. Wittgenstein, 'On Certainty', Oxford, Basil Blackwell, 1974.

6 P. Winch, 'The Idea of Social Science', London, Routledge & Kegan Paul, 1959.

7 As an example of a radical critique of Piaget, see V. Walkerdine and C. Venn, 'Ideology and Consciousness', vol. I, Oxford, I and C publications.

8 T. Mischel, in T. Mischel (ed.), 'Cognitive Development and Epistemology', London, Academic Press, 1971.

9 D.W. Hamlyn, in Mischel, 'Cognitive Development'. See also N. Malcolm, in the same volume.

10 J. Piaget, 'Genetic Epistemology', New York, Columbia University Press, 1970.

11 J. Piaget, 'Structuralism', London, Routledge & Kegan Paul, 1971.

12 Hamlyn, in Mischel, 'Cognitive Development'.

13 A. Montefiore, Catching the Continental Drift, 'The Times Higher Education Supplement', 13 February 1981. See also W. Quine, Two Dogmas of Empiricism, 'Philosophical Review', 1951.

14 Hamlyn, 'Experience and the Growth of Understanding'. See also the discussion between D.E. Cooper, R.K. Elliott and D.W. Hamlyn in 'Journal of Philosophy of Education', 14 (1), 1980.

Part 9

Social psychology

15 Social cognition: the case for Piaget

George Butterworth

INTRODUCTION

In its most general sense, social cognition can be defined as 'knowledge of others'. The study of its development not only involves cataloguing the social content of children's minds, but also it encompasses a variety of theories on the acquisition of social understanding. Thus, social cognition is concerned both with the content and the mechanisms of knowledge. In this paper, the aim is to defend Piaget against the criticisms that he was unconcerned with the social content of experience and that his 'individualistic' approach ignores the contribution of social factors to cognitive development. It will be argued that such criticisms simply dichotomize explanatory principles that are actually inter-related. The issues I shall be mainly concerned with are distinctions between physical and social objects and the dichotomy between individual and social approaches to the development of knowledge. However, I have no wish to defend his theory in all respects, and I shall eventually give examples of where I consider his totally constructivist approach to the development of knowledge to be wrong. This I believe to have led to a profound misconception of the nature and functions of egocentrism and of the role of sensory perception in the acquisition of knowledge.

Thus, I am for the theory in the sense that I support the general, dialectical approach and in the sense that I consider it amenable to empirical test and to be falsifiable. I also believe that it will be from an epigenetic framework that a viable account of the development of social cognition will eventually emerge and that this will be Piaget's real contribution.

Before addressing the criticisms in detail, it may be as well to attempt a more precise definition. Barker and Newson (1980) define social cognition as: 'how children of different ages construct a relation between themselves and the social objects of knowledge'.

Their definition presupposes a dialectical theory of cognitive growth, i.e., that knowledge of others necessarily requires parallel forms of self-knowledge, and it also shares Piaget's insistence on construction. Given such a definition, there seems no reason why a Piagetian approach should not be applied to any of the myriad problems of social development, except perhaps for lack of time. Yet much of the recent literature on social cognition not only fails to apply Piagetian theory but seems to be motivated by a thorough disenchantment with it (e.g., Kuhn, 1978; Damon, 1979; Chandler, 1977). What could have given rise to this state of affairs, and is it reasonable?

PIAGET ON THE SOCIAL CONTENT OF CHILDREN'S MINDS

The complaint that Piaget ignores the social context of experience is exemplified in a variety of ways. For instance, Kuhn (1978), on the basis of a study of the literature of the later 1970s, asks whether cognitive and social development actually comprise one psychology or two. She contrasts Piaget's organismic approach, with its emphasis on 'hidden' cognitive structures, with the prevalent social learning, or 'mechanistic' approach, where the emphasis is on observable events in the social environment. She complains that Piagetian theory tends to ignore the structure of the social environment while social learning theory tends to be bereft of any mention of cognitive structures brought by the child to the social situation. However, as she shows later in the same paper, there is no reason why Piaget's theory cannot be applied to issues that have concerned social learning theorists. Here the fundamental difficulty lies in reconciling the Piagetian and the behaviourist approaches to the same problem; one is simply confronted with a paradigm clash between an epigenetic structuralist theory and the environmentalist, empiricist approach of behaviourist learning theory.

A second aspect of the accusation that Piaget ignores the social dimension of experience can be discerned in the way in which his theory is sometimes presented as if he considers the child a social isolate, whose solitary interaction with the physical universe is both necessary and sufficient for the acquisition of knowledge. Damon (1979) pinpoints this criticism in one of Piaget's own anecdotes, the one about the child's discovery of number conservation. A child, in solitary play on a beach, discovers the invariance of number by arranging and rearranging a group of pebbles at his feet. Damon points out that the anecdote illustrates the criticism that Piagetian children not only apparently learn in social isolation, but also that they are more engaged in the acquisition of logico-mathematical knowledge than of social knowledge. From this characterization alternatives to Piaget become dichotomized into logical versus social reasoning, learning versus teaching, the individual versus the collective, and physical versus social knowledge. But are these dichotomies an appropriate basis for an evaluation of his theory concerning the child's knowledge of other minds?

If we consider the criticism at its most mundane level, namely that Piaget ignores the social content of experience, even his opponents must concede that no one can be expected to study everything. So, if it is the case that he devoted relatively more effort to so called 'cold-blooded' than to social cognition, this would simply be a matter of choice, and may reflect his purpose in tracing the origins of knowledge to its biological roots. But even at this level, Piaget clearly was concerned with the social content of experience, as many of his writings and those of the Genevan school attest. For example, his work on the emergence of symbolism (1951), his theory of the acquisition of concrete operations in the course of peer interaction (1932), his writings on sociology (1966) and the application of Piagetian theory to cross-cultural studies (Berry and Dasen, 1971) all speak to a concern with social factors. So the charge that Piaget is 'acultural and ahistorical' cannot be made to stick at the level of content; but perhaps the criticism is appropriate at the level of the mechanisms of cognitive development? This is a question to which we shall return when we consider Piaget's 'individualism' in relation to Vygotsky's collectivism in a later section.

THE DICHOTOMY BETWEEN PHYSICAL AND SOCIAL OBJECTS OF KNOWLEDGE

Among the various criticisms that have been made of Piaget, one technique is to dichotomize the cognitive processes necessary for knowledge of physical and social objects. Here the basic assumption is that different cognitive processes are required to know people and things; an extension of the assumption that there is a natural opposition between mind and matter. Of course, Piaget's reply would be that the logico-mathematical structures he describes are perfectly general and consequently are applicable both to the physical and social objects of experience. Indeed, in some cases the child's knowledge of social objects may be in advance of his or her knowledge of physical objects (a horizontal 'décalage'), but this is not because radically different cognitive processes are involved, but simply because the social object may afford greater opportunity for learning. One example is the décalage between person permanence and object permanence in infant development described by Piaget (1954). Another example of the application of Piagetian theory to social cognition is given by Youniss (1978), who interprets the child's comprehension of social relations in terms of a developing operativity. So it is certainly not the case that Piaget's theory is limited to the acquisition of physical concepts. Rather, in the dialectical account offered by him, the child's developing conception of the physical universe is paralleled by changes in concepts of self and of social objects.

A quite different solution to this problem of the distinction between the physical and the social is to assert that the necessary cognitive processes do not differ because all cognition is intrinsically social. Damon (1979) has argued that concept formation never occurs in total isolation from all social influences; therefore he maintains that all knowledge must in some sense be 'co-authored'. This seems to be a social determinist approach to the acquisition of knowledge, in which physical objects comprise a subsidiary distinction within a social world. Social objects are characterized by mutual intentionality; physical objects are those which lack this property - where intentionality is, so to speak, distinctly one-sided. So, on this view of the development of social cognition, the capacity to perceive objects as social depends upon knowing their actions to be intentional.

Again, criticisms based upon this distinction are weak, not least because Piaget himself described the development of intentionality in infancy around eight or nine months, with the co-ordination of secondary circular reactions, and it is perfectly possible to erect a Piagetian account distinguishing physical and social objects based on intentionality as the criterion (see, e.g., Frye, 1980). The main disadvantages of such an approach, however, concern the definition of intentionality itself (see, e.g., Bower, Broughton and Moore, 1970, or Bruner and Lyons, 1968, for quite a different account of the emergence of intentional action). If the definition of the social depends upon the definition of intention, the danger is that the confusion manifest in dichotomizing physical and social objects will simply be transferred to defining intentionality.

As Broughton (1978) has clearly stated, the physical and the social are not mutually opposed realities, but aspects of experience that interpenetrate. Piaget was correct not to render them mutually exclusive; on the other hand, they are not totally mutually inclusive and the question that becomes critical to any theory of social cognition is, what is the basis for separately categorizing people and things, as well as all the intermediate categories of animate objects, whose actions may or may not be social? Instead of the criterion of mutual intentionality, it may be useful to consider reciprocity to be the defining criterion of social objects. Reciprocity is dependent upon some degree of awareness of mutual relationship, and from this point of view, certain relations among humans may be considered intrinsically social, even though the young infant, for example, may lack the self-conscious knowledge or the concepts to define these relations as such.

Mutual intentionality, defined in Piagetian fashion, may therefore rest upon an earlier form of mutuality, which authors such as Trevarthen (1981) consider to be 'built in' to the behavioural repertoire of the infant as basic human motives. However, this criterion for distinguishing the merely physical from the social (and physical) requires the child to stand in conscious relation to something perceived as 'not self', while at the same time recognizing the similarity between 'self' and 'not self'. If the recognition of like by like distinguishes what is personal from what is sub-personal, it may prove difficult for Piaget's unrevised theory to accommodate these requirements. So, the second issue to which I should like to return among Piaget's basic assumptions about social cognitive development is the question of solipsism.

In summary, Piaget cannot be effectively criticized merely by pitting knowledge of the social world against knowledge of the physical. However, it may be legitimate to reconsider Piaget's theory in the light of evidence about the nature of interpersonal relations that may exist prior to the development of intention as Piaget defines it, to establish whether there may exist a form of mutuality or reciprocity that is independent of the capacity for reflection upon the physical and the social world but that may contribute to its development.

THE DICHOTOMY BETWEEN THE INDIVIDUAL AND THE SOCIAL

Perhaps the most basic dichotomy revealed in criticisms of Piaget's theory is that between individual and social approaches to knowing. Here the danger is that biological, psychological and sociological levels of explanation are being set in opposition, although certain theorists, notably Vygotsky (1962, 1966), are pursuing not so much a theory of social knowledge as a social theory of knowledge. What is interesting here is that one has to follow through various contrasts for a very long way before one comes to the heart of the matter, and even then, the disagreements can be resolved only with respect to evidence concerning starting assumptions.

Perhaps the best known example is the debate between Piaget and Vygotsky on the nature of egocentrism, Vygotsky is widely believed to have argued that cognitive growth is socially determined, that it proceeds from the social to the individual level. What he actually said was that, in the child's acquisition of higher mental functions, defined as those mental processes that depend upon speech and language, every function appears twice: first on the social level and then on the individual level, first between people and later as internal to the child's cognitive system (Vygotsky, 1966). So, the first thing to be noted is that Vygotsky was not offering a social determinist account of intellectual development in general; rather, he gave a special status to language among other intellectual processes, which of course Piaget did not share (although some researchers in the Genevan tradition are now beginning to reappraise the role of language in cognitive development: Karmiloff-Smith, 1979).

Vygotsky also disagreed with Piaget over the child's acquisition of scientific concepts. He argued that scientific concepts are part of the cultural heritage, the learning of which is rather like acquiring a foreign language. The child will learn through instruction, reading and a laborious effort to share, at least in part, in the fruits of scientific knowledge. The cultural heritage connects with the child's intellectual development through struc-

tures that are common to science and to the child's spontaneous
concepts, acquired in everyday social interaction. These
'content-filled' spontaneous concepts gradually become more
abstract until they eventually form the anchoring point for
social transmission of culturally stored knowledge. Piaget's
(1962) reply was that he never denied that young children
possess social concepts (or for that matter that they have a
figurative content to any of their stored experiences), but that
the child is not aware of the relations or operations implicit in
knowing, for example, that he has a brother. The transition
from preoperational reasoning to concrete operations involves
becoming aware of reciprocal and reversible relationships -
an awareness of the relations themselves, not simply a knowledge of their content - and this is fundamental to the development of scientific reasoning.

A similar rapprochement was offered by Piaget with respect
to the question of egocentrism. Vygotsky's position was that
egocentric speech does serve a communication function, and he
criticized Piaget for making it appear as if the child is not
attempting to communicate when engaged in monologue. In his
reply, Piaget makes it clear that the child is not speaking to
itself, but is speaking for itself, in the sense that often what
he or she says results in no effective communication. Again,
Piaget's position is that the child requires reversible and
reciprocal intellectual operations for rational communication and
co-ordination of viewpoints in order for communication to be
effective, and that these operations are most likely to be
developed in the context of peer interaction (Piaget, 1932).

Thus, it is not the case that the Piagetian child must be
considered to construct knowledge on its own. The child's
knowledge could be the outcome of an interaction; it could
involve the contribution of others, whether from symmetric
relations as in peer groups or asymmetric relations as with the
adult. Thought processes don't have to develop in social
isolation, even though they go on inside the head. The real
problem is that there is nothing in Piaget's theory that would
allow the mind of another to be transparent to the child. Knowledge of other minds is as much of a construction from scratch
as is any other kind of knowledge, and this is at the crux of the
problem of social cognition. And it is worth noting that this
criticism applies as much to the studies of Doise (1978), who
has insisted on the role of co-operative interactions in the
acquisition of concrete operations, as it does to Piaget, whom
Doise criticized.

Finally, problems arise in determining precisely what is meant
by the 'intermental level' from which Vygotsky claims all higher
mental processes are to be derived. Some of his interpreters have
considered it as a sort of conjoint cognitive process that occurs
only between individuals, with no counterpart within the
individual. Adult and child are considered as a unit, and the
danger is that the relation will be characterized in such a way

that the adult does all the cognitive work and the child simply becomes the passive recipient of whatever is socially transmitted. This we have already discussed and found unsatisfactory. Another way of thinking about the intermental level is as an emergent property of the interaction between individuals. Now this is useful because it recognizes the fact that the structural properties of a system in interaction may be greater than the sum of its parts. On the other hand, the danger is that the discontinuity between cognitive processes in the individual and cognitive processes that arise as a function of agreement on shared symbol systems will be stressed, at the expense of the continuity between biological and individual psychological processes that give rise to the semiotic function (see Massimo Piatelli-Palmarini, 1980, for all the ramifications of this). A third possibility is that all that is being asserted is that, at some fundamental level, similar cognitive processes occur in individuals when they are placed in the same context, and that the meaning and transmission of language occurs in relation to this totality.

If the latter is the case, then it is simply a logical assertion that development proceeds from the inter- to the intramental level. How could it be otherwise if the use of words depends upon some measure of agreement upon their meaning? In the most elementary case, the meaning of a word may be given only by social interactions in relation to a particular context, so to talk of a mental level at all is simply to acknowledge commonalities of perception and action (see MacNamara, 1972). It is only with cognitive growth that words come to carry their meaning autonomously. Stated in these terms, the question of the intermental reduces to questions about the role of language in cognitive development. That language acquisition is a social process is surely not in dispute. In summary, criticisms of Piaget's theory made in terms of individual versus social contributions to cognitive growth leave it possible that theories put forward as mutually exclusive may simply be dealing with opposite sides of the same coin. At least, this is how Piaget (1962) characterized his disagreement with Vygotsky, and he similarly characterized his disagreements with Wallon (Piaget, 1973) as a 'dialogue of the deaf'. So, as far as Piaget would have been concerned, the charge that his dialectical approach is acultural cannot be made to stick at the level of content or of mechanism.

INDIVIDUALISM AND SOLIPSISM IN PIAGET'S THEORY

Having attempted to defend Piaget against some of the criticisms levelled at his theory, it would be inconsistent with what I have written elsewhere (Butterworth, 1978) if I did not concede that I believe there are fundamental problems with his account of cognitive development, which have implications for theories of social cognition.

The fundamental problem as I see it is that he offers a totally constructivist account of cognitive development, such that even the most elementary levels of sensory experience are always mediated by action or by operations of the intellect. His is a 'representational realist' theory as opposed to the 'presentation-alist' realism of theories of direct perception, such as that pro-pounded by J.J. Gibson (1966) (see Blackmore, 1979). It is this constant necessity for mediation, for experience to be rendered objective, in Piaget's theory that leads to the indivi-dualism of which he is so often accused.

Perhaps I can briefly expand this argument in the context of some data on infants, although I think the evidence may have implications for the whole process of cognitive development. How does the infant come to know others as social objects? According to Macmurray (1933), this requires recognition of similarity between self and other; the origins of social knowledge lie in elementary forms of self-knowledge and vice versa. According to Piaget, however, the infant begins life as a solipsist, unable to distinguish 'self' from 'non-self' or to recognize the equivalence between self and other except in terms of patterns of circular reaction. The social world has no objective existence, since Piaget's theory precludes any direct perception of social or physical objects. Since perception is always mediated, admittedly by organizations of action at different levels of complexity, the path of development must be from the individual to the social. Piaget's individualism is rooted in the assumptions he makes about the nature of sensory perception, which locks the develop-ing child into a private world. Consequently, the notion that egocentrism consists in 'taking as the sole reality the one that appears to perception' emphasizes the private, subjective and somehow incoherent nature of experience. I believe that it was with this aspect of Piaget's theory that Vygotsky and Wallon had their fundamental disagreement, but, at the time, the evidence was not available to choose between their dialectical approach and Piaget's.

Recent studies, however, have amassed a great deal of evidence that Piaget's assumptions about the nature of early sensory perception may have been mistaken (for reviews see Bower, 1974; Butterworth, 1978), and in general the data are more consistent with a 'presentationalist' than a 'representation-alist' realist position. With respect to social perception, Meltzoff (1981) showed that human neonates can imitate tongue pro-trusion and mouth opening, behaviours consistent with the view, earlier put forward by Wallon (1973), that the first form of social relation is a symbiotic one whose mechanisms do not have to be constructed but are innately given and which allow proto-social contact from the outset. This formulation allows both for autonomy of the individual participants in the symbiotic relation and for emergent properties of their interaction.

With respect to the nature of infant egocentrism, Scaife and Bruner (1975) showed that babies from two months can follow an adult's line of regard, thus suggesting that even very young babies are aware that others have points of view. In a series of subsequent experiments I was able to show that babies are not solving this problem by a simple process of circular reaction (Butterworth and Cochran, 1980; Butterworth and Jarrett, 1980) such as would be necessary on Piaget's theory, since they do not simply turn until their gaze is interrupted by a visual target but seem to seek out a definite object of reference. However, there is a curious limitation on the infant's ability, which is that, even as late as eighteen months, babies behave as if they are unaware that there exists a space behind them. When the mother looks in that region, the infant turns in the appropriate direction but scans the space within its own visual field; it is as if the infant takes the other person's point of view, but only from its own point of view. We can see that what is egocentric about this behaviour is that the infant assimilates the adult's line of regard to its own visual field. On the other hand, the baby is not behaving solipsistically, since its behaviour credits the adult with a point of view. The infant, like a naive realist, behaves as if its own visual space is common to others, which of course, it is. It is this built-in assumption of the objectivity of experience, of its externality and its shared nature, that I believe to lie at the root of social cognition.

The child's assumption of the objectivity of sensory experience may offer a clue to explaining some of the phenomena recorded by Piaget and by some of his critics. There is only time briefly to mention two examples. The first concerns Piaget's (1951) famous anecdote about his daughter's inability to comprehend individual identity (p. 225). When out on a walk, Piaget and Jacqueline pass two slugs in quick succession and the child exclaims 'Encore la limace', which is interpreted by Piaget as if the child is saying 'There's that slug again'. As Karmiloff-Smith (1979) has pointed out, however, the child might just as easily be saying 'There's another slug' and relying on the presumption of a common history of experience for the adult to interpret her utterance appropriately. This explanation seems the more appropriate, since infants at Stage IV of Piaget's sensorimotor progression can be shown to individuate objects in relation to contextual cues (Butterworth, Jarrett and Hicks, 1982), demonstrating that the principle of individual identity is available.

The second example makes the inverse point and concerns the child's interpretation of the adult's utterance. This is the well-known study of number conservation by McGarrigle and Donaldson (1974-5), where it was demonstrated that the intentional actions of the experimenter seem to influence the child's judgment of number in a conservation of equivalence task. When the adult deliberately lengthens one row of counters the child is prepared to change its mind about equality, yet when the same transformation is brought about accidentally by a 'naughty teddy' the child sticks with the judgment that the number of counters in the two rows are equal. This suggests that the child interprets the adult's question in relation to the context and particularly in relation to whatever aspect of the display the adult's intentional action seems to pick out as the referent of the utterance. The child's assumption of a common context for experience, which ordinarily serves to disambiguate the adult's utterance, serves in the standard Piagetian task to mislead or place the child in a conflict. From a direct realist perspective, such examples do not indicate the presence of concrete operational reasoning in the preschool child. Rather, as Broughton (1978) has suggested, things have an obvious quality for the child; their reality is obvious, knowledge is presumptive, and the child's major problem may be to comprehend why the question should be asked at all.

Thus, when the child falls back on direct experience or relies on the context to disambiguate an event or an utterance which he or she has not fully understood, it falls back on a level of experience common to adult and child, and in that sense instantiates a social relation to maintain communication where more abstract means have failed or are simply unavailable. Egocentrism reflects the assumption that child and adult share a public world. It is not a retreat into privacy and solipsism.

CONCLUSION

In conclusion, there has been a tendency in the study of social cognition for explanatory principles to be polarized, and where criticisms have been addressed to Piaget's theory, I feel they have often been made at an inappropriate level. Rather than attempting to take sides, I should like to suggest that it may be more appropriate to apply the strength of the genetic method, which Piaget advocated and pioneered, than to test the basic assumptions inherent among various alternative theories of social cognitive development. For the discipline to advance further, it may be time to adopt a systems theory approach, such as that advocated by Glassman (1973), which does not deny that there are individual contributions to the social structure or that the social structure will have properties not observable at the level of individual behaviour. The problem of mechanism in social cognitive development is to establish how stability is achieved in living systems at different levels of complexity from the cell, through the organism, the group and society.

From this perspective, it seems unlikely that the direction of effect in social cognitive development will be a one-way traffic from the individual to the social or vice versa. Similarly, feedback from both physical and social experience may contribute to cognitive growth. The problem in social cognition is to choose among alternative dialectical theories. Fortunately, Piaget's theory incorporates a method to allow the psychologist to choose.

REFERENCES

Barker, W.D.L. and Newson, J.L. (1980) The Development of
Social Cognition Definition and Location, in S. Modgil and
C. Modgil, 'Toward a Theory of Psychological Development'.
Windsor: National Foundation for Educational Research, pp.
233-66.
Berry, J.W. and Dasen, P.R. (1971) 'Culture and Cognition:
Readings in Cross-cultural Psychology'. London: Methuen.
Blackmore, J. (1979) On the Inverted Use of the Terms 'Realism'
and 'Idealism' among Scientists and Historians of Science, in
'British Journal of the Philosophy of Science', 30, pp. 125-34.
Bower, T.G.R. (1974) 'Development in Infancy'. New York:
W.H. Freeman.
Bower, T.G.R., Broughton, J.M., and Moore, M.K. (1970)
Demonstration of Intention in the Reaching Behaviour of
Neonate Humans, in 'Nature', 228, pp. 679-80.
Broughton, J.M. (1978) Development of Concepts of Self, Mind,
Reality and Knowledge, in 'New Directions for Child Develop-
ment', 1, pp. 75-100.
Bruner, J.S. and Lyons, K. (1968) The Growth of Human
Manual Intelligence. I. Taking Possession of Objects. Unpub-
lished study, Centre for Cognitive Studies, Harvard
University.
Butterworth, G.E. (1978) Thoughts and Things: Piaget's Theory,
in A. Burton, and J. Radford (eds), 'Perspectives on Think-
ing'. London: Methuen.
Butterworth, G.E. and Cochran, E. (1980) Towards a Mechanism
of Joint Visual Attention in Human Infancy, in 'International
Journal of Behavioural Development', pp. 253-72.
Butterworth, G.E. and Jarrett, N. (1980) The Geometry of Pre-
verbal Communication. Paper presented to the Developmental
Psychology Section of the British Psychological Society,
Edinburgh.
Butterworth, G.E., Jarrett, N. and Hicks, L. (1982) Spatio-
temporal Identity in Infancy: Perceptual Competence or Con-
ceptual Deficit? in 'Developmental Psychology', 18(3), pp. 435-49.
Chandler, M.J. (1977) Social Cognition: A Selective Review of
Current Research, in W. Overton and J. McCarthy Gallagher
(eds), 'Knowledge and Development', vol. 1. 'Advances in
Research and Theory'. New York and London: Plenum.
Damon, W. (1979) Why Study Social Cognitive Development?
in 'Human Development', 22, pp. 206-11.
Doise, W. (1978) 'Groups and Individuals: Explanations in Social
Psychology'. Cambridge University Press.
Frye, D. (1980) Developmental Changes in Strategies of Social
Interaction, in M.E. Lamb and L.R. Sherrod (eds), 'Infant
Social Cognition: Empirical and Theoretical Considerations'.
Hillsdale, NJ: Lawrence Erlbaum.
Gibson, J.J. (1966) 'The Senses Considered as Perceptual
Systems'. Boston: Houghton Mifflin.

Glassman, R.B. (1973) Persistence and Loose Coupling in Living Systems, in 'Behavioural Science', 18, pp. 83-98.

Karmiloff-Smith, A. (1979) 'A Functional Approach to Child Language'. Cambridge University Press.

Kuhn, D. (1978) Mechanisms of Cognitive and Social Development: One Psychology or Two? in 'Human Development', 21, pp. 92-118.

Macmurray, J. (1933) 'Interpreting the Universe', London: Faber and Faber.

MacNamara, J. (1972) Cognitive Basis of Language Learning in Infants, in 'Psychological Review', 79, pp. 1-13.

McGarrigle, J. and Donaldson, M. (1974-5) Conservation Accidents, in 'Cognition', 3, pp. 307-11.

Meltzoff, A. (1981) Imitation, Intermodal Coordination and Representation in Early Infancy, in G.E. Butterworth (ed.), 'Infancy and Epistemology'. Brighton: Harvester Press.

Piaget, J. (1932) 'The Development of Moral Judgment in the Child'. London: Routledge.

Piaget, J. (1951) 'Play, Dreams and Imitation in Childhood'. London: Routledge.

Piaget, J. (1954) 'The Construction of Reality in the Child'. New York: Basic Books.

Piaget, J. (1962) 'Comments on Vygotsky's Critical Remarks Concerning the Language and Thought of the Child and Judgment and Reasoning in the Child'. Cambridge. Mass.: MIT Press.

Piaget, J. (1966) La Psychologie, les relations interdisciplinaires et le système des sciences, in 'Bulletin de psychologie', 254, pp. 242-54.

Piaget, J. (1973) The Role of Imitation in the Development of Representational Thought, in 'International Journal of Mental Health', 1 (4), pp. 67-74.

Piattelli-Palmarini, M. (1980) 'Language and Learning: The Debate between Jean Piaget and Noam Chomsky'. London: Routledge & Kegan Paul.

Scaife, M. and Bruner, J.S. (1975) The Capacity for Joint Visual Attention in the Infant, in 'Nature', 253, p. 265.

Trevarthen, C. (1981) The Primary Motives for Cooperative Understanding, in G.E. Butterworth and P.H. Light (eds), 'Social Cognition: Essays on the Development of Understanding'. Brighton: Harvester Press.

Vygotsky, L.S. (1962) 'Thought and Language'. Cambridge, Mass.: MIT Press.

Vygotsky, L.S. (1966) Development of the Higher Mental Functions, in A. Leontyev, A. Luria and A. Smirnov (eds), 'Psychological Research in the USSR', vol. 1. Moscow: Progress Publishers, pp. 11-44.

Wallon, H. (1973) The Psychological Development of the Child, in 'International Journal of Mental Health', 1, pp. 29-39.

Youniss, J. (1978) Dialectical Theory and Piaget on Social Knowledge, in 'Human Development', 21, pp. 234-47.

16 Social cognition and Piaget: a case of negative transfer?

Paul Light

George Butterworth and I have just finished editing a book on social cognition (Butterworth and Light, 1982), and this experience has brought home to us what a very elastic expression 'social cognition' is. What I've tried to do in this paper, therefore, is to clarify some of the senses in which the term is used and to examine the relationship of each of these 'versions' of social cognition to Piagetian theory.

For the sake of economy I have decided to make do with only three 'versions', which I shall designate simply as I, II and III. Social cognition I refers to the attempt to characterize social aspects of development in cognitive terms. Although this accounts for by far the largest proportion of the relevant literature, I shall give it only a cursory treatment here because its relationship to Piagetian theory seems relatively straightforward. Social cognition II refers to the contribution of social (in the sense of interpersonal/reciprocal) processes to the growth of knowledge. Social cognition III also deals with the contribution of social processes, but here taking social in the sense of cultural - I refer to the study of the growth of knowledge envisaged as a process of enculturation. This is at the same time the least researched aspect of social cognition and the most challenging one from the point of view of Piagetian theory.

In a further attempt to simplify things I shall restrict my comments throughout to the preschool and early school age period which Piaget has characterized in terms of concrete operational thought.

SOCIAL COGNITION I

The contents pages of journals such as 'Developmental Psychology' over the last ten years bear witness to a very considerate expenditure of research effort on the study of children's social knowledge. Topics such as friendship, person perception, empathy, altruism, communication, co-operation and morality

have been approached in terms of the child's developing understanding.

There is a certain sense in which the prevalence of such
studies represents a reaction against Piaget, but at the same
time this research typically draws very heavily upon Piagetian
theory. Social cognition I is a reaction against Piaget only in the
sense that Piaget's own empirical work is seen to be overly biased
towards the study of the child's knowledge of the physical world,
the world of physical objects, space, time, causality and so on.
This is a bias Piaget himself admitted, and indeed he expressed
his regret (e.g., Piaget, 1971) that his emphasis on such
'impersonal' concepts had led to a neglect of knowledge in its
social aspects.

However, it is clear that Piaget did not anticipate that the
study of the development of social knowledge would require
significant modification of his account of cognitive development.
He argued that the cognitive processes available to the child in
his dealings with the social world must be just the same processes
as are available to him in his dealings with the physical world.
Such a claim seems uncontentious, and in the light of it social
cognition I has developed largely as an application of concepts
drawn from Piaget's account of the growth of operational thinking to the study of developing social knowledge. Other contributors to this volume have touched on some of these (e.g.,
moral judgment, communication), and it is clear that the success
of such extrapolations of Piagetian theory is open to question.
But for present purposes it is enough to note that, from this
standpoint, the only complaint against Piaget seems to be that
he didn't comprehensively research all topics of interest
in developmental psychology. I think we should be grateful to
him for that!

SOCIAL COGNITION II

I have accepted, with Piaget, that the basic features of cognition
at any stage of development are largely indifferent to their field
of application. But an adequate psychological theory of cognitive
development needs to do more than merely describe the basic
features of cognition as it develops. It needs to provide an
indication of the factors promoting that development, and of the
processes involved in it. I have designated as social cognition II
that body of research which is concerned with the role of interpersonal interactions in the development of cognition. The
criticism of Piaget's theory from the standpoint of social cognition
II is that it inadequately reflects the role of such interpersonal
processes in cognitive development.

It is necessary here to distinguish between Piaget's early and
later work. In his early writing (e.g., 1932) we do find specific
suggestions on the role of interpersonal interactions in individual
intellectual development. He took the view that recognition of

inter-individual reciprocity was necessary to overcome egocentrism, and that such recognition was achieved directly
through social experience. Thus the decentring of thought
depended on the decentring of social relation, which was achieved
through social interaction. He emphasized interactions in the
peer group on the grounds that 'discussion is only possible
among equals' (1932, p. 409).

So in these early writings Piaget offered a conceptualization
of the role of interpersonal interactions, and seemed to open the
way to empirical research on the question. Such research never
materialized, however, and the question lay dormant for nearly
half a century. Only very recently has it become a lively research
topic, perhaps the most obvious example being the work of Willem
Doise and colleagues (e.g. Doise, Mugny and Perret-Clermont,
1975) on peer interaction and learning, which directly addresses
the question of whether and how inter-individual conflict of
centrations produces cognitive gain by the individual. Other
researches using similar paradigms have begun to explore in some
detail the factors involved in intellectually productive and
unproductive interactions between children (e.g. Russell, 1979;
Glachan and Light, 1982).

At the same time, studies have been made of the influence of
mother-child interaction patterns on the child's ability to
'decentre' in, for example, visual perspective taking tasks
(Light, 1979) or in communication tasks (Bearison and Cassel,
1975). These seem to show that, while Piaget's emphasis on
equality was justified, his stress on the necessary asymmetry of
the adult-child relationship was not. This recent empirical
literature identifies as effective in stimulating decentration just
those styles of interaction in which the mother treats the child
in terms of a 'constructed' equality.

So Piaget's early writings find echoes in this recent research.
But why has there been a delay of forty or fifty years in
researching these questions, which seem to be of the clearest
psychological interest? I want to suggest that some of the
responsibility must be laid at Piaget's door, in that the neglect
of these issues is a reflection of the character and the influence
of Piaget's later work on operational thinking.

What we see in the post-war work is an implicit (though not,
I'd like to stress, explicit) rejection of any crucial role for
social experience in the genesis of reflective thought. Karmiloff-
Smith makes the point nicely (1979, pp. 18-19):

> The fact that for several decades Piagetian theoretical and
> experimental work has placed main emphasis on the child's
> constructive interaction with his physical environment does
> imply that herein lies for Piaget the privileged source of inter-
> action for the child's cognitive development. Had Piaget
> hypothesised that . . . the child's cognitive growth stemmed
> from his constructive interactions with his socio-cultural
> environment, then presumably his . . . experimental con-

siderations would have explicitly conveyed this. A theory reflects its . . . research emphases, even if its epistemological foundations do not preclude shifting these emphases.

In other words, neglect can be tantamount to negation, and Piaget's failure to consider the ways in which interpersonal experiences 'feed into' cognitive development has, I think, been largely responsible for the retardation of research in this area.

Piaget's neglect of the role of social experience has been justified by some commentators as merely an aspect of a more general unconcern with the role of any specific experience in fostering cognitive development, and this position has been defended by distinguishing epistemological from psychological questions. Thus, for example, Barker and Newson (1980, p. 240) suggest that:

> Piaget's theory of operative development describes and analyses the emergence of the structural aspects of thinking, and while certain areas may be more influenced by discussion with peers, and development in others most encouraged by the manipulations of objects . . . this is not the epistemo-logical question to which the author addressed himself . . . in fact it is not really an epistemological issue of any great significance at all.

However, they continue (p. 241):

> Psychologists, immersed in the contingency of fact . . . cannot be satisfied with philosophical theory and are led to ask different sorts of questions.

Barker and Newson may (and I stress the 'may') be right about the epistemological insignificance of these issues; they are certainly right to recognize that these issues are far from insignificant psychologically. Unfortunately, Piaget's theory has been widely mistaken for an adequate psychological theory of cognitive development, and we have not been led to ask the 'different sorts of questions' to which Barker and Newson refer. As Karmiloff-Smith (1979, p. 1) puts it:

> Despite the fact that he is widely regarded as *the* psychologist of the twentieth century, for Piaget psychology has always been simply a means for establishing a biologically based epistemology.

If we have allowed our developmental psychology to be narrowed and stunted through a failure to recognize this, the mistake, perhaps, is ours rather than Piaget's.

SOCIAL COGNITION III

I want under this heading to focus on research concerned not with symmetrical, reciprocal interpersonal interactions, but with just those asymmetrical interactions in which the child is exposed to the knowledge instantiated in his language and culture.

Here Piaget's position is more straightforward. In advocating a constructivist theory of the development of knowledge, he directly opposed this to an alternative view in which the child is the passive recipient of culturally elaborated knowledge transmitted via language. This distinction between a 'constructivist' theory and a 'copy' theory was drawn in terms so black and white (white and black?) that any suggestion regarding the role of language and of the community of other 'knowers' tended to be taken as an advocacy of cultural determinism, and as a threat to the theory. I want to approach this topic indirectly through a brief consideration of the structuralist character of Piaget's theory.

Although Piaget avowed a concern with the function of intelligence, with intelligence as adaptation, with accommodation, assimilation and equilibration, these functional concepts were never really put to work in his account of the growth of operational thought. Instead, the core of this account is a structural model of cognitive development: a model couched in terms of a formal set of elements and relations with which the child's reasoning could be characterized. Piaget's search has been for ways of moving from the particular to the general - for more and more general ways of characterizing the operations involved, with less and less significance attaching to specific content and context.

The 'concrete operations' of Piaget's theory are of course elements within this model. Despite his own emphasis that the child's theories are as much a property of the knower as of the known, Piaget has little reservation in treating the elements of his own structural model as 'actual psychological activities' (1957, p. 7) going on in the child's head.

The child's thought is to be interpreted, therefore, in terms of his 'possession of' certain operational competences. However, in everyday situations we can only fleetingly glimpse these underlying competences, since they tend to be obscured by all manner of local and particular aspects of the context. Since Piaget's concern was with emerging operational competences rather than with the factors which influence the expression of these competences in performance, he moved towards relatively formal experimental procedures. These were offered as effective diagnostic tests for the various hypothesized operational structures. This method, with the associated image of a clear-cut underlying 'form' below the untidy surface of actual behaviour, came to dominate the study of cognitive development for several decades. And it is this approach which has come under attack in what may be seen as a recent reassertion of an older, more functionalist approach to intelligence (cf. G.H. Mead, 1934).

While Piaget's structuralism has concerned itself with the abstract epistemic subject, a functionalist approach has to be concerned with uses and outcomes, and thus with the context in which the child is pursuing his functional interests.

This is where culture comes in, since the culture represents both an instantiation of shared human functional interests and the effective context for their satisfaction in the individual. By 'culture', I mean to refer to those largely tacit understandings and agreements which are implicit in our various forms of social exchange, and most clearly in our language. A concern with culture in this sense, and with its place in the development of thought in the individual, is the hallmark of social cognition III.

Piaget, in rejecting the conception of the child's mind as a bucket into which the culture pours knowledge, has gone to the opposite (and equally unhelpful) extreme. His theory is ahistorical and acultural. It envisages the child as, in effect, reinventing logical and scientific thinking on his own. At best he may have 'a little help from his friends' in overcoming ego-centrism. The fact that logical, mathematical and scientific ways of thinking have a history, and are embodied in the life and language of the child's community, is almost totally ignored. Consequently the theory offers no way of understanding how individual and cultural aspects of knowing interact in ontogenesis.

What, then, has social cognition III to offer, and how does the conflict with Piaget show itself in practice? A brief consideration of the significance of language and context in cognitive development will, I hope, bring out some of the issues.

Piaget's treatment of the role of language in operational development is in line with his general treatment of cultural transmission. He characterizes language simply as a collection of conventional signifiers existing ready-made in the culture. This view of language as a set of static significations, either known or not, underlies Piaget's claim that operational thinking cannot be understood in terms of language acquisition, and likewise underlies Sinclair's (Inhelder, Sinclair and Bovet, 1974) evidence for the irrelevance of language to the genesis of the operations.

Any suggestion that the problem lies in the language is interpreted as a claim that certain lexical items are not in the child's repertoire. Thus for example, (Piaget, 1928, p. 9):

> Between the ages of 6 and 9, when the relationship indicated by *because* is incorrect, one can always assume that reasoning is at fault: the word 'because' is used spontaneously by the child from 3 or 4 onwards.

This conception of language, in which word mastery is the name of the game, and which is an all-or-none affair, is important in Piaget's theory precisely because it allows him to treat language as transparent. As soon as the child 'knows' a word, his use of it allows one to see through to underlying cognitive competence. Any move towards recognition of the dynamic and flexible aspects of language use threatens this 'access' to 'competence', but it is in just this direction that recent research is moving.

Take for example the studies by Donaldson, Lloyd and McGarrigle (Donaldson, 1978) concerning 'all' and 'more' and employing toy cars and garages. In some sense the children concerned clearly understood these words (if asked, for example, whether 'all' the garage doors were shut or which of two rows had 'more' cars in). But given three cars and four garages, they frequently denied that all the cars were in the garages - the expression 'all the cars' seemed to be taken to refer to all the cars which ought to be there. Again, given a row with four cars in four garages and a row with five cars in six garages, when the children were asked which row had more cars in many of them got it wrong. These and other similar findings suggest that young children's understanding of a question is highly dependent upon what's taken for granted at the time it's asked. Learning the meaning of a word, far from being an all-or-none affair, may be a gradual process of mastering contextually appropriate uses.

The importance of this issue of context can be brought out in relation to the situations Piaget himself used for testing the child's cognitive competences (Neilson and Dockrell, 1982, provide a clear review). Take Rommetveit's (1978) demonstration that, in a Piagetian class inclusion problem (cups, glasses, things to drink from), errors were still common in eight-year-olds, but were almost completely eliminated by asking the question before presenting the (pictured) objects. This suggests that, as soon as the materials were presented, they created in the children an expectation which led them to mis-interpret the reference of the question. McGarrigle, Grieve and Hughes (1978) have shown that, in the same situation, changing the materials to render the superordinate class more salient improved performance, and again they interpret the child's problem as one of locating the intended referent. Reviewing class inclusion studies, Grieve and Garton (cited in Neilson and Dockrell, 1982) suggest that we are here dealing with 'a lack of effective communication between adult and child rather than a lack of ability on the child's part' (p. 220). I want to suggest that this line of research should in fact lead us to question the distinction between 'a lack of effective com-munication' and 'a lack of ability on the child's part'.

Conservation figures centrally in Piaget's account of oper-ational thinking, and conservation tests have been prominent in recent studies of context and cognition. Probably the best known of these is McGarrigle and Donaldson's (1975) - Conser-vation Accidents - paper. Here, young children who typically gave non-conserving answers in the standard conservation procedure gave conserving responses when the transformation of materials was achieved 'accidentally' by an errant teddy bear.

This study has been replicated (Dockrell, Neilson and Campbell, 1980) and shown to be generalizable to quite different kinds of 'accidents' (Light, Buckingham and Robbins, 1979). The effects of such variations in logically irrelevant aspects of the task are sometimes very large. In our study (Light, Buckingham and Robbins, 1979) we found a shift among five-year-olds from 5 per cent conservation in the Piagetian version to 70 per cent conservation in a modified version.

McGarrigle and Donaldson offered their study as evidence that we have underestimated the child's competence using standard Piagetian procedures. They saw children's failure in the standard condition as reflecting misleading features of the context, i.e., as false negatives. But this argument is two-edged; if contextual cues can generate false negatives, they can on the same argument also generate 'false positives' – the young children succeeding on the modified tasks can be seen as being 'led into' correct responding by the context, rather than as revealing any underlying logical competence. I have recently tried to highlight this point in a study with Amanda Gilmour (in press) which demonstrated that similar contextual modifications can increase the frequency of conserving responses even where the property being considered (area within a fixed perimeter) is not in fact conserved.

The Piagetian response here would be to agree that these are false positives and to argue that 'psuedo-conservation' is being mistaken for 'true' conservation because inappropriate or insufficient criteria are being applied. This tack has provoked a good deal of unproductive debate and research which has been, in Brown and Desforges (1979, p. 61) terms, 'either bogged down in, or joyously preoccupied with, the criterion problem'.

There is no doubt that the judgments of, say, ten-year-olds do differ from those of, say, four-year-olds. If we stick with conservation as our example, the older children seem able to attend to the questions they are asked even when these questions are contextually unlikely ones, and to offer conserving judgments in contexts which would mislead the younger children. But instead of arguing about what are and what are not the hallmarks of 'true' conservation, we might do better to consider the developmental relationship between the later relatively decontextualized judgments and the earlier context-dependent ones.

The argument for attending to the issue of contextual support for cognitive judgments does not in my view rest on any supposed advantages of 'ecologically valid' tests which make 'human sense' to the children and thus provide better indices of their abilities. It rests on the hypothesis that the interactional context, supporting a particular 'reading' of the speaker's intention, has a vital part to play in the attainment of shared reference to complex concepts. In the case of the conservations, the problematic concepts are, for example, amount, weight and number, and the rather special sense of 'same' as it is used in relation to concepts of this kind. The attainment of conservation must involve the child coming to agree with others as to how these terms are to be used. Not 'nothing but' this, you will note, if for no other reason than that the achievement of such agreement presupposes all manner of other commonalities. But I should like to follow Russell (1978) in arguing that children do not first learn what we mean by amount, weight or number and only later learn that these are conserved across certain kinds of transformation. The conservations are intrinsic properties of these concepts, the reason being that these concepts have their functional roots in the human activities of sharing, counting and so on. The language we use thus embodies cultural agreements, and these agreements in turn rest on shared functional interests.

I have bracketed as social cognition III those approaches to individual cognitive development which have tried to focus on the child in interaction with his culture or, in Walkerdine and Sinha's (1978) terms, have considered cognitive development as 'a complex interaction between the individual and the social context in which he exists, in which the medium of language plays a central and strategic role' (p. 173). It would appear that attending to the role of language need not involve resorting to a 'passive copy' model. The child is not simply taught his language; he learns it, through an active and continuing effort to interpret the others' meaning, working from context towards text. Neither should it be supposed that any attempt is being made here to ground all intelligent behaviour in such inter-subjective agreements.

With these reservations, however, it does seem to me that these recent attempts to understand the ontogenesis of knowledge as a process not of invention but of 'guided reinvention' (cf. Lock, 1980), hold much promise. And the case I want to argue here is that such limited progress as has been made in this direction has been made despite, and not because of, the massive influence of Piaget's theory.

To sum up, then, social cognition I represents the positive transfer case, the extension of Piaget's account from the cognitive to the social domain being a matter of fleshing out the skeleton he provided (Modgil, Chapter 1 above). Social cognition II is a mixed case, drawing on Piaget's account of operational development but having to struggle against his generally negative treatment of experiential factors in development. Social cognition III has the same problems and more, since it opposes a concern with performance and function to Piaget's concern with competence and structure. Here, I think, a case for negative transfer can indeed be made. However, even here there is perhaps enough common ground to make the disagreement profitable.

REFERENCES

Barker, W. and Newson, J. (1980) The Development of Social Cognition: Definition and Location, in S. Modgil and C. Modgil

(eds), 'Towards a Theory of Psychological Development'.
Windsor: National Foundation for Educational Research.

Bearison, D. and Cassel, T. (1975) Cognitive Decentration and
Social Codes: Communicative Effectiveness in Young Children
from Differing Family Contexts, in 'Developmental Psychology',
11, pp. 29-36.

Brown, G. and Desforges, C. (1979) 'Piaget's Theory: A
Psychological Critique'. London: Routledge & Kegan Paul.

Butterworth, G. and Light P. (eds) (1982) 'Social Cognition:
Studies of the Development of Understanding'. Brighton:
Harvester Press.

Dockrell, J., Neilson, I. and Campbell, R. (1980) Conservation
Accidents Revisited, in 'International Journal of Behavioural
Development'.

Doise, W., Mugny, G. and Perret-Clermont, A.-N. (1975)
Social Interaction and the Development of Logical Operations,
in 'European Journal of Social Psychology', 5, pp. 367-83.

Donaldson, M. (1978) 'Children's Minds'. Glasgow: Fontana.

Glachan, M. and Light, P. (1982) Peer Interaction and Learning:
Can Two Wrongs Make a Right? in G. Butterworth and P. Light
(eds), 'Social Cognition: Studies of the Development of
Understanding'. Brighton: Harvester Press.

Inhelder, B., Sinclair, H. and Bovet, M. (1974) 'Learning and
the Development of Cognition'. London: Routledge & Kegan Paul.

Karmiloff-Smith, A. (1979) 'A Functional Approach to Child
Language'. Cambridge University Press.

Light, P. (1979) 'The Development of Social Sensitivity'. Cambridge University Press.

Light, P., Buckingham, N. and Robbins, A. (1979) The Conservation Task as an Interactional Setting, in 'British Journal of
Educational Psychology', 49, pp. 304-10.

Light, P. and Gilmour (in press) Conservation or Conversation?,
in 'Journal of Experimental Child Psychology'.

Lock, A. (1980) 'The Guided Reinvention of Language'. London:
Academic Press.

McGarrigle, J. and Donaldson, M. (1975) Conservation Accidents,
in 'Cognition', 3, pp. 341-50.

McGarrigle, J., Grieve, R. and Hughes, M. (1978) Interpreting
Inclusion, in 'Journal of Experimental Child Psychology', 26,
pp. 528-50.

Mead, G.H. (1934) 'Mind, Self and Society', ed. C.W. Morris.
Chicago and London: University of Chicago Press.

Neilson, I. and Dockrell, J. (1982) Cognitive Tasks as Interactional Settings, in G. Butterworth and P. Light (eds),
'Social Cognition: Studies of the Development of Understanding'. Brighton: Harvester Press.

Piaget, J. (1928) 'Judgement and Reasoning in the Child'.
New York: Harcourt, Brace.

Piaget, J. (1932) 'The Moral Judgement of the Child'. London:
Routledge & Kegan Paul.

Piaget, J. (1957) 'Logic and Psychology'. New York: Basic Books

Piaget, J. (1971) 'Biology and Knowledge'. Edinburgh University Press.

Rommetveit, R. (1978) On Piagetian Cognitive Operations, Semantic Competence, and Message Structure in Adult-child Communication, in I. Markova (ed.), 'The Social Context of Language'. London: Wiley.

Russell, J. (1978) 'The Acquisition of Knowledge'. London: Macmillan.

Russell, J. (1979) Children Deciding on the Correct Answer: Social Influence under the Microscope. Paper presented to the Annual Conference of the Developmental Section of the British Psychological Society, Southampton, September.

Walkerdine, V. and Sinha, C. (1978) The Internal Triangle: Language, Reasoning and the Social Context, in I. Markova (ed.), 'The Social Context of Language'. London: Wiley.

Part 10

Sociology

17 Towards a Piagetian theory of social development

Peter Kutnick

The following paper is presented to illuminate Piagetian theory applied to sociology. As Piaget's broader sociological writings remain only partially accessible in the original French and the main body of his theory concerns the genesis of the 'individual', this paper cannot be given without some serious qualifications. Rather than a macro-view of society, Piaget's work can only be associated with a micro-view.

In avoiding macro-issues, this paper will avoid casting Piaget's theory into the functionalist or Marxist fields of sociology. The theory does not describe the broad structure of society. Nor does it attempt to explain economic relations and constraints as the basis of social order and its inevitable conflicts.

Piaget's sociological view, if one can extract it from his sociological and other writings, is reductionist to the extent that the microcosm fulfils his structural principles. The theory is anti-phenomenological, yet bounded by rules and regulations within cultures. The theory is based upon the four factors responsible for cognitive development, which Piaget distinguished as: biological factors, equilibration factors, social factors of interpersonal co-ordination, and factors of education and cultural transmission. All four factors are influenced by the social environment to some extent – certainly by its presentation, opportunity for stimulation and cultural values. (In his reliance on cultural values, Piaget may be accused of being Durkheimian.) The most obvious environmental effects have been explored in the educational and cultural transmission factor. This curiously under- and over-explored factor is central in validating criteria of the theory, and as such, discussion of this point will be reserved for a later part of the paper. The biological/adaptive system will be accepted as given. Equilibration and social factors are central in drawing out the main elements of Piaget's diverse theory.

Piaget's micro-view centres on the types and generation of relationships between individuals and groups, operations and context. In turning to Piaget's early books, one can draw out points to gain an understanding of the generation of social

relationships. Basic reference will be made to 'Moral Judgment
of the Child', 'Play Dreams and Imitation', and logical-mathematical development, with qualifying reference made to
'Language and Thought of the Child' and 'Judgment and
Reasoning'. An amalgamation of the above writings rests on
bases of structural theory, stressing the development of
qualified stages, organismic interaction, schemes and context.
Concurrent with the generation of (close) social relationships,
the necessity of underlying (or perhaps 'deep') logical-
mathematical and social authority structures will be described.
Mays (1980) has provided an historical explanation/background
for Piaget's writings cited above, and has further drawn
attention to: (1) cognitive and affective parallels in development,
based on psychoanalytic and therapeutic criteria; (2) Piaget's
view of the self as a social product, citing Hegelian criteria;
and (3) respect, characteristic of relationships, that is generated
within relationships.

In his 'Etudes sociologiques', Piaget specified that 'structures
of intellectual operations are identical to structures underlying
social interactions involving values and exchanges of ideas'
(from Doise, Mugny and Perret-Clermont, 1975, p. 368). Structure implies an equilibrium of a common scale of values/language,
conservation and reversibility. Social and individual logics go
hand in hand. For Piaget (and others), it was impossible to
establish a causal link. While cognitive operations are often
referred to for their individual character, social relations and
'valeurs' have been stressed as fundamental to the theory.

If pushed, relationships can be seen as the antecedents to
social processes and functional structure of society. Relationships, especially in their archetypical forms, have characteristic
interactions, schemes and contexts. Relationships involve the
individual with society. 'Archetypes' of social relations were
originally identified in 'Moral Judgment of the Child' as 'constraint' and 'co-operation'. Both relations represent a distribution
of power/authority between people, obligations and rights.
Extracting the above points from Piaget, a theory of social
relationships can be structured and extended to provide explanation of social phenomena as political socialization.

For brevity I shall assume basic knowledge of logical-
mathematical stages/development. Further, I shall not debate
but assume the existence of stage/structural theory. I shall
concentrate on major social developmental aspects often overlooked
or given limited light in Piaget's early writing.

'Moral Judgment of the Child' overtly describes stages of moral
development, justice, equity and rules. James Youniss (1978)
has researched deeper into the volume and noted seven aspects
which he considered to form the social development basis in
Piaget:

(1) children are born in social relationships, often holding several positions;
(2) once the infant achieves permanency, then persons play a direct role in the construction of order;
(3) order is derived from interactions when the child constructs rule systems;
(4) a division between self and others becomes evident in a rational rule system within the social network;
(5) any relationship can develop in that either party can reconstruct the social order;
(6) through development, the self and others become relativistic concepts with a multiplicity of views; and
(7) concepts of persons are open to change as relationships develop.

Further points to be drawn from 'Moral Judgment' include:

(1) autonomous moral judgments or the stage of autonomy is possible only after moralities of constraint and co-operation are acknowledged;
(2) both constraint and co-operation are based on authority or some division of power between individuals and groups;
(3) authority relations (whether of constraint or co-operation) are reciprocal, noted by power assertion and obedience or mutuality – that is, obligation of partners characterizes authority;
(4) early development of constraint (and later co-operation) have sensorimotor and pre-operative bases – the development of schematic understanding that Piaget noted as the 'Law of conscious realization';
(5) further development of constraint shows concrete and formal operational aspects of thought (which will be discussed later in reference to research by Damon); and
(6) the social context of development both limits and promotes movement towards autonomy.

'Moral Judgment of the Child' holds much more for the reader than a description of simple stages of moral development. Piaget places moral and social development in a social relational context. Social relations are based upon reciprocal authority relationships and obligations. Development has an underlying (deep) structure based on logical-mathematical schemes and social understanding. Rule systems are, initially, constructions of social order/authority. It is a simple deduction (to further qualify) that groupings within a society and societies themselves represent and are representative of the authority 'archetypes' of constraint and co-operation. Hence individuals within groups and societies will adapt differing moral/social outlooks – dependent on their context of development.

The initial/fundamental stage of close social relationship development, according to Piaget, was sensorimotor. He briefly mentioned that stage in two respects in 'Moral Judgment of the Child', expanded on qualities of the stage in 'Play, Dreams and Imitation', and referred to it in 'Etudies sociologiques'. Piaget discussed sensorimotor development in relation to the development of constraint. Schemes described by the constant repetition of behavioural action preceding cognitive awareness were referred to in the 'law of conscious realization'. The unusual aspect of sensorimotor schemes (especially in the first half-year of life) is that these actions are not solely initiated by the infant – they may be (and often are) initiated by care-giver and others. (Actions/behaviour in this early stage of development may be separated from cognition; or knowledge/understanding of the action.) The initiation and maintenance of actions is bounded by availability of persons, objects and ritual; that is, actions are limited by context.

An example of context is the (necessary) development of constraint structured through Western family upbringing practices. What ties the Western child to constraint? Piaget answers by pointing to two phenomena:

(1)   The strongly egocentric stage of early childhood; this limits intellectual and social action to the perceived uncritical acceptance of the here-and-now. On the social/moral level of interpretation, the child is constrained by an unequal power relationship with care-giver:
(2)   Acceptance of the relationships is associated with early affective development described in 'Play, Dreams and Imitation'.

In stating that affect was parallel in development to cognition, Piaget further describes qualities of sensorimotor (SM) affective schemes. Early emotional development expands in pre-operative, concrete and formal operation schemes. But affect differs from cognition in that it does not generalize: the child's emotional relations are confined to a few individuals. Piaget explained this phenomenon by citing the limited number of tactile caring/ physical contacts in the early SM substages, centring on the secondary circular reaction. (As an aside, this substage is noted by Yarrow (1972) as the foundation of the attachment relationship.) The lack of generalizability of affect demonstrates: (1) this stage of the theory is rooted in SM development; (2) affective, social and cognitive development are 'intertwined'; (3) affective development can be discussed from two perspectives: (a) the development of emotional relationships with various types of individuals, and (b) the developing (cognitive applied to affect) ability to reflect and describe affect by the individual. The amalgamation of cognitive, social and affective development underlies the separation of close social and social relationships, the qualities of these relationships and their generation.

Further developmental qualifications and extensions have been explored in 'Language and Thought of the Child' and 'Judgment and Reasoning'. The transition from a mainly egocentric to a sociocentric perspective was described and discussed in 'Language and Thought'. The role of the peer group was very important in that it provided the stimulation and cognitive conflict for the transition. The transition was again discussed in 'Judgment and Reasoning' in the Three Mountains and National Identity studies. 'Judgment and Reasoning' stressed the generation of cognitive/ intellectual and social operations having qualities such as reversibility and conservation. The child's social knowledge paralleled individual knowledge.

Table 17.1 Damon's early authority levels

Level 0-A   Authority is legitimized by attributes that link the authority figure with the self, either by establishing affectional bonds between authority figure and self or by establishing identification between authority figure and self. The basis for obedience is a primitive association between authority's commands and the self's desires.

Level 0-B   Authority is legitimized by physical attributes of persons – size, sex, dress and so on. The specific attributes selected are those which the subject considers to be descriptive of persons in command. These legitimizing attributes may be used in a fluctuating manner, since they are not linked logically to the functioning of authority. The subject recognizes the potential conflict between authority's commands and the self's wishes, and thinks about obedience in a pragmatic fashion: commands are followed as a means of achieving desires, or to avoid actions contrary to desires.

Level 1-A   Authority is legitimized by attributes which enable the authority figure to enforce his commands (physical strength, social or physical power, and so on). Obedience is based upon subject's respect for authority figure's social or physical power, which is invested with an aura of omnipotence and omniscience.

Level 1-B   Authority is legitimized by attributes that reflect special talent or ability, and that make the authority figure a superior person in the eyes of the subject. This special talent or ability is no longer associated simply with power, but is rather indicative of the authority figure's ability to accomplish changes that subordinates cannot. Obedience is based on reciprocal exchange; subject obeys because authority figure has helped him in the past, or because authority figure otherwise 'deserves' his obedience.

Level 2-A   Authority is legitimized by prior training or experi-
            ence related to the process of commanding. Authority
            figure therefore is seen as a person who is able to
            lead and command better than subordinates. Obedience
            is based on subject's respect for this specific leader-
            ship ability and on the belief that this superior leader-
            ship ability implies a concern for the welfare and the
            rights of subordinates.
Level 2-B   Authority is legitimized by the co-ordination of a
            variety of attributes with specific situational factors.
            Subject believes that a person might possess attri-
            butes which enable him to command well in one situ-
            ation but not in another. Authority, therefore, is
            seen as a shared, consensual relation between parties,
            adopted temporarily by one person for the welfare
            of all. Obedience is seen as a co-operative effort
            which is situation-specific rather than as a general
            response to a superior person.

While Piaget has not written or described the stages of social
relationships, several researchers have adopted his paradigm
and provide us with interesting examples. William Damon's
(1977) Early Authority Levels describe development of legitimacy
and obedience (see Table 17.1). Further, Damon found that
these levels were highly correlated to, and parallel in development with, logical-mathematical (L-M) development (especially in
classification, perspective taking and compensation). Other
researchers such as Kohlberg (1976) and Selman (1976) have
discussed the necessary-but-not-sufficient L-M qualities underlying moral/social development. The example of development of
social perspective-taking clearly relies on social decentring
ability, reciprocity and, generally, conservation. Development
of social reasoning/understanding then has a parallel and
underlying L-M basis.

But L-M thought is not limited to the reasoning ability of the
child. Piaget wrote of these stages in schematic terms which
associate action, behaviour and cognition. In terms of the
development of relationships, Mueller and Lucas (1975) observed
preschool toddlers. From their observations they discussed
sensorimotor to conservation schemes in the progression of play
relations. Lee (1975) wrote of similar physical and social schemes,
culminating in the conservation of social partnerships among
peers. The author (Kutnick, 1980) observed children's interactions with and knowledge of teachers. In reviewing what and
how this knowledge became known, pre-operative (action preceding cognition) and concrete operative (action and cognition
taking place simultaneously) schemes were described.

This review of social development from a Piagetian perspective
has stressed stages, and parallel and underlying cognitive
qualities - especially schemes. There are numerous examples

which further this explanation (see, e.g., Connell, 1971; Weinreich, 1975). But before stages of social relationships can be fully discussed, two further qualifications need to be made. First is an expansion of the limited attention given to the sensorimotor stages by most of the above researchers. Second is the alternate authority relation to the constraint so characteristic of Western society; the placement of co-operation, not in its often-quoted stage sequence (after constraint), but as a social authority relationship whose appearance is governed by social structure.

The sensorimotor period is better referred to as sensorimotor-affective. The concept of permanence has both cognitive and social implications. Permanence is necessary for the development of the focused relationship of attachment according to Yarrow (1972); which is generated in the sensorimotor circular reactions. Attachment is important in that it is characterized by trust, security and dependence between child and care-giver. Antecedents of constraint also lie in the assimilative actions of the early circular reactions. The child adapts early physical, social and affective repetitions. Among the repetitions are interactions with care-giver which provide support and comfort - physically, physiologically and psychologically. The care/comforting relationship places the infant in a ritualized position of obedience. Attachment is thus a reciprocal relationship between unequals - the root of the authority relationship of constraint. A similar phenomenon was described by Hoffman (1976) in the development of empathy and altruism in the sensorimotor infant. The sensorimotor stage is far more dynamic than most researchers give it credit. The infant establishes the reciprocal (dominant-submissive) relationship of constraint, develops and demonstrates attachment, begins (physiologically and psychologically) emotional development, and is thus dependent on the ordered and repetitious stimulations of the environment.

The main alternate authority relation to constraint is co-operation, according to Piaget. Co-operation is the power relationship among equals. Co-operation has been characterized by mutuality and reciprocity. The earliest exposure of the child to co-operation is in interaction among peers, although co-operation is not limited solely to peer relations. The existence of co-operation (or the development of co-operative social relations) is, in part, defined by the structure of society. Studies of upbringing practice of the Israeli kibbutz and educational practices in the Soviet Union focus on the building-in of co-operative activities. By negation, Western upbringing and instructional methods are lacking in the extent and importance of co-operation; placing emphasis on constraining and individualistic skills. The structure and availability of peer group activity is an artefact of society. The role of the peer group is very important, though. Peers have been noted as promoting cognitive, social and moral development. Doise (1978) has speculated about the role of group cognition - especially

Table 17.2 Development of social relationships, with logical–mathematical, moral and social perspective (developmental) parallels

	Social development	Logical–mathematical	Moral	Social perspective
(1)	Reflex behaviour/neo-natal capacities			
(2)	Sensorimotor–affective schemes	Sensorimotor	Autistic	
(3)	Development of dependent relationship		Heteronomous	Egocentric
(4)	Early rule/authority application, reflective egocentric understanding	Pre-operational		
(5)	Concrete and rational rule/authority application; self-reflective questioning			
(6)	Involvement with peers, reflective mutual social development	Concrete operational	Co-operative	Sociocentric
(7)	Reflective ability to balance and apply constraining and/or co-operative principles	Formal operational	Autonomous	

in the transitional advance from pre-operations to concrete operations. Qualities of loyalty and obligation to the group are not dissimilar in structure to similar qualities of constraint. The similarity is not surprising as they are both archetypical authority relationships; their underlying structure is undoubtedly the same. Considering the authority/power/obligation relations among the individuals and groups, Piaget identifies axis of authoritative relationships (see Figure 17.1) with an individual's position being governed by social, individual and intellectual development and social/cultural context.

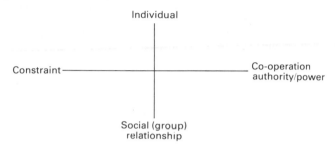

Individual

Constraint ———————————— Co-operation
authority/power

Social (group)
relationship

Figure 17.1 Authoritative relationships axis

Given the above exposition of the development of social relationships, with cognitive, moral and affective qualifications, one can now (reasonably) put together a stage/structural sequence adapted from Piaget – and test for validity using his own criteria. Stages can be extracted from the above review of the child's social development; it would include cognitive, behavioural and affective elements and would follow in this order (see Table 17.2 for parallel logical-mathematical, social and moral development):

(1) reflex behaviour and neo-natal capacities – drawing the infant into close physical contact with care-givers;
(2) sensorimotor-affective schemes – incorporating primary and secondary circular reactions:
 (a) realization of sensory schemes;
 (b) recognition of care-giver;
 (c) trust/dependence of care-giver;
 (d) initial realization of dependence and obedience;
(3) development of dependent relationship while realizing self is different from environment; behavioural interactions with peers;
(4) early rule/authority application and reflective egocentric understanding:
(5) concrete and rational rule/authority application, with self-reflective questioning of the rule basis;
(6) involvement with peers and reflective mutual social development;

(7)   reflective ability to balance and apply constraining and/or
      co-operative principles (in moral judgment, friendship,
      affiliation, political development, etc.).

It is noted by the author that the stages as presented have a
Western (nuclear family) bias. Communal upbringing practices
would necessarily move interactions with peers to an earlier stage
(presumably 2), creating a sense of mutual obligation much
earlier - as with corresponding collective commitments. Additionally, because peer relations in Western societies occur at a late
stage of development, the children's interactions may start on
a pre-operational or concrete operational basis. While the late
start does not hinder communication and expression, it does
lack the sensorimotor/obligation basis - thus social construction
makes most peer relations qualitatively distinct from child-parent
relations.
   In review thus far, I have brought together relevant aspects
from Piaget's theory. The biological, equilibrium personal and
educational/cultural factors are mainly descriptive aspects of
the theory. More relevant/testable criteria are the uniqueness of
stage, invariant sequence, hierarchical and universal qualities,
and Piaget's establishment of 'social operations' and archetypes
of interpersonal relationships. As the research reviewed has
been stage-expositions of development, I have not focused on a
progressive development critique of the theory. The uniqueness
of stages in social development is, I think, self-evident,
qualified by the different types of relationships to which the
child adapts and logical-mathematical qualifications which underlie the ability to reflect about these stages and schemes of
adaptation. Reciprocal understanding of obligation, reciprocity,
reversibility and conservation are evident in both social relations
and social thought. And the invariance of sequence in social
thought/understanding is predicted and upheld by both logical-
mathematical and social (from ego to sociocentric) development.
There have been numerous examples of this progression in the
literature - in work by Damon and Selman and others. But while
the progression appears to exist, it is qualified in rate of
development by type and amount of early exposure to peers and
adults dictated by social context. An element of confusion within
the social-logical sequence is the logical ability to reflect about
a relationship (as co-operation) as opposed to the socio-emotional
'being' of the relationships (an example of this is a primary
schoolteacher telling a class to divide into groups and 'co-
operate' on a project). The splitting into logical v. socio-
emotional relations is the difference between social and close
social relationships. Hierarchical ordering and integration extends
the logical-socio-emotional split and parallel development argument. I have already given the example of 'thinking about' as
opposed to 'being' in a relationship. For further evidence I must
retreat to separate verifications of logical-mathematical and
social developmental stages discussed in earlier papers. The

search for universal support strongly qualifies the context of upbringing, social/familial patterns, and societal structure. Without reintroducing the cross-cultural debate, I must draw upon and qualify several aspects. In the volume edited by Dasen (1977), logical and social development have been verified cross-culturally. Piaget (1959) stated that 'the social environment, even more, in a sense, than the physical environment . . . affects intelligence through three media of language, the content of interaction and rules imposed on thought (collective logical or pre-logical norms)'. In being aware of social and cultural differences between societies and underlying structural similarities, the more obvious conclusion of Piaget's sociological writings is that he provided the qualities and structure, but did not attempt an integration of the work. While noting logical and social developments, the main societal qualification is the existence and type of interpersonal relationships (to this end the role of co-operation as well as constraint are essential factors), whose existence is defined by social structure and social construction.

In putting together a stage-structural sequence of authoritative relationships, one can apply the sequence to the better understanding of social phenomena as political socialization. The main point of this brief statement is that Piaget's writings do provide a useful tool of analysis. Recent political socialization reviews bring out a contradiction. 'Classic studies', such as Hess and Torney (1967) and Greenstein (1975), provide evidence of the progression of knowledge of authority figures and social constructions, based on socio-emotional and logical development. But recent work by Tapper (1978) indicates inability to change/adapt in the political climate, leading to stable political party affiliations within families, or apathy. While the individual effectively 'learns' of politics, he/she is also constrained by the 'learning process'. Political ideology described in these studies undoubtedly lies in the individual hemisphere in the Authoritative Relationship Axis; that is, a quasi-social centration, a phenomenon similar to Piaget's nationalistic egocentrism in 'Judgment and Reasoning'. A similar phenomenon is found in Garbarino and Bronfenbrenner's (1976) comparison of moral development in Western and communist societies, in which Western adolescents display an individualistic orientation and communist adolescents display a collectivist orientation. This analysis by relationship centration/decentration is a useful analytic tool, but still requires more research.

In summary, Piaget's sociological theory is really his theory applied socially. Elements of adaptation, structure, equilibration and interaction are fundamental elements. The social context and social relationships are further fundamental elements, as well as organizing features as operational thought. Piaget provides tools for the analysis of social/societal understanding. It is a pity that the elements described in his early writings were only taken up in the 'Etudes sociologiques' and not more generally. Piaget's approach and breadth of understanding will

certainly stimulate if not facilitate our understanding of self and
society.

REFERENCES

Connell, R. (1971) 'The Child's Construction of Politics'.
Melbourne University Press.
Damon, W. (1977) 'The Social World of the Child'. San Francisco:
Jossey Bass.
Dasen, P. (ed.) (1977) 'Piagetian Psychology: Cross-cultural
Contributions'. New York: Gardiner Press.
Doise, W. (1978) 'Groups and Individuals'. Cambridge University
Press.
Doise, W., Mugny, G. and Perret-Clermont, A. (1975) Social
Interaction and the Development of Cognitive Operations, in
'European Journal of Social Psychology', 5, pp. 367-83.
Garbarino, J. and Bronfenbrenner, U. (1976) The Socialization
of Moral Judgement and Behavior in Cross-cultural Perspec-
tive', in T. Lickona (ed.), 'Moral Development and Behavior'.
New York: Holt, Rinehart & Winston.
Greenstein, F. (1975) The Benevolent Leader Revisited, in
'American Political Science Review', 69, pp. 1371-98.
Hess, R. and Torney, J. (1967) 'The Development of Political
Attitudes in Children'. Chicago: Aldine.
Hoffman, M. (1976) Empathy, Role-Taking, Guilt and Develop-
ment of Altruistic Motives, in T. Lickona (ed.), 'Moral
Development and Behavior'. New York: Holt, Rinehart &
Winston.
Kohlberg, L. (1976) Moral Stages and Moralization, in T. Lickona
(ed.), 'Moral Development and Behavior'. New York: Holt,
Rinehart & Winston.
Kutnick, P. (1980) The Inception of School Authority, in
'Genetic Psychology Monographs', 101, pp. 35-70.
Lee, L.C. (1975) Towards a Theory of Cognitive and Social
Competence, in M. Lewis and L. Rosenbaum (eds), 'Friendship
and Peer Relations'. New York: Wiley.
Mays, W. (1980) Affectivity and Values in Piaget, in S. Modgil
and C. Modgil (eds), 'Towards a Psychological Theory of
Development'. Windsor: National Foundation for Educational
Research.
Mueller, E. and Lucas, T. (1975) Peer Interaction Amongst
Toddlers, in M. Lewis and L. Rosenbaum (eds), 'Friendship
and Peer Relations'. New York: Wiley.
Piaget, J. (1929) 'Judgment and Reasoning'. London: Routledge
& Kegan Paul.
Piaget, J. (1951) 'Play, Dreams and Imitation in Childhood'.
New York: Norton.
Piaget, J. (1959) 'The Language and Thought of the Child'.
London: Routledge & Kegan Paul.
Piaget, J. (1965) 'Moral Judgment of the Child'. New York:

Free Press.
Piaget, J. (1967) 'Études sociologiques'. Geneva: Droz.
Piaget, J. and Inhelder, B. (1969). 'Psychology of the Child'.
London: Routledge & Kegan Paul.
Selman, R. (1976) Social Cognitive Understanding, in T. Lickona
(ed.), 'Moral Development and Behavior'. New York: Holt,
Rinehart & Winston.
Tapper, T. (1978) 'Education and the Political Order'. London:
Macmillan.
Weinreich, H. (1975) Kohlberg and Piaget, in 'Journal of Moral
Education', 4, pp. 201-13.
Yarrow, L. (1972) Attachment and Dependency, in J.L. Gewirtz
(ed.), 'Attachment and Dependency'. Washington: V.H.
Winston & Sons.
Youniss, J. (1978) The Nature of Social Development, in H.
McGurk (ed.), 'Issues in Childhood Social Development'.
London: Methuen.

18 Piaget in a social context: views from the left

Janet Strivens

This paper is concerned with a number of critiques of Piaget's work informed by broadly similar interests in the social context in which the theory has developed and the influence it exerts on important fields of practice within society. However, before these can be discussed, it is necessary to take a more general look at the nature of the relationship between sociology and psychology and to point out certain trends which have changed the nature of that relationship. It is hoped that this will provide a clearer context for the discussion following, and assist in evaluating the significance of the objections raised.

In most branches of psychology in the past decade there has been a growing awareness of the social context in which the discipline has developed, and the social effects of the uses to which it has been put (Armistead, 1974; Israel and Tajfel, 1972; Buss, 1979). At the same time, a radical critique has emerged to claim serious attention, a movement which has also occurred in sociology and philosophy. There is however an important difference: whereas the radicalization of sociology may have transformed the discipline, changing the nature of the questions to be asked, the radical critique of psychology comes close to denying any validity at all to the psychological enterprise. This section will briefly explore two questions: first, why it should be the case that an increasingly sociological perspective on psychological 'knowledge' and practice should be so closely (if not completely) identified with the radical position; and second, why the radical critique in psychology is so threatening to the premises upon which the discipline operates.

Although it can be argued that efforts at integrating the two disciplines have not had a marked effect on the development of either, it is possible to look back to a time when sociology and psychology existed side by side in a comfortable complementarity.[1] This absence of conflict can now be seen as an indication of a basic congruence of values and beliefs, a shared consensus model of society and allegiance to a positivistic view of scientific method. The radicalization of sociology under the growing influence of phenomenological, and later of neo-Marxist, perspectives has undermined this relationship, and over the same period the gulf between the two disciplines has widened. (This is particularly marked in those areas where they are forced into contact, in the confrontation of issues of policy and practice in the welfare services, criminology and education; see for example Esland, 1977; Corrigan and Leonard, 1978; Taylor, Walton and Young, 1973.)

Within sociology, current fashions tend to emphasize the divisions within the subject, but as O'Donnell (1981) points out, these divisions overlie a considerable degree of consensus about the concerns which sociologists share. Both traditional and radical sociology accept the importance of structural analyses of society, which involves an account of both the distribution of various attributes within a population and the form of relations existing between the categories thus created. The categories are not groups in the social psychological sense; there is no assumption of a shared consciousness of their communality. Consciousness may be 'shared' in another sense, however, in that it is socially constructed; the categories through which people perceive and interpret reality express the social relations and conditions which they experience. Thus, what counts as 'knowledge' is not universal and unchanging, but relative to different forms of social experience.

Social structure and the social construction of knowledge and consciousness are not in themselves radical assumptions; they are part of the stock-in-trade of sociologists. It is when one begins to see the structural relations in society in terms of dominance and oppression rather than hierarchy, in other words, in the movement from a consensus to a conflict model of social structure, that a transformation occurs in the way in which questions are formulated. From a recognition of the oppressive nature of structural relations, one is led to question the oppressive nature of the social construction of knowledge, and to ask why certain forms of knowledge dominate our thinking.

It could be argued that the radical critique in psychology started from the recognition of the oppressive nature of certain psychological practices for which it was led to seek explanations. In consequence we have what appears to be a convergence, if not an identity, of sociological and radical perspectives. The question of why the radical position threatens the whole enterprise of psychology is more complex, and can be touched on only briefly here. It rests on the supposed centrality of the concept of the individual (Adlam et al., 1977):

> Both humanistic and biologistic psychologies, grounded in an essentialism, retain as their central category the concept of 'the individual'. They thus ignore that crucial break which Marx formulates in his sixth thesis on Feuerbach, that 'the human essence is no abstraction inherent in each individual. In its reality it is the ensemble of social relations'. . . . Psychology . . . takes this individual as its focus and its

origin. . . . There can be no such thing as a *materialist psychology*. It is an impossibility, a contradiction in terms.

In these comments, the concept of the individual in psychology is inextricably bound up with a belief in the existence of a human 'essence', an idealist notion which is unacceptable within a Marxist approach. However, not all radicals are Marxists, and many psychologists might question the characterization of psychology offered above.[2] While 'the individual' remains an ambiguous and highly suspect concept for both sociologists and radicals, it is not yet clear that it singlehandedly undermines the pursuit of psychology.

A final distinction which seems useful in reviewing critiques of psychology is that made by Adlam et al. (1977) between psychology as 'theoretical product' and as a 'practical effect'. Critiques of the 'practical effect' take the problem of psychological theorizing as it informs, sustains or transforms social practice, and in consequence are likely to be grounded in empirical research. When the practice under examination involves the sorting of people into groups, as is often the case with the application of psychometric techniques, it seems a relatively straightforward matter to demonstrate socioeconomic, racist or sexist bias in the results, and adduce a correspondence with relations of power in society. The value of such research has been widely recognized.[3] However, when psychological theorizing is meant to inform a process, such as education, treatment of the mentally ill or social work method, then issues become clouded. In the first place it is not clear to what extent 'theory' of any recognizable kind enters into the practitioner's daily decisions (Carew, 1979; McNamara, 1976). Second, such research quickly raises intractable problems of relating macro-analyses to the observations of micro-interactions. It is hardly surprising to find that the majority of radical/sociological critiques focus on psychology as theory.

Critiques of psychology as theory tend by their nature to be analyses of the language used. In general, the problem taken is the demonstration of a relationship between the language of the discipline, or specific approach within the discipline, and a social context in which certain forms of explanation and certain concepts gain currency. The borderline with philosophy is crossed, or dissolves. This borrowing of philosophical categories has one unfortunate effect in making such critiques somewhat inaccessible to many psychologists. A more serious problem of such efforts is that they tend to throw up contradictory results. Terms used by the 'founding fathers' of the different approaches are reinterpreted in the light of the critic's own allegiances.[4] This may be due to the rather cavalier way in which the philosophical categories are sometimes used, but it helps to encourage the attitude that such arguments are little more than elaborate word-games which can be safely ignored as psychologists go about their business.

With this thought in mind, let us take a look at a number of recent critiques of Piagetian theory and the ways in which they pose their problems and dissatisfactions.

THREE 'MARXIST' COMMENTARIES ON PIAGET

Commentators are necessarily selective, particularly with a subject as extensive as Piagetian theory. The process of selection involves them in making their own interpretation of key concepts, which they sometimes fail to make explicit. It is helpful, in contrasting the views of the authors reviewed here, to note a series of almost polarized constructs through which they locate their concerns.

In his chapter, Piaget, Marx and the Political Ideology of Schooling, Kaufman (1979) takes constructivism as the central distinguishing feature of Piagetian psychology. He opposes constructivism to scientific materialism, which he claims forms the basis of both behavioural psychology and contemporary monopoly capitalism. Furthermore, he stresses the dialectical nature of Piaget's theory, loosely defined in this context as qualitative change in development rather than continuous growth, which makes the theory 'consistent with the ideology of socialism'. He finally opposes this 'holistic and dialectical model of development' to a 'reductionist and mechanistic view', as a desirable foundation for pedagogy.

Kaufman's central concern appears to be with educational practice. He believes that the practices which emanate from theories resting on different epistemological foundations must be mutually exclusive, and he seeks to demonstrate that an educational practice informed by what he takes to be the principles of Piaget's position is not compatible with the dominant values now current in society. In his alignment of capitalism with behaviourism, socialism with constructivism (in the form of Piagetian theory), he argues for a basic congruity between Piaget and Marx which has been perceived by other educationalists on the left (Francis, 1977).

Venn and Walkerdine (1978) totally reject this position. The object of their critique is Piaget's epistemology, although they refer briefly to the relationship between Piagetian theory and progressivism in education. In a detailed examination of Piaget's views on the nature of knowledge and scientific progress, drawn mainly from his writings on genetic epistemology and structuralism, they demonstrate the strong elements of idealism and positivism which situate the theory within the framework of bourgeois science (Venn and Walkerdine, 1978, p. 90):

(Piaget) seeks the common 'essence' in different natural processes: an idealist enterprise. The search for essence denies the analysis of precisely that which is the root of the real problem, namely the differences in reality, that is to say, the specificities in different cognitive formations. Piaget's history coincides with the history of formal transformations reduced to universal mathematical laws; it is a positivist interpretation of history.

A central feature of their criticism of Piaget's account of the development of thought is the tendency towards formalism with increasing abstraction, the ultimate separation between thought and action (ibid., p. 88):

The supercession of the real world in Piaget's formalism entails the loss of the real world and not its appropriation by conscious thought, because one cannot return to the real objects from the abstract mathematical form of expression of the experience which was their source.

Buck-Morss (1975) also finds fault with the formalistic emphasis in genetic epistemology, while recognizing that the development of the ability to think abstractly is absolutely necessary to human existence (p. 37):

Abstract formalism and abstraction are not the same thing. The ability to abstract is a cognitive skill fundamental to human-language competence . . . but formalism is a particular kind of abstraction. It is the ability to separate form from content and to structure experience in accordance with that distinction.

Buck-Morss uses this distinction between abstraction and abstract formalism to offer an explanation of the cultural and socio-economic bias in Piagetian tests, while at the same time avoiding a cultural relativism which would deny the reality of the technological dominance of Western culture. She points out the apparent contradiction in Piaget's thesis (also noted by Venn and Walkerdine) between the stress laid on the close inter-relation of organized action with the content of the physical environment in his studies of early infancy, and the direction of development towards increasing separation of thought and action in studies of older children (Buck-Morss, 1975, p. 40):

This is the same idealist propensity that neo-marxists criticise in all bourgeois philosophy; placing more value on the idea than the reality . . . for Piaget, the culmination of learning is when the child can 'do' everything in his head, that is, when he can divorce theory from practice.

In view of the widely differing assessments of Piaget among these writers, it is interesting to note that Kaufman deals summarily with the concept of idealism in his discussion. He sees idealism, materialism and dialecticism as three general models in Western philosophical thought, but leaves idealism out of his argument, since 'specific forms of theory and practice related to the idealist model are not widely found in contemporary Western society in the form of political ideologies or educational practice'.

Although there are of course areas of disagreement within Marxism, the apparent discrepancies in the viewpoints discussed above are perhaps more indicative of the different priorities of theoreticians and practitioners. Debate around the possibility of a Marxist psychology, and even more urgently a Marxist pedagogy, will no doubt continue for as long as both academics and practising teachers are actively contributing to the development of Marxist ideas.

INFLUENCE OF THE FRANKFURT SCHOOL

In a largely supportive commentary on Buck-Morss (1975), Buss (1977) attempts to resolve some of the contradictions he perceives in her Marxist interpretation of cross-cultural bias in Piagetian tests by introducing ideas drawn from the 'Critical Theory' of the Frankfurt School. Since Critical Theory has also been a strong influence on Buck-Morss's recent work, a brief introduction, however inadequate, is needed. The name applies to a group of German scholars working at various times at the Institute for Social Research at the University of Frankfurt. If it is possible to grasp a unifying idea linking the various talents, interests and values of these philosophers and social scientists, it is in the understanding of the nature of a 'critique' as perpetual re-examination of taken-for-granted categories of thought and knowledge. Connerton (1976), in his introduction to a useful selection of writings in Critical Theory, draws out the historical changes in usage which give the concept of the critique its richness, particularly in the context of German intellectual history. He traces the development in meaning from 'the art of informed judgment' appropriate to the study of ancient texts, through the increasing emphasis on clear and rational thought, to the acquisition of polemical overtones as the process of critique becomes a political activity.

The precise way in which Critical Theory is characterized here is necessarily limited, and concentrates on those aspects which can be set against the Piagetian thesis. One important strand, particularly in the work of Habermas, is a concern with the limitations of language. Habermas assumes the non-identity of the linguistic concept with the reality it denotes; in other words, language is an approximation to reality, a medium for conveying meaning which is only partially successful. Because we rely so heavily on language to convey our meanings (particularly in literate cultures; see Olson, 1975), it plays a central role in establishing the categories through which we perceive the world. Since language is a system, the constraints on our perceptions are systematic, leading to systematic distortions of reality. One effect of this systematic distortion in the communication of meanings is that certain constraining assumptions are withheld from critical reflection. This is the essence of the notion of 'false consciousness'. The most effective form of political repression is to exclude certain concepts from the arena of debate. In a superficial sense this can be seen in the control exercised over the media, but more profoundly, it permeates society through the categories of a common language.

This concern with the functions of language interconnects with another central theme, that of emancipation. Critical Theory implies a continual process of re-examination of the conditions of knowledge, in order to free ourselves from socially and historically imposed constraints. In present-day society the overriding problem is the status of scientific knowledge. Through the use of 'instrumental reason', the type of formal, logical thinking that underpins science and technology, human-kind has progressively won mastery over nature, but in the process, and through the same logic, has become alienated from nature. Science can be liberating, but when it comes to dominate thinking it can have the opposite effect. Critical Theory recognizes this tension, and its cultivation acts as both a test and a corrective of 'formal theory' while avoiding the dangers of an unreflective pragmatism.

To return to Buss and his attempt to rework Buck-Morss's argument using the framework of critical theory, his starting-point is the status of scientific knowledge in Piaget's own thinking. Refering to Habermas's (1971) discussion of 'scientism' in 'Knowledge and Human Interests', he claims that 'Piaget has slipped into that positivistic conceptual error of equating epistemology and philosophy of science.' For Piaget, as for Marx, philosophical speculation is unsatisfactory and inadequate as a road to 'truth'. But whereas Marx sought to transcend philosophy through human action in the world, Piaget turned to a formal, abstract model of scientific thought. His system is an example par excellence of the 'instrumental reason' to which the Frankfurt School opposes 'practical reason', reason grounded in human activity. When Buck-Morss's arguments are reinterpreted within this framework, the focus of analysis of the cross-cultural bias in Piagetian tests is shifted from the relations of production to the state of technological development in the different societies.

In a more recent article (1980), Buck-Morss herself has moved towards a reinterpretation of a Marxist analysis under the influence of Critical Theory. She takes Adorno's concept of 'negative dialectics', and in an extended discussion struggles to explain what it would mean to develop children's ability to think dialectically. Her difficulties illustrate the odd contradiction of attempting in written language to grasp and convey the act of paradigm-breaking and reformulation, when an essential part of the critique stresses the limitations of communication of meaning through language. In contrast to her previous academic style, she begins to illustrate her discussion with riddles and scraps of fairy stories. There is almost a flavour here of the enigmatic form of communication used by Zen masters in their teaching; one cannot grasp the meaning through rational analysis. Nevertheless, underlying her visionary tone is a clear message; the formal operational thought which is the culmination of the Piagetian model of development is 'less adequate than dialectical thinking, because it cannot reflect critically upon itself', and it cannot encompass the ambivalence of evaluating knowledge within a social context of differential power.

CONCLUSION

For those who find stimulation in a challenge to received forms of thought, the commentaries on Piaget's work reviewed here have much to offer. However, the implications for those working, and training workers, in applied fields are far from clear. None of the critics is concerned in any direct sense with an examination of practice which might be informed by a Piagetian theoretical framework. Since both Marxists and critical theorists are in principle committed to the grounding of knowledge in human action, there is a certain ambiguity about the value of such discussions. In the introduction to this paper it was suggested that social researchers operating within a radical social perspective tend to back off from those urgent questions which arise out of the experience of practitioners and their attempts at understanding their own actions. In different guises the gulf between theory and practice continues. This, rather than any specific psychological or sociological paradigm, should be the chief concern of the radical critique.

NOTES

1　Perhaps the best-known attempts are those by Parsons and Shils (1962), and Gerth and Mills (1954). As recently as the early 1970s, 'American Sociology' carries a surprising number of papers showing a positive interest in Skinner's work.

2　Including Piaget (1971, p. 68):
There are thinkers who dislike 'the subject', and if this subject is characterized in terms of its 'lived experience' we admit to being among them. Unfortunately, there are many more for whom psychologists are by definition concerned with 'subjects' in just this individual 'lived' sense. We do not ourselves know any such psychologists; if psychoanalysts have the patience to attend to individual cases in which the same conflicts and complexes show up again and again, it is once more with a view to discovering common mechanisms.

3   See for example Bowles and Gintis (1976); Kamin (1974).
4   For a discussion of such opposing interpretations of
    Skinner's operant psychology, see Strivens (1981).

REFERENCES

Adlam, D., Henriques, J., Rose, N., Salfield, A., Venn, C.
    and Walkerdine, V. (1977) Psychology, Ideology and the
    Human Subject, in 'Ideology and Consciousness', 1, pp. 5–61.
Armistead, N. (ed.) (1974) 'Reconstructing Social Psychology'.
    Harmondsworth: Penguin.
Bowles, S. and Gintis, H. (1976) 'Schooling in Capitalist
    America'. New York: Basic Books.
Buck-Morss, S. (1975) Socio-economic Bias in Piaget's Theory
    and its Implications for Cross-cultural Studies, in 'Human
    Development', 18, pp. 35–49.
Buck-Morss, S. (1980) Piaget, Adorno and the Possibilities of
    Dialectical Operations, in H.J. Silverman (ed.), 'Piaget,
    Philosophy and the Human Sciences'. Brighton: Harvester
    Press.
Buss, A.R. (1977) Piaget, Marx and Buck-Morss on Cognitive
    Development: A Critique and Reinterpretation, in 'Human
    Development', 20, pp. 118–28.
Buss, A.R. (ed.) (1979) 'Psychology in Social Context'. New
    York: Irvington.
Carew, R. (1979) The Place of Knowledge in Social Work
    Activity, in 'British Journal of Social Work', 9 (3).
Connerton, P. (ed.) (1976) 'Critical Sociology'. Harmondsworth:
    Penguin.
Corrigan, P. and Leonard, P. (1978) 'Social Work Practice
    under Capitalism: A Marxist Approach'. London: Macmillan.
Esland, G. (1977) 'Diagnosis and Testing' (Unit 21, OU course
    E202). Milton Keynes: Open University Educational Enterprises.
Francis, M. (1977) Piaget goes Left, in 'Radical Education' no. 8.
Gerth, H. and Mills, C. Wright (1954) 'Character and Social
    Structure'. London; Routledge & Kegan Paul.
Habermas, J. (1971) 'Knowledge and Human Interests'. Boston:
    Beacon Press.
Israel, J. and Tajfel, H. (eds). (1972) 'The Context of Social
    Psychology: A Critical Assessment'. London: Academic Press.
Kamin, L. (1974) 'The Science and Politics of IQ'. Hillsdale,
    NJ: Lawrence Erlbaum Associates.
Kaufman, B.A. (1979) Piaget, Marx and the Political Ideology of
    Schooling, in P.H. Taylor (ed.), 'New Directions in Curriculum
    Studies'. Brighton: Falmer Press.
McNamara, D. (1976) On Returning to the Chalk Face: Theory
    Not Into Practice, in 'British Journal of Teacher Education',
    2 (2), pp. 147–60.
O'Donnell, M.H. (1981) 'A New Introduction to Sociology'.
    London: Harrap.

Olson, D.R. (1975) The Languages of Experience: On Natural Language and Formal Education, in 'Bulletin of the British Psychological Society', 28, pp. 363-73.

Parsons, T. and Shills, E.A. (eds) (1962) 'Towards a General Theory of Action'. New York: Harper and Row.

Piaget, J. (1971) 'Structuralism'. London: Routledge & Kegan Paul.

Strivens, J. (1981) The Use of Behaviour Modification in Special Education: A Critique, in L. Barton and S. Tomlinson (eds), 'Special Education: Policy, Practices and Social Issues'. London: Harper and Row.

Taylor, L., Walton, P. and Young, J. (1973) 'The New Criminology'. London: Routledge & Kegan Paul.

Venn, C. and Walkerdine, V. (1978) The Acquisition and Production of Knowledge: Piaget's Theory Reconsidered, in 'Ideology and Consciousness', 3, pp. 67-94.

Part 11

Conclusion

19 Piaget's struggle and the struggle about Piaget

Peter Bryant

It is hard to summarize a collection of papers about a man as great as Piaget, because much of his greatness lies in his diversity, which is breathtaking. It is impressive enough to set out, as he did, to build a bridge between biology and philosophy: but to succeed as well in influencing subjects as disparate as psychology, social anthropology, education, sociology and, in the end, as Maggie Boden shows us, artificial intelligence is flexibility par excellence. This variety is reflected in the many different topics and approaches which are found in the various chapters of this book. It is a marvellously variegated picture, but how on earth does one sum it up?

Perhaps the best way is to appeal to the device around which the editors formed first the conference and then this book. They plumped for contradiction – one view for and the other against – and it turns out to be a subtle ploy. For the idea of contradiction lies at the heart of Piaget's theory. It is contradiction which makes the equilibration model work, and it is equilibration which pushes the child through all the various Piagetian stages: the child changes, and changes, again and again for the same basic reason. He has two different and incompatible views about the same thing. They contradict each other and they do so because both are inadequate. The only solution for the child – the only possible solution – is to resolve this inner conflict by changing his intellectual structures. The result is a new and more adequate view which removes the conflict. Equilibrium is restored, and in the process a new intellectual stage is reached. So contradiction leads to new things and to better things.

Perhaps it was the editors' faith in this model which led them so generously and so open-mindedly to provide space for the critics as well as for the supporters of Piaget's theories. Perhaps this was why the two kinds of view – for and against – were so openly juxtaposed. Certainly, looking again at the different pairs of contributions, it is easy to see how together they produce new insights which would have been out of the question if just one or the other view had been presented on its own.

So, is Piaget's emphasis on contradiction justified? Strangely, in a book so full of contradiction, very little is said here about this side of his theory. Let us look for a while at the question of contradiction and Piaget's equilibration model. His views are set out most clearly in two of his last books, 'The Development of Thought' (1978) and 'Experiments in Contradiction' (1980).

First, what are contradictions? They can happen, according to Piaget, for a number of reasons. One is that what seems to the child to be the same action can lead, on different occasions, to quite different results, and this provokes a dilemma which the child solves only by understanding eventually that not one, but two or more different actions, are involved. Another is that the child does not categorize classes properly, and a third is due to his making incorrect inferences. In each case the child can resolve the inconsistency only by adding new and more effective logical moves to his repertoire. The contradiction arises only because of some intellectual inadequacy or other (in what inferences, etc.), but its existence speaks of a process which leads to a new developmental stage, where the inadequacy and the contradiction exist no longer. Let us see how this process works.

The story that Piaget tells is complex and somewhat abstract. It involves a series of hypothetical steps for which, as far as I can see, there is no direct evidence. The first of these steps is a perturbation or disturbance - which is an inner upheaval directly caused by the contradiction. What happens according to Piaget is that the contradiction actually impedes the child's behaviour, so that he does not fulfil some goal. He is frustrated, and this leads to the perturbation or disturbance which is itself motivating. It motivates the next step, which is regulation: this is the modification of a particular piece of behaviour. Once the child has begun to modify what he does, the next Piagetian step, compensation, is possible. To compensate is to find and perform the opposite action - the one that cancels out the effect produced by the first action. Thus the child is experimenting with actions which produce and which cancel out particular effects, and his experimenting finally leads to the final and most important step in this chain of events. It is equilibration. Piaget tells of different types of equilibration, but of these only one need concern us here. That is 'equilibration majorante'.

This is how Piaget describes the emergence of a new and more advanced logical structure, which allows the child to understand the events which at the beginning of the process had seemed capricious and incomprehensible. Thus the original disturbance is removed, and at the same time the child has taken an intellectual step forward.

I suppose that one could quite reasonably ask two separate questions, one about the empirical evidence for the theory and

the other about its cogency. They are separable questions since
the theory could be inherently convincing even if there were no
good evidence for it, simply because it is very hard to get good
convincing evidence about the causes of developmental change.
And it is certainly true that the evidence offered by Piaget's
colleagues for his suggestion that contradiction or conflict lead
to intellectual upheavals and improvements is very, very weak.
The 'conflict' which Inhelder, Sinclair and Bovet (1974) induce
is a discrepancy between what the child expects to happen and
what actually does happen, and it is difficult to reconcile this
contradiction with those which Piaget himself describes as important. But even if Piaget and his colleagues did not contradict
each other about contradictions, the actual experiments cannot
be taken seriously. They are training experiments, and training
experiments need proper controls, a very boring point but a
basic one, and one entirely ignored by Inhelder, Sinclair and
Bovet (Bryant, 1981).

But quite apart from this empirical difficulty, the theory has,
too, a serious conceptual problem. It creates a system which
tells the child what is wrong, but tells him no more than that.
To have two contradictory views about the same thing tells the
child that either one or both of those views is wrong. It does
not tell him what is the correct solution, and it does not tell
him how to 'transcend', to use Piaget's own term, the contradiction. 'Regulation' and 'compensation' certainly do not help
much: they are vague terms and only give us a vague picture of
a child dimly aware that something is wrong and blindly trying
out new things until he hits on the right way. How ironic that
a model supposedly so at odds with learning theory should resort
in the end to something suspiciously like trial and error. But
it has to, because the equilibration story does not provide a
guide to show the right way; it only propels the child away from
what is wrong.

Is there an alternative? I have proposed one (Bryant, 1982)
which is the opposite of contradiction. My hypothesis is that
children realize that a strategy is right when they see that it
consistently produces the same answers as another strategy does.
It is agreement, according to my hypothesis, not conflict, that
causes developmental change, and as evidence for this I have
reported a series of experiments on measuring (Bryant, 1982)
which seems to show that children begin to measure as a result
of seeing that measurement produces the same answers as do
direct comparisons. Conflicts, on the other hand, either between
measurement and other comparisons or between different types
of direct comparison, produced no change at all.

So there is some evidence, albeit rather scanty, that agreement
between strategies can cause a developmental change. But it
may be that it works hand in hand with conflict; conflict telling
the child that something is seriously wrong with the way that
he is setting about things and agreement showing how to solve
the problems.

One thing to note about Piaget's causal ideas is that they internalize the Hegelian dialectic (which, incidentally, seems originally to have given Piaget the ideas for his causal model). The thesis and antithesis takes place inside the child, and the eventual synthesis which represents the new and more advanced intellectual stage is for the most part self-generated. In fact, some of Piaget's colleagues (e.g., Perret-Clermont, 1980) have begun fairly recently to work on the possibility that the important conflicts are public, not private. Their experiments look at the possibility that disagreements between children could produce developmental stages. Their experiments are interesting, but show almost as great a neglect as did Inhelder, Sinclair and Bovet (1974) for the right kind of controls.

I mention this new work partly because it is an interesting development and partly because it brings me back to the main theme of this book, in which the conflicts are between rather than within people. One author holds one view, the other the opposite view, and the editors hope for a synthesis. In fact, the opposing views in this book are not for the most part about the question which I have discussed so far – the causal question. Most of the chapters are about the other side of Piaget's theory, the side which deals with the nature of intellectual development.

Here the issue is straightforward and reasonably familiar. Piaget, on the whole, emphasized children's logical incapacities, and most of his experiments are attempts to show that younger children lack this or that logical ability, which quite clearly is part of the intellectual repertoire of older children. The list of experiments which make this point hardly needs rehearsing. Conservation, transitivity, class inclusion and seriation are the best known, but they are only some of Piaget's tasks in which young children flounder to a quite surprising degree. They fail to solve logical problems, and Piaget argues that they are therefore to some extent a-logical. This is the thesis: it really is as simple as that.

The antithesis has been around for ten years or so. A number of experimenters have managed to show that children who fail hopelessly in Piaget's tasks succeed none the less in closely similar problems which apparently – or at any rate to the satisfaction of these experimenters – make exactly the same logical demands. Examples such as the experiments by Bryant and Trabasso (1971) about transitivity, by McGarrigle and Donaldson (1975) about conservation, and by Markman (1979) about class inclusion are now very easy to find. If these experimenters' conclusions are correct, Piaget must be wrong. The antithesis is as simple as the thesis.

What is one to do with a disagreement of this sort? An obvious possibility is to assume that either the thesis or antithesis is right, and therefore, according to which one thinks correct, that Piaget is completely right or completely wrong. It is at this level that most of the controversy about Piaget has remained.

There is nothing misguided about this, and there is certainly every reason for questioning very closely whether these new experiments really do test conservation, transitivity and class inclusion (Bovet et al., 1981; Breslow, 1981; Smith, 1982). The thesis, so to speak, can strike back.

But there is another possibility which is surely Hegelian enough to have tickled Piaget's fancy. It is to transcend the two views, and to treat each as part of a greater synthesis. Piaget does certainly demonstrate some curious failure on the part of young children in logical tasks. These failures cannot be ignored. On the other hand, as I have said, there is growing evidence that the same children do often succeed in closely similar tasks. Put together, or synthesized, these two kinds of results suggest that the children often possess the logical structures in question, but do not always know when to use them. So the problem may be one of the deployment of logical skills, and not of their existence, in young children.

Indeed, there is some direct evidence that this is so. Measuring, it seems, is something which children are not willing to do when a more direct comparison between the quantities in question is not possible (Bryant and Kopyntynska, 1976). They can measure, but often do not at times when it is the most appropriate thing to do. They have logical skills but do not always deploy them properly.

So the argument can take a seriously new turn, which not only incorporates Piaget's work but would have been quite impossible without it. His work is an essential part of a greater story: and it started that story off and pushed it on a very long way.

Among the obvious qualities which were responsible for his stupendous achievement - his intellectual breadth, his extraordinary originality, his energy - we can discern something slightly less tangible, and that is a strong and persistent optimism. For though he saw human rationality, to which the whole of this work is a resounding tribute, as the product of a struggle, it was a struggle which could be relied on to produce in the end the right results. We should remember that he once was deeply and personally affected by another kind of cataclysm - the First World War - and yet overcame his troubles. Perhaps his experiences then convinced him that struggles can be transcended. His was a resilience for which we should all be grateful.

REFERENCES

Bovet, M., Parrat-Dayan, S. and Deshusses-Addor, D. (1981) Peut-on parler de precocité at de regression dans la conser vation? I Precocité, in 'Archives de Psychologie', 49, pp. 289-303.
Breslow, L. (1981) Re-evaluation of the Literature on the

Development of Transitive Inferences, in 'Psychological Bulletin', 89, pp. 325-51.

Bryant, P.E. (1981) Training and Logic, in M.P. Friedman, J.P. Das, and N. O'Connor (eds), 'Intelligence and Learning'. New York: Plenum Press.

Bryant, P.E. (1982) The Role of Conflict and Agreement between Intellectual Strategies in Children's Ideas about Measurement, in 'British Journal of Psychology', 73.

Bryant, P.E. and Kopyntynska, H. (1976) Spontaneous Measurement by Young Children, in 'Nature', 260, p. 773.

Bryant, P.E. and Trabasso, T. (1971) Transitive Inferences and Memory in Young Children, in 'Nature', 232, pp. 456-8.

Inhelder, B., Sinclair, H. and Bovet, M. (1974) 'Learning and the Development of Cognition'. London: Routledge & Kegan Paul.

Markman, E.M. (1979) Classes and Collections, in 'Cognitive Psychology', 11, pp. 395-411.

McGarrigle, J., and Donaldson, M. (1975) Conservation Accidents, in 'Cognition', 3, pp. 341-50.

Perret-Clermont, A-N. (1980) 'Social Interaction and Cognitive Development in Children'. London: Academic Press.

Piaget, J. (1978) 'The Development of Thought'. Oxford: Basil Blackwell.

Piaget, J. (1980) 'Experiments in Contradiction'. University of Chicago Press.

Smith, L. (1982) Class Inclusion and Conclusions about Piaget's Theory, in 'British Journal of Psychology', 73.

Name index